Palgrave Studies in Risk, Crime and Society

Series Editors
Kieran McCartan
Department of Criminology
University of the West of England
Bristol, UK

Philip N. S. Rumney
University of the West of England
Bristol, UK

Nicholas Ryder
University of the West of England
Bristol, UK

Risk is a major contemporary issue which has widespread implications for theory, policy, governance, public protection, professional practice and societal understandings of crime and criminal justice. The potential harm associated with risk can lead to uncertainty, fear and conflict as well as disproportionate, ineffective and ill-judged state responses to perceived risk and risky groups. Risk, Crime and Society is a series featuring monographs and edited collections which examine the notion of risk, the risky behaviour of individuals and groups, as well as state responses to risk and its consequences in contemporary society. The series will include critical examinations of the notion of risk and the problematic nature of state responses to perceived risk. While Risk, Crime and Society will consider the problems associated with 'mainstream' risky groups including sex offenders, terrorists and white collar criminals, it welcomes scholarly analysis which broadens our understanding of how risk is defined, interpreted and managed. Risk, Crime and Society examines risk in contemporary society through the multidisciplinary perspectives of law, criminology and socio-legal studies and will feature work that is theoretical as well as empirical in nature.

More information about this series at
http://www.springer.com/series/14593

Sarah Wright Monod

Making Sense of Moral Panics

A Framework for Research

palgrave
macmillan

Sarah Wright Monod
Victoria University of Wellington
Wellington, New Zealand

Palgrave Studies in Risk, Crime and Society
ISBN 978-3-319-61820-3 ISBN 978-3-319-61821-0 (eBook)
DOI 10.1007/978-3-319-61821-0

Library of Congress Control Number: 2017945793

Cover credit: Malcolm Fairman/Alamy Stock Photo

Printed on acid-free paper

This Palgrave Macmillan imprint is published by Springer Nature
The registered company is Springer International Publishing AG
The registered company address is: Gewerbestrasse 11, 6330 Cham, Switzerland

For Joe, and Chilla

Preface

This book has a number of beginning points. One of these was my captivation with the idea of moral panic. Another was my frustration at not knowing where to start if I wanted to explore one. And another one was the need for some clarity about what 'moral panic' referred to: an abstract concept to unpack social phenomena? Or material on-the-ground-happening reactions that emerge in real life social situations? Perhaps the most significant beginning point, however, was in the latter months of 2002, as I witnessed a young boy being actively demonized by the news media in New Zealand where I live, and my experience of being a voyeur who could do nothing to mitigate the consequences for his life-chances that I suspected would follow. I later felt that the directions in which the scholarship of panic has been headed over the past decade were too narrow. I thought that despite the good intentions to extend the capacity of the concept of panic by connecting it with theory, it was too soon.

We live in a time when we need moral panic more than ever. We don't need more material on-the-ground-happening moral panics (though they do perform a function, as will be discussed). We need the abstract concept, or at least *a* concept, or even *a number of* concepts, that can help us to think critically about how and why issues are presented to us in the ways that they are, and why we respond to only some of them. We live at a time when the leader of the free world wants to build a wall to keep his nearest neighbours out, uses social media to vilify officials and journalists and denies that climate change exists. My senior colleague, Professor John Pratt, argues that this moment in time marks 'the end of reason'.

Making sense was written to assist with the practice of doing panic research, with a view to rekindle thinking about the shape of the analytical concept. It is a book for students and scholars interested in both *moral panics* (material on-the-ground-happening panics) and *moral panic* (the analytical concept). It focuses on the relationship between the two articulations. It prepares readers to investigate a panic and supports them to contribute their findings to moral panic scholarship.

I have loads of people to thank. Firstly, to my colleagues at the Institute of Criminology at the Victoria University of Wellington, especially Fiona Hutton, Lizzy Stanley, John Pratt and Kim Workman. You have all been tremendously instrumental in my thinking and in the directions in which my work has gone (and is going). I also owe so much to the following people for their wisdom and guidance: Mike Hill, Mike Rowe, Rob White, Allison Kirkman, David Pearson, Brigitte Bonisch-Brednich, Chamsy el-Ojeili, Jan Jordan, Venezia Kingi and Heather Day.

My dear friend Amanda Rohloff deserves a special mention. What an outstanding mind! She made some deep impressions in my work and challenged me often. I miss you, Mandy.

A massive thanks to my family who put up with me. Jake, you are my everything. Paul, you rock my world. Diana, I can't be without you. Peter, you are always there for me. Mike and Nikki, we got this thing called life! Arohanui Shannon, Jesse, Bri and Kairo.

Big, big thanks to my RA's Josh Barton, Jordan Anderson and Samantha Keene, and to the students in CRIM326 in 2016. You lot smoothed out the rough edges.

Lastly, a shout out to my postgraduate students: Madeleine, Sarah, Megan, Danny, Hannah, Jordan, Ange and Sophie, each of whom I have been privileged to see blossoming into remarkable criminologists.

Wellington, New Zealand Sarah Wright Monod

Contents

1
Introduction

This book is about the concept of moral panic. The idea of moral panic was first used by cultural theorist Marshall McLuhan in *Understanding media: The extensions of man* (1964). Jock Young (1971) then used the idea in his study of the social reaction to drug-taking in Notting Hill in the late 1960s. However, it was Stanley Cohen (1972) who developed panic into a definitive analytical concept in relation to his analysis of the Mods and Rockers phenomenon, which unfolded in the mid-late 1960s Britain. Cohen's book *Folk Devils and Moral Panics* (1972) is now considered to be a classic study of the complex interplay between deviant action and social reaction that all students of sociology, criminology and related subjects should ensure they become familiar with. Cohen (1972, p. 1) defines a panic as follows:

> A condition, episode, person or group of persons emerges to become defined as a threat to societal values and interests; its nature is presented in a stylized and stereotypical fashion by the mass media; the moral barricades are manned by editors, bishops, politicians and other right-thinking people; socially accredited experts pronounce their diagnoses and solutions; ways of coping are evolved or (more often) resorted to; the condition then disappears, submerges or deteriorates and becomes more visible.

S. Wright Monod, *Making Sense of Moral Panics*, Palgrave Studies in Risk, Crime and Society, DOI 10.1007/978-3-319-61821-0_1

> Sometimes the object of the panic is quite novel and at other times it is something which has been in existence long enough, but suddenly appear in the limelight. Sometimes the panic is passed over and forgotten, except in folklore and popular memory; at other times it has more serious and long-lasting repercussions and might produce such changes as those in legal and social policy or even in the way a society perceives itself.

Cohen was writing at a time when criminologists and sociologists of deviance were focused on unpacking the social and political practices of creating and legislating against 'outsiders'. The labelling perspective, in particular, was making tidal waves in criminology, and scholars were sensitized to the work on behalf of 'moral entrepreneurs' and the role of self-fulfilling prophecies in developing deviant identities. In the UK, the spotlight was firmly placed on the relationships between the media, the state (and its agents), and those defined as 'deviant' as scholars there filtered the understandings of labelling through a critical lens (see Garland, 2008; Rohloff, Hughes, Petley, & Critcher, 2013; Young 2011). In a study into a reaction about 'muggings', Hall, Critcher, Jefferson, Clarke and Roberts (1978), for example, saw panic as a tool by which powerful groups could manage public perceptions and protect their interests. They found that anxieties about threats that young black men posed to law and order in the early 1970s had been set off by elite groups who were keen to distract the English public from a potential economic crisis in the early 1970s. Sometime later, and across the Atlantic, Goode and Ben-Yehuda (1994) saw panics emerging from several beginning points. For them, the concept of moral panic captured a particular form of social problem construction that largely stemmed from the claims-making work of interest groups and other moral entrepreneurs.

Many other scholars have since employed the concept of moral panic to understand and unpack practices of creating outsiders. Indeed, there is now a vast array of case studies in the literature. There are panics about the media (video nasties, cyberbullying, sexting and online gaming), about sexual abuse (paedophilia and satanic ritual abuse); health panics (AIDS, SARS and Ebola), panics about consumption for leisure (alcopops, Ecstasy and Ritalin) or about the effects of consumption on health (obesity); about violent youth (gangs, school shootings and boy racers) and dissident youth (Goths); about political outsiders (terrorists and asylum seekers) and political undesirables (welfare teens and squatters); about animals (dangerous dogs and foxes); about fictional characters (Harry Potter, Batman and Slender Man); about music (death metal and hip-hop); and items of clothing (hoodies). The list, as Altheide (2009) observes, is almost limitless. In fact, so many issues have been labelled 'panics' that scholars no longer agree where the concept's analytical parameters lie (Goode & Ben-Yehuda, 2011). Are they really all *moral* reactions? Can they really all be called moral *panics*? (see Jewkes, 2015; Rohloff et al., 2013; Thompson, 1998).

Additionally, moral panic is one of the very few social science concepts that has made its way into public discourse. Notably, and somewhat ironically, media professionals have used the term as a way to assure their audiences to *not panic.* All sorts of different forms and magnitudes of social reaction have been dismissed by the media as 'just another moral panic' (Altheide, 2009; Cohen, 2002; Hier, 2002; Hunt, 1997; Jewkes, 2015; Thompson, 1998). Concerns about Ebola, for example, have been linked to similar (debunked) concerns about swine flu and the HIV/AIDS epidemic by some journalists (maxreidjournalism, 2014; Gilman, 2010; Petrow, 2014). The media has also denounced reactions to issues such as campus rape (McArdle, 2015), the game Minecraft (Kemp, 2015) and the paracetamol challenge, where young people dare each other to take lethal amounts of paracetamol in one sitting (Dewey, 2015), as panics. Simon Jenkins of the British newspaper *The Guardian* has gone so far as to denounce moral panic as the 'mad publicity disease' (Jenkins, 2007).[1]

There are also a number of criticisms that have been directed at moral panic. Underpinning the concept, for example, is an assumption of *disproportionality.* Indeed, a reaction is defined as a panic as it is thought to be all out of proportion to an empirical—or any rational sense of—reality (Garlands, 2008). However, critics have questioned how social scientists can realistically measure, and make judgements about, a human being's *emotional* response to something (see Cohen, 2002). Another key criticism is that the media, key to the development of most panics, is markedly different to what it was in the 1960s and 1970s when Young (1971) and Cohen (1972) were developing the concept. How relevant, then, can their understandings of how a panic develops possibly be today? Who is actually doing the panicking is a further area of dispute. Is it the public, or is it the press? Panic scholars also tend to be too quick to blame 'social anxiety' or 'ontological insecurity' for an incidence of panic. But if we are living in an *age* of anxiety and insecurity, and presumably everyone is subject to some degree of each, why do panics occur only in *some* spaces and about only *some* things?

Anyone picking up a contemporary article or text about panic will note that most authors will open their accounts just as I have done here. They will offer a brief explanation about the formative studies (and most will quote, as I have, Cohen's opening paragraph), they will discuss panic's prolific use and they will describe at least two of panic's critic's concerns. Thereafter, studies will tend to do one of two things. They will either present a case study of a moral panic that has occurred (drawing on the work of Cohen, Hall et al. or Goode and Ben-Yehuda) or they will consider what kinds of practices the concept is describing and consequently where its focus is, or should be. This latter exercise is normally executed in one of two ways. Scholars will either consider how shifts across the global political and cultural landscape (mainly the notion that we are in a 'risk society') challenge the idea of moral panic or they connect the concept with a broader theoretical idea (notably the literature on moral regulation). There are benefits and risks of doing more case studies and of considering where the focus of the concept is (or should be). Further case studies make for an ever more diverse field, which may in turn contribute to more quarrels about the efficacy of the panic concept to explain social reactions of a particular sort. Considering where the focus of panic is (or should be) has much promise in that it can address some of the critiques as well as extend, or reinstate, the value of the concept. There is some concern, however, that some of the efforts in this vein are simply 'hooking it [panic] up to whatever theoretical model is currently fashionable' (Best, 2013, p. 76; see also Dandoy, 2014), and that the practical application of the concept to understand a case may be compromised as a result.

This book argues that despite the range of debates that have come to mark the field of panic study, the concept of moral panic remains to be an important idea for the social sciences, and for criminology in particular. Indeed, a concept that can be used to unpack volatile social conflicts that give rise to untenable practices of exclusion and excessive practices of criminalisation has perhaps never been more essential. Critcher (2003, 2006), over a decade ago now, reasoned that the marked increases in social plurality, together with the development of the public sphere and the decline of class alignments since the turn of the twenty-first century, brought with it more fervent contests over morality than ever seen before. We can now add to these social shifts the impending threats stemming from climate change, alarming levels of social and economic inequality and the divisions in social consciousness that Brexit and the election of Donald Trump both testify to. All of these issues may be said to be profound existential ones that give rise to substantial challenges to the ways by which communities are currently organized. What is more, many of us are now immersed within a globalized culture that is dependent on mobile digital technologies and where understandings are cultivated and circulated in unregulated spaces of social media. The times, they are a-changing.

This book argues for an approach to the study of panic that combines the two types of studies described above: case studies of panics *and* considerations of where the focus of the concept of panic is (or should be). It makes a case for this approach by drawing on a range of evidence and demonstrates its efficacy by examining two episodes of moral panic. It describes a framework that can be used to study moral panics, which pays particular heed to the way by which Cohen developed *Folk Devils and Moral Panics*. The processes of panic described by Cohen (1972) in *Folk Devils* were intimate with their subject matter—the Mods and Rockers—and his idea for a concept that could deconstruct the nuances of other cases was drawn from these processes. Given the diversity of the field today *and* the impetus to consider where the focus of panic is (or should be), it is critical that panic scholars establish (as far as it is possible to do so) some common ground about the shape of the concept of moral panic, and how it can be used in the present day. To achieve this, I propose that the study of panic should always be a study of a material situated reaction *in a first instance*. Researchers examining an episode of moral panic should use the concept as a guide but approach the case inductively and let the data 'speak' (so to speak) as much as possible.

Researchers should then locate that episode within its particular social, cultural and political context. The main idea here is that the on-the-ground-happening processes of panic are too specific and socially and historically bound for one analytical concept to capture entirely, even though quite separate panics *may* resemble each other at a more abstract level. Research needs to begin at the material, on-the-ground level, regardless, and let 'the case decide the concept' (Becker, 1998), as Cohen did with his study of the Mods and Rockers. Researchers should then identify what aspects of this particular episode are *not* captured by the parameters of the model of moral panic (the analytical concept) as they are currently understood. What explains these variances? Are these critical to understanding the unfolding of this particular social reaction? Would a model based on this particular episode look dramatically different to Cohen's one?

If this inductive approach is practiced across many types of material panics, three things could be achieved. First, it would allow for a view of what features of panic remain salient across all cases and where the model may need adjusting. Second, it would enable us to 'group' cases that have similar variations about them and to decide whether another analytical concept might be more appropriate for the analysis of these, whether another level of abstraction is required or the inclusion of another idea might be helpful. Third, a developed understanding about the contexts in which material panics emerge can help to inform an *explanation* about what a conceptual model reveals (see Dandoy, 2014). It may indeed be, as the scholars considering where the focus of the concept is suggest, that studies of material moral panics (the on-the-ground-happening panics) have the potential to tell us much more about these short-lived volatile social reactions than the concept, in its current shape, allows them to realize. An understanding of the specific contexts in which these reactions unfold could, I argue, allow for a much more stable connection with broader ideas to be made. Cohen (2002) maintained that the whole point of studying deviance and social control was to identify and understand the complex relationship between social objects and events and their interpretation. A comparative analysis of moral panics, each of which has been investigated as a situated material episode, would enable scholars to see why a set of conditions could set off a panic in one community (or at one time) but not another with the same condition (Cohen, 2002). How, then, can researchers study moral panics in an inductive way, whilst remaining relatively comparable? Below, I outline the framework that I propose can facilitate inductive case study moral panic analysis.

A Framework for Doing Moral Panic Research

As panics are constructed through talk and depend on mediation, they can be understood as 'discursive events' (Critcher, 2009; Maneri, 2013). Indeed, both the Mods and Rockers and the mugging episodes were deconstructed by how they were 'talked about' (Cohen, 1972; Hall et al., 1978). A completed panic might be seen as the achievement of a discursive formation about a particular phenomenon or happening, and an analysis of a material panic can be seen as an investigation of how patterns of meaning have emerged and developed and given rise to this achievement. An inductive investigation of moral panic needs to employ open-ended questions (to trace the material patterns of meaning and locate them in their specific socio-historical context) as well as a set of analytical reflective questions (to observe the relationship of these material patterns with the conceptual processes). This mixture of different question types is similar to that outlined for a *discourse tracing* approach to textual data (see LeGreco & Tracy, 2009). The panic research will begin with an inkling that something out of order has occurred (something akin to moral panic) and this sense should be made transparent and formalized in an initial phase of the research. In total, there would be five research phases, each of which would attend to several questions:

Phase 1: *Justifying and guiding questions*

- Why does the analyst believe a case of moral panic is at hand? What has happened: that is, what events have triggered a reactive sequence in motion? Is there a folk devil? Is there evidence of disproportionality? Is there a reaction by powerful bodies?
- What model is guiding, but not limiting, the research?

Phase 2: *Open-ended questions of a material panic*

- What is the panic about? What meanings are developing and across what spaces? How are they developing?
- Who are the claims-makers and what are their interests?

Phase 3: *Contextual questions of a material panic*

- What, at this place and time, is made visible with the development of these meanings?
- What, in this place and time, supports the development of these meanings?

Phase 4: *Probing questions of a conceptual relationship*

- How do the features of the conceptual model capture the meanings of this episode?
- What meanings are not captured? How might they be captured?

Phase 5: *Imaginative questions for a connection with social theory*

- What is the nature of the contextual features of this episode?
- What ideas can shed light on this nature?

The primary data sample for most panics will be the news media and will include hard news articles (including photographs); editorials and letters to the editor in the printed press; news broadcasts, film footage, interviews and social commentary on television and radio; and news items and social commentary on the Internet (including independent media). Cohen's (1972, 2002) primary sample was documentary sources, the bulk of which was media text. Cohen also administered questionnaires to trainee probation officers, teachers and students and conducted interviews with Members of Parliament, editors, hoteliers, shop assistants, bus drivers, taxi drivers, newspaper sellers and members of the public. However, he did this in 1964 and in 1965, at the very time, the episode of the Mods and Rockers was unfolding. Most contemporary panic analyses will be retrospective, and so the ability to capture 'on-the-ground' assessments from people in the community where the said panic is occurring is likely to be more difficult than it was for Cohen. Moreover, the reality is that most scholars don't have the time nor the funding to conduct multi-year semi-ethnographic studies into a panic episode in the same way that Cohen did. Nevertheless, in the first phase, a researcher should cast the net wide so as to capture the content and significance of panic discourse emerging elsewhere. Other publically accessible data sites should be included where it is appropriate and possible to do so (examples might include website pages of interest groups or transcripts of parliamentary debates). Where a said case calls for it, sites like Wikipedia and Reddit, commentary on behalf of J-Bloggers as well as comments made by the public on online news sites and the Facebook pages of news corporations should be included. Tweets and comments made on personal Facebook pages may also be critical and could additionally be a valuable 'social sensor net' for a researcher (Williams & Burnap, 2015). Researchers should be aware of the complexities of ethical issues when using data from online forums, and in particular from personal social media sites, however (see Langer & Beckman, 2005; Moreno, Goniu, Moreno, & Diekema, 2013; Zimmer, 2010).

The primary unit of analysis for a panic is *text*. Patterns can be examined by looking at how words, combinations of words, connections between sentences and the structures of passages give rise to and shape meaning (Fairclough, 1995). An inductive analysis of text should be circular and iterative, and involve repeated readings to identify initial patterns and to then build on these by re-examining them in relation to their location in the overall sample and to other emerging patterns (Gill, 2000; Taylor, 2001). Multiple meanings will be found, though some of these will be less completed than others. The presentation of the data will therefore only be a summary of selected findings that are chosen by the analyst to best illustrate the patterns of meaning found (Taylor, 2001).

This framework will be demonstrated in action in this book, with the study of two quite different cases of moral panic that have emerged in the New Zealand context. Each of these panics can be viewed as typical moral panics, yet each of them also follows a unique trajectory. The features of the contexts in which they emerged allowed me to suggest, tentatively, some interesting connections that might be made between moral panic and social theory.

Chapter Outline

The book is comprised of eight chapters. This Introduction is the first chapter. Chapter 2 documents the development of the concept of moral panic in what can be seen as the foundational studies or the 'original project' of panic. These works are Cohen's (1972) *Folk Devils and Moral Panics*, Hall et al.'s (1978) *Policing the Crisis* and Good and Ben-Yehuda's (1994) *Moral Panics: The Social Construction of Deviance*. Chapter 3 examines and evaluates the nature of the critiques directed at moral panic since its inception and the responses to these by Cohen (2002, 2011) and other key scholars in the field. Chapter 4 critically examines the considerations of where the focus of the moral panic concept is (or should be) and the connections made between panics (material panics and the concept of panic) and broader shifts and ideas in the efforts to achieve this. The inductive approach to moral panic that is of focus in this book will be positioned in relation to these works. Chapter 5 discusses the central role of the news media in panic development as conceived of by Cohen and his contemporaries. The media in the early accounts was seen as critical in the construction of folk devils, to the mobilization of action and reaction, and for 'right-thinking' people and other interested parties to be heard. This chapter discusses how later analyses saw the media as a means for those at risk of being criminalized to 'fight back' (McRobbie, 1994), and how, today, we need to be conscious of features of new media ecosystems. Chapter 6 illustrates the inductive approach to moral panic with an examination of a case of moral panic that occurred in relation to a murder of a pizza delivery man in Auckland, New Zealand in 2001. This is a case that has all the ingredients of a typical moral panic: a heinous crime committed by a group of young people (including a child); sensationalist media coverage; a plethora of opinions, diagnoses and remedies; and the development of a proposal to make a knee-jerk law change. Chapter 7 describes another seemingly 'typical' case featuring a trigger event involving a 23-hour long standoff between police and a lone gunman; dramatic media accounts of unfolding events; an array of sentiments and analyses from politicians, editors, blogging communities and gun lobbyists; and the establishment of an urgent governmental inquiry. Though both cases can be seen as classic panics, approaching them as situated material episodes illustrates that each followed a unique trajectory and that each of these directions had something to offer in terms of thinking about where the panic concept might be adjusted, as the trajectories of all material panics potentially do. Each of the specific contexts in which they occurred also has something to offer for thinking about connections between moral panic and social theory. Chapter 8 brings the discussion to a close by considering some of those connections and reflecting upon the efficacy of the inductive approach for panic study.

Note

1. Garland (2008) notes with some irony that the very same media professionals often work to escalate or 'stoke a panic' to boost their readership.

References

Altheide, D. (2009). *Terror post 9/11 and the media* (Vol. 4). New York: Peter Long Publishing.

Becker, H. (1998). *Tricks of the trade: How to think about research while you are doing it.* Chicago: The University of Chicago Press.

Best, J. (2013). The problems with moral panic: The concept's limitations. In C. Krinsky (Ed.), *The Ashgate research companion to moral panics* (pp. 67–78). Surrey: Ashgate.

Cohen, S. (1972). *Folk devils and moral panics.* Herts: Paladin.

Cohen, S. (2002). *Folk devils and moral panics* (3rd ed.). London: Routledge.

Cohen, S. (2011). Whose side were we on? The undeclared politics of moral panic theory. *Crime, Media, Culture, 7*(3), 237–243.

Critcher, C. (2003). *Moral panics and the media.* Buckingham: Open University Press.

Critcher, C. (Ed.). (2006). *Critical readings: Moral panics and the media.* Berkshire: Open University Press.

Critcher, C. (2009). Widening the focus: Moral panics as moral regulation. *British Journal of Criminology, 49,* 17–34.

Dandoy, A. (2014). Towards a Bourdieusian frame of moral panic analysis: The history of a moral panic inside the field of humanitarian aid. *Theoretical Criminology, 19*(3), 416–433. doi:10.1177/1362480614553522.

Dewey, C. (2015, May 29). What was fake on the internet this week: The paracetamol challenge, Tinder causing STDs and human trafficking at Hobby Lobby. *The Washington Post.* Retrieved from http://www.washingtonpost.com/news/the-intersect/wp/2015/05/29/what-was-fake-on-the-internet-this-week-the-paracetamol-challenge-tinder-causing-aids-and-human-trafficking-at-hobby-lobby/.

Fairclough, N. (1995). *Media discourse.* London: Edward Arnold.

Garland, D. (2008). On the concept of moral panic. *Crime, Media, Culture, 4,* 9–30.

Gill, R. (2000). Discourse analysis. In G. Gaskell & M. Bauer (Eds.), *Qualitative researching with text, image and sound: A practical handbook for social research* (pp. 172–190). Thousand Oaks, CA: Sage.

Gilman, S. L. (2010). The art of medicine: Moral panic and pandemics. *The Lancet, 375,* 1866–1867.

Goode, E., & Ben-Yehuda, N. (1994). *Moral panics: The social construction of deviance.* Oxford, England: Blackwell.

Goode, E., & Ben-Yehuda, N. (2011). Grounding and defending the sociology of moral panic. In S. Hier (Ed.), *Moral panic and the politics of anxiety* (pp. 20–36). New York, NY: Routledge.

Hall, S., Critcher, C., Jefferson, T., Clarke, J., & Roberts, B. (1978). *Policing the crisis: Mugging, the state, and law and order.* London: MacMillan.

Hier, S. (2002). Conceptualizing moral panic thought a moral economy of harm. *Critical Sociology, 28*(3), 311–334.

Hunt, A. (1997). Moral panic and the moral language in the media. *British Journal of Sociology, 48*(4), 629–648.

Jenkins, S. (2007). Forget bird flu: Mad publicity disease is much more scary. *The Guardian.* Retrieved from http://www.theguardian.com/commentisfree/2007/feb/14/comment.politics1.

Jewkes, Y. (2015). *Media and crime* (3rd ed.). Los Angeles: Sage.

Kemp, L. (2015, April 7). Don't indulge in Minecraft "moral panic". Something new isn't something to be feared, its something to be understood. *WalesOnline*. Retrieved from http://www.walesonline.co.uk/lifestyle/lifestyle-opinion/dont-indulge-minecraft-moral-panic-8990304.

Langer, R., & Beckman, S. C. (2005). Sensitive research topics: Netnography revisited. *Qualitative Market Research: An International Journal, 8*(2), 189–203.

LeGreco, M., & Tracy, S. J. (2009). Discourse tracing as qualitative practice. *Qualitative Inquiry, 15*(9), 1516–1543.

Maneri, M. (2013). From media hypes to moral panics: Theoretical and methodological tools. In C. Critcher, J. Hughes, J. Petley, & A. Rohloff (Eds.), *Moral panics in the contemporary world* (pp. 171–192). New York: Bloomsbury.

Maxreidjournalism. (2014, November 24). Ebola: A crisis or just another moral panic? Retrieved June 27, 2015, from https://maxreidjournalism.wordpress.com/2014/11/24/ebola/.

McArdle, M. (2015, January 28). Moral panics won't end campus rape. *Bloomberg View*. Retrieved from http://www.bloombergview.com/articles/2015-01-28/moral-panics-won-t-end-campus-rape.

McLuhan, M. (1964). *Understanding media: The extensions of man* (1st MIT Press ed.). Cambridge, MA: MIT Press.

McRobbie, A. (1994). Folk devils fight back. *New Left Review, 203*, 107–116.

Moreno, M. A., Goniu, N., Moreno, P. S., & Diekema, P. (2013). Ethics of social media research: Common concerns and practical considerations. *Cyberpsychology, Behavior and Social Networking, 16*(9), 708–713.

Petrow, S. (2014, October 16). "Fearbola": The eerie echo of the early years of Aids. *Stuff*. Retrieved from http://www.stuff.co.nz/world/africa/62459069/fearbola-the-eerie-echo-of-the-early-yearsss-of-aids.

Rohloff, A., Hughes, J., Petley, J., & Critcher, C. (2013). Moral panics in the contemporary world: Enduring controversies and future directions. *Moral panics in the contemporary world* (pp. 1–29). New York, NY: Bloomsbury.

Taylor, S. (2001). Locating and conducting discourse analytic research. *Discourse as data: A guide for analysis* (pp. 5–48). London: Sage.

Thompson, K. (1998). *Moral panics*. London, England: Routledge.

Williams, M. L., & Burnap, P. (2015). Cyberhate on social media in the aftermath of Woolwich: A case study in computational criminology and big data. *British Journal of Criminology*. doi:10.1093/bjc/azv059.

Young, J. (1971). *The drugtakers: The social meaning of drug use*. London, England: Paladin.

Young, J. (2011). Moral panics and the transgressive other. *Crime, Media, Culture, 7*(3), 245–258.
Zimmer, M. (2010). "But the data is already public": On the ethics of research in Facebook. *Ethics and Information Technology, 12*(4), 313–325.

2
The Development of the Moral Panic Concept

This chapter explores the studies of Cohen (1972), Hall, Critcher, Jefferson, Clarke, and Roberts (1978) and Goode and Ben-Yehuda (1994) that were foundational to the development of the concept of moral panic. Together, they can be seen as one 'original project' of moral panic insofar as it is these studies that were first to apply and extend the concept of panic in relation to material cases. The objective of the chapter is to identify the common elements between each of their case studies as well as to view how the models they developed in relation to these cases were subject to the social, cultural and historical contexts from which they were drawn.

Folk Devils and Moral Panics

In 1964, at Clacton, during a cold and miserable Easter, two adolescent groups known as the Mods and Rockers scuffled on and off over a period of two days. The media went about sensationally over-reporting the events of these incidents, the police increased their vigilance and overzealously employed crowd control tactics at Clacton and at other nearby beachside towns, and local people urged that the

S. Wright Monod, *Making Sense of Moral Panics*, Palgrave Studies in Risk, Crime and Society, DOI 10.1007/978-3-319-61821-0_2

authorities should 'do something' about vandalism and mob violence amidst rumours that vigilante squads were being formed by tradesmen seeking to protect their property. Editors articulated their opinions about what should be done about out-of-control youth, interest groups and members of parliament argued for increased disciplinary measures and stiffer sentences, and the courts imposed unusually severe sanctions upon arrestees in an effort to 'clamp down' upon the volatile disturbances that had come to appear to be happening ever more frequently.

For PhD student Stanley Cohen, this series of events demanded scholarly interpretation. The 'episode' would become the topic of his dissertation and later the subject of his influential text *Folk Devils and Moral Panics.* Informed by the 'transactional' or 'interactionist' approach to deviant behaviour (see Becker, 1963; Lemert, 1951), his analysis developed in relation to an emphasis on the set of reactions to the Mods and Rockers: how were they identified, labelled and controlled? Why did the reaction take particular forms? What were the myths, stereotypes and methods of control that erupted from the interaction between the deviants and society?

Cohen (1972) observed that the information about the activities of the Mods and Rockers was mostly received via the media. As a result, much of his analysis is devoted to understanding the role of the media in the development of the episode. He was especially concerned to understand the ways by which the two groups were constructed into deviants, or *folk devils*, and to comprehend how the information in the media served to increase the deviant acts *as well as* the societal reaction to the acts. To assist in developing his understanding, he drew upon Wilkins' (1964) 'deviance amplification cycle' which describes how an initial act of deviance can set off a societal reaction, which in turn increases the deviance, followed by another increase in the reaction and so forth. Cohen (1972) illustrated how the media exaggerated the seriousness of what had occurred at Clacton by way of a number of practices that are characteristic of crime reporting. Sensational headlines and melodramatic language were employed to describe the events and those involved in them, for example. Phrases such as 'riot', 'battle' and 'screaming mob' created an image of a town under siege. Other more subtle journalistic practices were also evident, such as the use of plurals to describe a single event and reporting the same event many times, which gave the impression that it had occurred more than once. Headlines were also frequently misleading. The term 'violence' would appear in headlines but the article attached to those headlines would report that *no* violence had occurred. Rumours were also reported as if they had some factual basis. What is more, the media suggested that the events at Clacton were likely to happen again, urging the public to be alert. The media would print statements from police or local councillors about what they would do 'next time', with descriptions of any immediate precautions that had already been put in place. Interviews with Mods or Rockers themselves about their plans for 'revenge' against their rivals would also be printed. Cohen (1972) argued that these 'predictions' operated to *trigger off* events of a similar order by preparing the public to be ready and by offering the potential Mod or Rocker the symbols and stage directions with which and upon which he/she was to perform. Even when no such event transpired where it was expected to, the media would write stories about the kinds of things that *could* have happened and were narrowly missed. What Cohen (1972) detected was that the 'reaction' to the Mods and Rockers had become something more than the amplification cycle was able to explain. Indeed, the key processes of the media as described by Wilkins (exaggeration, distortion, prediction and symbolization) appeared to be having an amplification effect *independent* of actual events.

Cohen (1972) observed a set of phases in the episode: first, there was the *initial deviance* (the events in Clacton). This was followed, second, by an *inventory phase* where the seriousness of the event and subsequent episodes were talked about in the media in exaggerated terms. Third, the public, the police and the press were then *sensitized* to reinterpret neutral or ambiguous stimuli as potentially or actually deviant as they formed opinions and attitudes about the issue in a sense-making phase. These opinions and attitudes would interact and augment each other to produce an *overestimation* of the deviance which then led to an *escalation* of control towards the Mods and the Rockers in a rescue and remedy phase. Cohen (1972) identified that each phase had a larger problem before it and a sharper idea of what the problem exactly was than the preceding phase had, as each phase circulated around and interacted with each of the other phases (the inventory with the sense-making phase; the sense-making phase with the rescue and remedy phase and so forth). As each phase passed, the 'problem' became more removed from what was really happening. Moral panic could be conceptualized, as a result, as a reaction to a condition, person or group of persons that is or who are defined as a threat that is *out of proportion* to any actual threat it or they may pose.

Folk Devils is often called to account for its emphasis upon describing 'what' happened in the Mods and Rockers episode and 'how' it came to be seen as a much larger problem than it actually was at the expense of addressing 'why' it occurred (see Jefferson, 2008; Shuker, Openshaw, & Soler, 1990). But the 'why' *was* attended to in the study, albeit briefly. Cohen (1972) interpreted the clashes on the beaches as a response to an emerging consumer culture which was characterized by high wages and a commercial youth movement that embraced fashion and idolized wild pop heroes (such as *The Rolling Stones* and *The Who*). The newly affluent teenagers (the Mods) could revel in this emerging scene, but for working-class teens (the Rockers), there were still structural barriers to participation. These teens (the Rockers) would rebel against their situation and create their own excitement on the beaches, where their rivals (the Mods) would join them. Cohen (1972) located the response to these clashes (the ensuing moral panic) as a retort by the older generation to the permissive post-war society that had allowed for this consumer culture (and its differential access) to develop. Other social changes, such as the abolishment of conscription from 1961 in the UK, may be seen to have deepened the sense of concern about youth having no discipline when compared with their parents and grandparents.

Policing the Crisis

Cohen's (1972) moral panic is understood largely as an unintended and unanticipated construction. In part, this reflects the influence of theories of social constructionism that were still dominant in criminological thinking in the early 1970s. Further towards the end of the decade, a group of scholars from the Centre for Contemporary Cultural Studies at the University of Birmingham employed the concept to understand how a brutal robbery of an Irishman by a group of black youths in Handsworth, England in 1972, had initiated a resounding press, judicial and public response about a 'frightening new strain' of crime known only to date in America—mugging. Yet, the event, though horrific, was neither new in its character nor particularly unusual.

Sceptical about the speed in which the idea of mugging took hold, and about the re-articulation of old forms of street crime under this new and imported label, Stuart Hall, Chas Critcher, Tony Jefferson, John Clarke and Brian Roberts (1978) observed that a set of relations between the media and elite bodies was important in the development of how mugging was represented. They found that the media turn to 'accredited experts' in order to maintain the news values of 'impartiality' and 'objectivity', and these experts, in turn, become *primary definers* in that they are able to frame how events will be reported upon by the media. Hall et al. (1978) also saw that the media became *secondary definers* as they transformed these primary definitions into everyday language as they 'spoke' to the public. The media also 'spoke back' to elites, claiming to speak *for* the public. Primary definers who would call upon this voice as evidence that further assertions about the threats of mugging were required (or desired), and these assertions would then be used to support additional secondary interpretations. In other words, the amplification cycle that would create an *ideological closure* around the issue of mugging would be set in motion by virtue of *routine news practices* and the *structural reciprocal relations* between the media and their institutional sources (see Jefferson, 2008).

Hall et al. (1978) also examined the significance of the folk devil (the mugger) in the panic in a more extensive way than what Cohen (1972) did. To do this, they looked at what was happening in the wider socio-political environment at that time. Drawing from the work of Antonio Gramsci, they argued that the early 1970s was a period where hegemony—consent to authority—was in crisis and that this was due, in large part, to the economic recession. They concluded that the specific concern about mugging would operate to redirect social anxieties away from the real issue to one about 'law and order'. In order for dominant interests to remain dominant, the periodic failure of capitalism needed to be shielded from popular view, and this was achieved by 'whipping up' an issue as a problem that could be held responsible for the deprecation of a respectable work ethic (which was related to a decline in jobs) at the same time as it would unite the lower and middle classes. This issue would be *race*. Indeed, the response evolved into a notion that the British 'way of life' was at threat and installed a perception that the weak liberalist position that Britain had taken on law and order issues in the post-war period was to blame. In turn, this would justify a series of severe control measures that were directed at black inner city youth who were seen to be responsible for the wholesale denigration of the moral fabric.

Effectively, *Policing the Crisis* reworked the understanding of power in a moral panic insofar as the official reaction was seen as not just reactive, but 'part of the circle out of which "moral panics" develop' (Hall et al., 1978, p. 52). Moral panic is defined (or redefined) as an ideological event in which a specific and historical crisis is developed and managed, which in turn suggests that there is a necessary collusion between each party involved in its construction: the government, interest groups and the media. It also suggests that there will be, or *can* be, very little opposition. This all sounds very conspiratorial in today's climate. The UK government has tried very hard in the recent past to undermine the BBC, and the BBC itself publically states and defends its independence from political interests (Kanter, 2014). Thus, any suggestion that there might be a relationship between the two would be a contested one. The American context, where President Trump actively calls out journalists for presenting 'fake news', definitely dismisses any collusion between the press and political elites there. And the idea that panic could be 'whipped up' by those in power has certainly had some implications for how *Policing the Crisis* has been received. I consider these implications in detail in this chapter where I discuss the critiques directed at moral panic.

The Social Construction of Deviance

In this section, I take a look at moral panic as it has been conceived in the American context through the work of Eric Goode and Nachman Ben-Yehuda (1994a, 1994b). For these two scholars, the set of phases that Cohen (1972) observed were not particularly conducive for understanding the development of panics that emerged in the USA. There, the media are less centralized and tend to rely less on sensationalist journalism than do the British press (Critcher, 2003; Victor, 1998). Therefore, the ways by which a local event is transformed into a general problem depend more upon the rhetorical activities of interested parties and their access to the appropriate channels. To account for this nuance, Goode and Ben-Yehuda (1994a, 1994b) situated the trajectory of moral panic within a collective behaviour framework, defining the concept as an irrational group reaction or 'a kind of fever … characterised by heightened emotion, fear, dread, anxiety, hostility and a strong sense of righteousness' (1994a, p. 31). Like in Cohen's (1972) work, there is a concern for the processes of definition, but there is astutely more of a focus on organized interests and the role of claims-makers, their alliances and the ways in which they seek to gain public attention (and support). For Goode and Ben-Yehuda (1994a, 1994b), a panic can be distinguished from other, more general social problems with the identification of five 'criteria'.[1] First, there must be a heightened *concern* over the behaviour of a group and the consequences this behaviour poses for wider society. We can measure the manifestation of this concern through opinion polls, proposed legislation, interest group calls for action to be taken, social movement activity and by public commentary by way of media attention (Goode & Ben-Yehuda, 1994b). Second, a dichotomization occurs between 'them' (the folk devils) and 'us' (the responsible and law-abiding citizens). The behaviour of the folk devils (them) is seen to be threatening to the values, interests and, possibly, the very existence of society as 'we' know it, and there is *hostility* towards this outsider. Often this involves identifying the deviant in terms of a stereotype (the Mod or the Rocker and his style of dress and demeanour; the 'mugger' and his ethnicity and/or class position). Third, there must be a *consensus* within society, or at least considerable segments of it, that the threat proposed is very real and serious: that inconceivable practices such as satanic ritual abuse, for example, not only exist but also are prolific across a nation's communities. Further, Goode and Ben-Yehuda (1994b) are firm that what characterizes a panic is *disproportionality*. In a panic, the threat, costs and figures proposed by claims-makers are wildly exaggerated and do not coincide with an objective reality. Finally, moral panics are *volatile*. They typically explode, reach a pitch and then subside just as suddenly. Some panics leave no impact on the legal, moral and social fabric, whilst others become institutionalized as organizations are established to deal with the 'problem'. Even so, Goode and Ben-Yehuda (1994b) argue that all panics leave informal traces which in effect prepare a community for later panics. Panics often create labels, for example, such as 'video nasty' and 'boy racer', which function to help name (and understand) new events and behaviours.

Goode and Ben-Yehuda (1994a, 1994b) further argued that panics could be usefully categorized in terms of three distinct models differentiated by dimensions of motive and responsibility. In a *grassroots* panic, it is the deeply felt attitudes and sentiments of a broad area of lay society that appear threatened, though concern may also manifest within other sectors such as the media or amongst political bodies. In an *interest group* panic, the cause tends to be ideological or moral *or* to do with advancing a material or status position of a group.[2] In an *elite engineered* panic, panic processes are employed by powerful groups to avoid a genuine solution to a real problem whose presentation would undermine elite interests. We might position Cohen's (1972) case study as an interest group panic and Hall et al.'s (1978) analysis of mugging as a classic example of an elite engineered one. However, all three are to be seen as 'ideal types' that when applied will illustrate different aspects of a given panic. Indeed, Goode and Ben-Yehuda (1994a) suggest further that no panic is explicable by means of a single configuration. The grassroots version, for instance, cannot take account of how raw concerns are intensified and mobilized, and so some insights from the other models are required in the analysis stage.

The Original Project

Virtually, all panic case studies have drawn on one or another of these three foundational works, and so collectively, they can be seen as the 'original project' of moral panic. It is a project with two different strands, however. Thompson (1998) argues that studies undertaken in the American context tend to favour analysis through Goode and Ben-Yehuda's (1994a, 1994b) interest group model, and so they focus on the work of claims-makers in panic development. Early works include Joel Best's research into understandings of victimized children (1990), Philip Jenkins' (1998) analysis of the construction of child molesters and Mary de Young's (2004) study of the satanic ritual abuse phenomenon. Research done elsewhere tends to draw more upon Cohen's (1972) and Hall et al.'s (1978) studies and their understanding of the media as a claims-maker *and* as the primary institutional vehicle for the dispersing of claims.[3] Critcher (2003) views two distinct formulations of panic within the original project: one argues for processes at work (Cohen; Hall et al.) whilst the other sees that there are attributes that can be identified (Goode & Ben-Yehuda). Correspondingly, he argues that we term the first a *processual model of moral panic* and the second an *attributional model of moral panic.* Critcher (2003) argues that in practice, it is the processual model that grasps the common features between panics (an issue emerges as a threat, moral entrepreneurs support it, experts pronounce diagnoses and the state institutes repressive measures) whereas some of the attributes of Good and Ben-Yehuda's model have proved problematic (concern and consensus, in particular, are noted to be difficult to measure). Moreover, Cohen's (1972) model is the most employed and best understood within the panic literature.

Implications

Cohen (1972, p. 172) ended *Folk Devils* with a prediction that there would be more episodes like the one he had studied and that other 'as yet nameless folk devils will be created'. Perhaps this is why he established some scaffolding for a panic 'model' in his opening paragraph. However, in the introduction to the second edition of *Folk Devils* (Cohen, 1980), he expressed concern that he might have conveyed that there was a sense of timelessness about the particular set of processes that he had observed. He noted that the recent developments in social theory to that date, particularly cultural studies and deviancy theory, were more attentive to issues of structure and culture, and that as a result, action undertaken by folk devils could be better understood as stemming from particular structural positions and as particular forms of resistance. Similarly, the reaction could be understood in the light of a society increasingly concerned with issues of law and order in an era marked by deep social crevices (i.e. Hall et al., 1978). In the introduction to his third edition in 2002, he noted that sophisticated understandings of claims-making practices (i.e. Goode & Ben-Yehuda 1994a, 1994b) and the conception of the modern era as a 'risk society' each offered key ways to extend the study of panics. Later, in 2011, he wrote that we could now make a distinction between old and new panics insofar as contemporary panics have new forms and features about them that are different from those of the past (Cohen, 2011). Old panics tend to be elite engineered whereas new panics are those initiated by social movements and victims' groups. Old panics would *sometimes* bring about new laws, whereas new panics *are likely to* result in fresh rules, regulations or criminal codes. Some new panics are about exposing denial, cover-ups and unjust tolerances. This to some degree speaks to the notion that there can be good panics and bad panics, which I examine more closely in Chap. 3.

Other theorists have also noted the changing shape of material panics. Goode (2012), for example, makes a distinction between macro-panics (where a whole society, or a good sized proportion of it, are up in arms) and micro-panics (where moral minorities and specialized interest groups are up in arms). In post-modern pluralistic society, Goode (2012) argues, it is increasingly difficult to arouse concern amongst large sectors of society. We need a concept that is at the same time microscopic (to help us view and unpack micro-panics) and able to cast a wide angle lens (to help us understand the connection between these micro-panics) (Goode, 2012). We might, he says, with lots of re-research and re-conceptualizing, come to think of panic quite differently to how we do at the moment.

What is clear from the enormous field of enquiry that has developed since *Folk Devils* is that a conceptual, transferable model of panic is valuable. Nonetheless, the intimacy with which Cohen (1972) developed the concept in relation to the Mods and Rockers, and the way by which Hall et al. (1978) exposed the structural relationship between the state and the civil sphere, identifying in course how political processes can operate in the distortion of reality in their analysis of the mugging phenomenon, demonstrates that the concept is relative to real-life, on-the-ground-happening events: *material* episodes of panic. Goode and Ben-Yehuda's (1994a, 1994b) identification of three models differentiated by the variables of motive and responsibility also supports the need for empirical assessments of material events, insofar as it understands that some of the attributes will be achieved via different means and others would play out according to who was driving the respective campaign. What is more, *context* matters when developing an abstract way to understand what is happening on the ground. That two distinct models have emerged, each designed to capture the nuances of episodes in two different contexts (the processual model for a British context; the attributional model for an American context—see Critcher, 2003), attests to this. These two observations, together with Becker's (1998) contention that the case should decide the concept, form the basis of the inductive approach to moral panic developed here.

Indeed, to reiterate, my central argument is that the study of panic should always be a study of a material reaction, situated within its particular social and historical context, *in a first instance.* Whilst an understanding of panic's established conceptual parameters, as developed by the scholars of the original project of moral panic, should guide empirical research, we need to move beyond ticking off stages and identifying criteria once and for all. We also need to have a way to approach *deviant* cases (such as terrorism—see Walsh, 2016), cases that extend beyond what the model is able to capture (such as Ecstasy—see Critcher, 2000) and cases that didn't quite fit (such as drug-facilitated sexual assault—see Moore, 2009). We further need to be able to answer questions about why this or that case, which had all the ingredients for panic, *didn't* eventuate (see, e.g. Jenkins, 2009; Wozniak, 2016). A framework that can enable us to study the materiality of on-the-ground-happening panics and social reactions that resemble panics, in whatever size or shape they come, but at the same time name them and connect them under the conceptual umbrella of 'moral panic', is long overdue.

Indeed, one of the main critiques directed at the concept of moral panic is that it is outdated and can no longer help us to 'make sense' of social reactions in a world that has undergone some radical changes since the 1960s and 1970s. In Chap. 3, I take a closer look at this criticism, as well as a number of others that have been raised.

Notes

1. Social problems are void of the folk devils upon whom the anxiety of the public is projected and lack the characteristic 'fever' of a panic. Moral crusades, on the other hand, are mobilized by specific moral entrepreneurs who adopt an issue to further their own interests. A panic may result from a crusade, but in the main, a panic will have a variety of interested parties, and either advertently or inadvertently will appeal to a wider and more diverse constituency (see Goode & Ben-Yehuda, 1994b; Critcher, 2003).
2. Although invariably, there is a "happy coincidence" of both principle and interest (Thompson, 1998, p. 9).
3. Jenkins (1992), for example, makes an outright denial that the media can create a panic.

References

Becker, H. (1963). *Outsiders: Studies in the sociology of deviance*. New York: The Free Press.

Becker, H. (1998). *Tricks of the trade: How to think about research while you are doing it*. Chicago: The University of Chicago Press.

Best, J. (1990). *Threatened children: Rhetoric and concern about child-victims*. Chicago: Chicago University Press.

Cohen, S. (1972). *Folk devils and moral panics*. Herts: Paladin.

Cohen, S. (1980). *Folk devils and moral panics* (2nd ed.). Oxford: Martin Robinson.

Cohen, S. (2011). Whose side were we on? The undeclared politics of moral panic theory. *Crime, Media, Culture, 7*(3), 237–243.

Critcher, C. (2000). "Still raving": Social reaction to ecstasy. *Leisure Studies, 19*(3), 145–162. doi:10.1080/02614360050023053.
Critcher, C. (2003). *Moral panics and the media*. Buckingham: Open University Press.
de Young, M. (2004). *The day care ritual abuse moral panic*. Jefferson, NC: McFarland.
Goode, E. (2012, November). *The moral panic: Dead or alive?* Seminar presented at the Revisiting moral panics: Moral panics and the family, University of Edinburgh.
Goode, E., & Ben-Yehuda, N. (1994a). *Moral panics: The social construction of deviance*. Cambridge, MA: Blackwell.
Goode, E., & Ben-Yehuda, N. (1994b). Moral panics: Culture, politics, and social construction. *Annual Review of Sociology, 20*, 149–171.
Hall, S., Critcher, C., Jefferson, T., Clarke, J., & Roberts, B. (1978). *Policing the crisis: Mugging, the state, and law and order*. London: MacMillan.
Jefferson, T. (2008). Policing the crisis revisited: The state, masculinity, fear of crime, and racism. *Crime, Media, Culture, 4*(1), 113–121.
Jenkins, P. (1992). *Intimate enemies: Moral panics in contemporary Great Britain*. New York: Aldine de Gruyter.
Jenkins, P. (1998). *Moral panic: Changing concepts of the child molester in modern America*. New Haven, CT: Yale University Press.
Jenkins, P. (2009). Failure to launch: Why do some issues fail to detonate moral panics? *British Journal of Criminology, 49*(1), 35–47.
Kanter, J. (2014, December 8). BBC News boss hits back at Government Criticism. *Broadcast*. Retrieved from www.broadcastnow.co.uk.
Lemert, E. (1951). *Social pathology*. New York, NY: McGraw-Hill.
Moore, S. E. H. (2009). Cautionary tales: Drug-facilitated sexual assault in the British media. *Crime, Media, Culture, 5*(3), 305–320. doi:10.1177/1741659009349242.
Shuker, R., Openshaw, R., & Soler, J. (1990). *Youth, media and moral panic in New Zealand: From hooligans to video nasties*. Palmerston North, New Zealand: Massey University.
Thompson, K. (1998). *Moral panics*. England: Routledge.
Victor, J. S. (1998). Moral panics and the social construction of deviant behaviour: A theory and application to the case of ritual child abuse. *Sociological Perspectives, 41*(3), 541–565.
Walsh, J. P. (2016). Moral panics by design: The case of terrorism. *Current Sociology* doi:10.1177/0011392116633257.

Wilkins, L. T. (1964). *Social deviance: Social policy, action and research*. London: Tavistock.

Wozniak, J. S. (2016). Missing the moral: Excited delirium as a negative case study of a moral panic. *Punishment & Society, 18*(2), 198–219. doi:10.1177/1462474516635885.

3
Critiquing Moral Panic

The concept of moral panic (in both its processual and attributional formulations) has been subject to a range of criticisms since its development. Goode (2012) argues that successful concepts tend to attract criticism as a decent debunking can bring about a good deal of academic esteem for the critic in question. This is not to say that the charges lodged against panic are all without warrant. Cohen (2002) himself, in the third edition to *Folk Devils*, attended to four 'recurring criticisms'. Rohloff and Wright (2010) later discussed three primary 'problems' with panic research. David, Rohloff, Petley and Hughes (2011), in turn, identify 10 'dimensions of dispute'. Two criticisms (problems/dimensions of dispute) in particular have been repeatedly discussed in the literature. The first of these is that the criterion of disproportionality is a normative, invested assessment made by left-leaning academics. The second is that a panic model (as devised by Cohen and his contemporaries) is appallingly outdated for examining the complexities of social reactions emerging in the present-day era. This chapter explores both of these critiques, placing particular emphasis on how the criterion of disproportionality has been both challenged and defended by panic scholars, as well as on the need for our panic studies to account for the power of

S. Wright Monod, *Making Sense of Moral Panics*, Palgrave Studies in Risk, Crime and Society, DOI 10.1007/978-3-319-61821-0_3

folk devils, the new media ecosystem and a risk-conscious public. I also consider the variable of public concern in a panic: is it really needed? Or is a perception of concern enough? I then argue that to better understand why individual panics happen we also need more attention paid to the study of specific contexts in which they emerge.

A Normative Concept?

> People may panic in a fire, but this does not imply that the building is not burning nor that there is no threat. (Waddington, 1986, p. 258)

As the above quote from Waddington (1986) suggests, the notion of 'panic' seems to imply that there is no (or very little) substance to a reaction. The challenge, therefore, is this: what qualifies the panic analyst to decide that there is no threat, if one is perceived and/or experienced? Indeed, the concept of panic is often accused of being a normative concept designed to challenge cultural politics and expose elite interests, rather than an analytical, deconstructive one able to shed light on phenomena in an objective way. This critique has been most eagerly directed at Hall, Critcher, Jefferson, Clarke and Roberts (1978) study of moral panic, with *Policing the Crisis* cast as far more of an exercise of neo-Marxist scholarship than a contribution to the sociology of deviance (see Jones, 1997; McRobbie & Thornton, 1995).[1] The criterion of disproportionality has since become something of an Achilles heel for researchers using the concept (Rohloff & Wright, 2010). Hunt (2011), for example, contends that in considering the 'appropriateness' of a reaction, panic analysts are effectively suggesting that claims made by interest groups and the actions of right-thinking people and the panicking public are at best 'misguided' and at worst 'crazy', especially where some level of concern might be warranted or at least empathized with (see also Garland, 2008; Jewkes, 2011). Panic scholars respond to this charge in different ways. Some, especially those aiming to extend panic in order to illustrate its broader sociological significance, agree that the notion of it as a normative assessment is a problem (Hier, 2002a, 2002b, 2003, 2008, 2011, 2016a; Rohloff, 2008, 2011). I discuss the work of these scholars in more detail in the next chapter. Other scholars are defensive about the political underpinnings of the concept (Cohen, 2002; Critcher, 2008, 2009a; Goode, 2008, 2012; Rohloff & Wright, 2010; Walsh, 2016; Wright, 2015; Young, 2009). And some studies have uncovered extreme levels of disproportionality. The satanic ritual abuse (SRA) panic is a case in point. In the first instalment of the SRA panic (over time, it would travel from its birthplace the USA to other countries such as New Zealand), children in day care centres everywhere were said to have suffered such atrocities as being held under water, being burnt with candles, being injected with needles, being buried in coffins underground, being defecated and urinated on and bearing witness to other children being tortured and killed, and all at the hands of day care workers (de Young, 2004; Jenkins, 1992; Pratt, 2005). With not one shred of corroborating evidence ever found, in any instalment, the SRA panic has been denounced as entirely fictional (see Hill, 2005). The case against asylum seekers in Australia is another good example. Martin (2015) argues that panic about Afghan boat people and their threat to border security challenges the national mythology of 'white Australia', which, in turn, serves to justify harms enacted as part of Australia's colonial past. Overstayers from Anglo countries, who present much more of a threat to border security, and of whom there are many more, are largely left alone by Australian authorities (Martin, 2015). They, unlike the boat people, don't disturb the 'white Australia' myth.

One response to this issue may be to point out that panic scholars tend to be focused on examining the *overall* reaction (the claims and responses inflamed and augmented via a cycle of amplification) and from a retrospective position. They tend not to be fixated on judging individual actions of people based upon what they know or feel in the midst of a panic, which could be interpreted to be rational, or at least be understandable (see Best, 2011; de Young, 2004). However, it nonetheless remains difficult to establish a definitive measure of proportionality against which a reaction might be argued to be in excess of. As Cohen (2002) argues, it is difficult to calculate emotion, symbolism and representation in quantitative terms. Indeed, it is only with a prior commitment to externally erected goals of social justice, human rights or equality we can expect to make an evaluation that R (the reaction) is an inappropriate response to A (the action) (Cohen, 2002). However, Cohen (2002) maintains that there are cases where measures of proportion *can* be made empirically. The evaluation of the rhetorical means of social problem construction is one example (see Best, 2008). Young (2009), on the other hand, suggests that analysts make a distinction between an *emotional* response to an event, which may be proportionate to a level of anxiety felt, and a *reasonable* response to an event, which someone without that same level of anxiety could be expected to make (see also Garland, 2008). Young (2011, p. 252) also calls to attention the effects of amplification, pointing out that because the fantasies about others often lead to the increased social monitoring of those others (thereby effectively *creating* deviants), the most appropriate question to ask is: 'is the reaction disproportionate to the problem if there had been no such social reaction in the first place?' If not, then: 'the answer will always be corrupted by the question' (Young, 2011, p. 252).

Cohen's (1972) intention to expose reactions that were not just out of proportion but *tendentious* (slanted in a particular ideological direction) and *misplaced* (aimed at something which was not the 'real' problem) has also lent weight to the notion that panic assessments are normative analyses. As Garland (2008, p. 22) observes: 'one reads of very few instances of "moral panic" analysis being applied to episodes where the underlying moral concern appears to be shared by the sociologists who invoked the term'. As Cohen (2011) notes, panic researchers have been (and still are) accused of 'taking sides'. From Hall et al. (1978), however, we might take that it is not necessarily the case that the analyst or the analysis is politically positioned but that the procurers of panic are. Indeed, McRobbie (1994b), whilst contesting that panics can be 'whipped up' in quite the same way as Hall et al. argued they could be during the 1970s, argues that a moral panic remains an effective way by which conservatives seek and secure support: it is their 'chief campaigning arm' (McRobbie, 1994b). She notes in particular how single mothers were scapegoated in the panic following the murder of James Bulger in the early 1990s and how this served to justify the conservative government's restrictions on welfare provisions. Emotional speeches by politicians connecting welfare dependency with the crime were instrumental in this practice of 'othering' (McRobbie, 1994b). Critcher (2006) too identifies that issues over the moral state enable those on the Right to distinguish itself, particularly if the Left can be seem to have adopted similar policies (economic policies especially) (see also Goode, 2012). The Right also has its concerns about panics seemingly 'whipped up' by the Left. Gene Healy of the Cato Institute—a conservative 'think tank' in the USA—wrote an article expressing his thankfulness that proposed gun restrictions which followed the massacre at Newtown, Connecticut, never materialized. The panic, he argues, that never quite got underway, posed to threaten the core foundation of freedom and the right to bear arms for US citizens (Healy, 2014). Indeed, the Left have been accused of pushing far too many 'politically correct' agendas that, according to 'liberal elites', are beyond the reason of common sense (Critcher, 2011).

From the other side of the coin, Left Realists have viewed panic analysts to be holding back critical knowledge with their focus upon inflated figures and the symbolic imagery of evil. Young (2007), for example, argued panics were triggered precisely because the increasingly 'squeezed' middle class felt moral indignation against those who appeared to them to be flouting the rules, particularly the underclass. An acute awareness that they (the middle class) might one day join this underclass in a modern precarious social order keeps the middle class permanently alert for any signs of trouble (see McLaughlin, 2014). Other critics argue that often an issue's candidacy for a moral panic can be regarded as trivial, especially when more significant and damaging events that could and perhaps should command social apprehension exist (see Jenkins, 2009; Jewkes, 2004). Young's (2011) response to this is that reactions are not so much about the instance of deviance in question but the deep cultural, structural and normative shifts that underlie it, to which the deviance in question is an illustration of. Cohen (2002, p. xxii) argues that the fact that many panics are about superfluous events and actions is exactly why interpretations of deviance need to be studied and how it is we are apathetic and indifferent to torture, political massacres and social suffering in distant places whilst becoming hysterical over such things as video 'nasties' and alcopops. Perhaps instead of exposing these 'bad' panics, Cohen (2002) argues, we as panic researchers might encourage the same inflammatory processes towards 'good' panics whereby we can then 'overcome the barriers of denial, passivity and indifference that prevent a full acknowledgment of human suffering' (Cohen, 2002, p. xxxiii). In a later paper, he suggests that the climate change movement is engaged in orchestrating a panic against climate change deniers (Cohen, 2011).[2]

The idea that there can be 'good panics' is an important one which is beginning to gather some steam. Hier (2016a), for example, argues that if we imagine panics as normatively ambivalent operations of power which emerge from negative reactions to putative harms *and* from positive relations of care and obligation, then the idea of a 'good panic' becomes viable. He argues that the reaction to the killing of Cecil the lion by an American dentist in South Africa derived from relations of care for non-human animals. He also argues that the outcry against racially motivated police violence in the USA stemmed from a social obligation to protect the rights of others. Each of these can be seen in terms of developing 'good panics'. I have also argued that a 'good panic' developed about the harmful actions of the New Zealand Government in opening up a marine mammal sanctuary for oil and gas exploration in 2014 (Wright Monod, 2016). No permits for oil and gas exploration were granted in the sanctuary in that year, which I attribute to the good panic that had emerged and developed over a six-week period. Unfortunately, in true panic style, this outcome was merely symbolic, as the sanctuary was again opened up for bids in 2016 (Wright Monod, 2016). Though studies like these show that there is considerable scope for a developing an understanding of 'good panics', there are some conceptual issues to be fleshed out. Hier (2016a) sees an abandonment of the criteria of disproportionality as critical to a conception of a 'good panic', for example. Others have argued that in cases where the outcome serves social justice ends, the terminology of 'panic' may need to be abandoned. Jenkins (Jenkins, 2009, p. 2) puts it this way: 'whoever heard of a *legitimate* panic, or of *well-founded* hysteria'? (original emphasis). Cohen's (2011) response to this is that there have been many a panic about child abuse, an issue that is irrefutably legitimate. On the other hand, a 'good' panic might challenge the understanding of the function of deviancy to reconstruct moral boundaries (see Durkheim, 1984; Cohen, 1972; Erikson, 1966; Jenks, 2011). An additional question is whether 'good panics' will occur only for 'hot button' issues or whether those who are subject to harm are the inherently vulnerable as well as the intrinsically endearing (majestic lions; cute dolphins; innocent children). What of, say, prison suicides or of practices that enact rape culture? What of issues such as poisoned rivers or the transference of e-waste from the Global North to the Global South? And what of the plight of asylum seekers who are often demonized in 'bad' panics? (see Martin, 2015).

Nevertheless, panic researchers need to be prepared that they will be scrutinized for making claims about social reactions they have deemed to be 'out of order'. Best (1993), with sympathy for the panic analyst, suggests that the scrutiny that panic researchers tend to be subject to is better directed at the enterprise of social science itself and its promise to improve the world once we have deconstructed and understood it. Nevertheless, if the data used are appropriate and the method sound, then one can defend one's assessment as valid (Garland, 2008). I suggest that researchers also locate themselves contextually (which enables a degree of situated insight about the 'appropriateness' of a reaction) as well as scholarly and politically (which enables transparency about the research undertaken). Indeed, Cohen (2002) suggests that there may be a continuum along which we view the relationship between moral panics and political ideology, from the abstract analytical to the invested critical (see also Miller, 2013; Rohloff & Wright, 2010). Nevertheless, panic researchers should not apologize for being concerned for social justice and for working to expose reactions that might have led to injustices done.

Folk Devils 'Fight Back'

> Moral panics are totalitarian products of democratic systems. (Critcher, 2006, p. 14)

One of the more astute criticisms of the original panic concept is that it dismisses folk devils as agentless; as 'hapless victims' (de Young, 2011). McRobbie (1994a) contends that the expansion of 'new moral minorities' (pressure groups, associations, voluntary organizations and other grassroots political bodies) in the 1990s gave folk devils the support networks through which they could 'fight back'. In de Young's (2004) assessment of the SRA phenomenon in the American context, she argues that the child care providers were able to resist the process of folk devilling through drawing on their social capital as nurturers. Additionally, instead of defensively arguing 'I didn't do it', they aimed to turn the dialogue around and offensively stated 'this is a media witch-hunt'. de Young (2004) argues that these two features were significant towards the exposure of the SRA panic as a purely constructed phenomenon. McRobbie and Thornton (1995) also highlighted that some folk devils might celebrate the status and perhaps view their attributed deviancy as part and parcel of their passage from adolescence to adulthood. Panic processes could also be employed by various marketing outlets as 'priceless PR campaigns' (McRobbie & Thornton, 1995, p. 565). Similarly, Walsh (2016) has illustrated how the folk devils of panics about terrorism actively exploit deviant images of them created by others in order to appear more threatening than they actually are. In this way, panic becomes 'the weapon of the weak' (Walsh, 2016). Each of these examples speaks to an aspect of Cohen's (1972) work that is often overlooked. Cohen (1972) argued that the character roles of the Mods and Rockers that were constructed by the media were subsequently entered into and enacted by actual youths who took pleasure in doing so. Many of the Mods and Rockers in the episode were simply young people who had heard about the scuffles and were keen to get in on the fun.[3] They appropriately posed for media photographs and wore the expected attire as they turned up to watch the anticipated (predicted) event. The agency of the folk devil won't always be as Cohen (1972), McRobbie and Thornton (1995) and de Young (2004) have described, however. Where an increased authority might be afforded to a particular interest group, a reaction might follow a very narrow trajectory in which the folk devil is afforded very little discursive space. In New Zealand in the early 2000s, a law and order interest group called the Sensible Sentencing Trust (SST) was given considerable agenda-setting power by the media. This, in turn, would see 'politicians running to catch up with their demands' in the general election of 2002, and a number of punitive law and order policies were enacted thereafter (Pratt & Clarke,

2005, p. 306). The SST was also instrumental in singling out a child who had been part of a group involved in a murder as 'public enemy number one' in 2002. I show how, specifically, in Chap. 6, where I examine the case of 'killer kids'. The point to be made here is that though there are exceptions, most folk devils are highly visible characters with little social status: They are *outsiders* in the sense that they are both structurally and politically weak (Cohen, 1972). Levi's (2008) analysis of why panics are difficult to erect and sustain against white-collar criminals, like bankers, illustrates that economic power and social status serve as barriers to demonization (see also de Young, 2004). Hier's (2002a) example of resistance from 'ravers' to the problematization of 'raves' as drug spaces also demonstrates that the socio-political position of the potential folk devil remains a crucial variable in their ability to resist the deviant label.

Changes in the Media

Another problem for the moral panic concept is the ways by which the media has undergone some radical changes. McRobbie (1994a, 1994b) made quite a splash in the field when she argued that the emergence of new media platforms in the 1990s meant that there were many more vehicles for 'right-thinking' people and other interested parties to voice their claims. She also suggested that a crowded media marketplace would mean that some media would routinely sensationalize the ordinary and/or position their respective publication as a moral guardian in order to gain a competitive edge. For McRobbie (1994b), either of these developments could (and would) independently create the prerequisites for moral debates and stimulate the conditions for panic (see also Aldridge, 2003). The use of a prescribed model of panic with sets of processes could not capture alternative pathways such as these. Critcher (2000) argued, however, that whilst insightful, the significance of the argument had been overdrawn. Drawing on findings from a study of a panic about Ecstasy use by young 'ravers' in the UK, he proposed that a collusion (intended or not) between the police, the tabloids and the governing party is an almost impenetrable force. Notions, therefore, that each and every folk devil can 'fight back' are not viable.

However, can we be so sure of this in the present day, in an era where the term 'media' no longer refers to 'the news' but digital, social and mobile media platforms through which 'networked publics' create and share content? Indeed, media theorists now speak of media *ecosystems* (Jewkes, 2015). What is particularly significant about media ecosystems is that the traditional boundary between media producers and media consumers has been demolished. Content is co-created. For some media criminologists, the nature of some of the new arrangements in media ecosystems presents ontological challenges to our understandings of the ways by which the media (that is, the *news* media) are able to define acts of deviance. Yar (2012), for example, argues that social media sites such as Facebook, YouTube, Twitter and Instagram restructure the traditional relationship between deviators and those who represent them insofar as media consumers are now also active media producers in these spaces. The Internet in this sense is both 'qualitatively remarkable' (Jewkes & Yar, 2010) and 'criminologically consequential' (Yar, 2012, p. 248). For others, the significance of social media platforms lies in their operation as 'social sensor nets' that enable criminologists to monitor social reactions to criminal events in real time (Williams & Burnap, 2015, p. 2). Maratea (2008) also argues that the blogosphere has emerged as a key influential public arena to which professional journalists and government officials go when they want indications of what the public think of a particular social issue or policy idea. In Chap. 5, I discuss in closer detail the relationship between moral panics and contemporary media ecosystems, paying particular attention to the affordances of social media and the implications of these for the development of moral panics. In Chap. 7, I examine how bloggers played a key role in constructing a panic about 'gangster guns' in New Zealand in early 2016.

Risk Issues or Moral Issues?

A quite different but just as pertinent issue as the challenges posed by the changes across the social and cultural landscape described so far is the appearance of 'risk' problems. Beck (1992) argues that modern society is a 'risk society' where social life is organized according to the prevention and management of potential harms. For Ungar (2001), this means that our sites of anxiety are changing, and therefore, new models for analysing social reactions are required.[4] For other commentators, the challenge is to see where risk and moral issues meet: how risk problems are politicized and how then the identification of an impurity or threat to 'the care of the self' is articulated in moral terms (see Critcher, 2003; Garland, 2001; Thompson, 1998). However, Cohen (2002) contends that the two orders (risk and moral) are analytically distinct, as the concept of risk does not capture the depth of emotion in a panic well. It pertains more to methods of prediction or can be seen in terms of a specific type of language that is employed by administrators, managers and other official agents when they are endorsing a particular course of action (see Moore, 2013). A sensitized media or anxious public will not be thinking about 'risk factors', for example, when there is a known sex offender on the loose. Second, understandings of what is risky or dangerous shift across time and context. However, others have pointed out that there are no objective 'scientific' categories of objective risk, and that technical issues (like risk) are often subject to processes of moralization as individuals are called upon to 'be responsible' (Hier, 2003; Rohloff, 2013). Falling victim to harm is evidence of a failure to manage one's risk—indicating *irresponsibility*, a moral affront. And, if we accept that a particular practice or space poses a risk to us, we will want to hold someone to account for that predicament. Who is it that is responsible for the levels of youth disorder in this community, or for the alarming levels of toxic waste in the waterways of that society? Cohen (2002) argues that the allocation of blame is something that is central to moral panic.

What each of these issues (the agency of folk devils; the new media ecosystem; a risk-conscious public) illustrates is that panic analyses need to account for aspects of our modern context that are remarkably different from the past. The media ecosystem is especially important to consider, given the centrality of the media to panic development in the majority of cases. It might bring with it new opportunities for panic analysis as well. One of the prospects that social media offers is a new avenue for capturing the public mood as a panic develops. That said, how to capture the public sentiment in a panic analysis, and indeed, *whether* to, has been the subject of some debate. This is the focus of discussion in the next section.

An Absent Public

> ...to take constructions of public opinion as evidence of consent is both intellectually and politically dangerous. (Stabile, 2001, p. 263)

Interestingly, Cohen's (1972) study documented that the reaction on behalf of the public was not necessarily congruent with the reaction of the media and social control agents, and that it was the actions of only particular publics (some moral action groups; some commercial interests; some individuals) and their varied interpretations of the problem that came to the attention of the legislators. Nevertheless, most panic analyses have a working assumption that the public (as a whole, or at least a significant segment of it) is involved in a panic and that the role of active and imaginative audiences is to comprise a significant part of the research agenda (Goode & Ben-Yehuda, 1994a; Miller & Kitzinger, 1998). In practice, however, public concern has proved difficult to establish and, as a result, tends to be inferred directly from sensationalist media coverage (see Goode & Ben-Yehuda, 1994b; Burns & Crawford, 1999; Welch, Price & Yankey, 2002 in particular). This has been seen as problematic for three reasons. First, it leans towards a view of the news media as an objective and non-commercial space for civil debate, where public opinion is reflected, which is a strange conclusion to come to when we consider that most media outlets are corporately owned and profit focused (Mitchell & Holcomb, 2016; Myllylahti, 2016). It is the kind of assumption that is made by politicians when trying to secure votes or argue for a particular course of action (see below). Second, it assumes that 'the media' is one unified entity. This was an understanding that McRobbie and Thornton (1995) pointed out was difficult to apprehend in an era of mass, niche and micro-media platforms, an argument that is only more pertinent now in the new media ecosystem. Following, and third, it presents 'the people' as an ignorant monolithic mass who are subject to media propaganda. This speaks to the 'transmission model' of communication, which has given rise to a variety of media effects theories (see Singer, 2016). Most theorists working with the media accept that whilst texts can and do affect, audiences can also resist (see Surette, 1988; Kitzinger, 2004). And, as argued, it is the *co-production* of content (and hence, of meaning) between producers and consumers that is significant about media ecosystems (Schirato, Buettner, Jutel & Stahl, 2010; Singer, 2016; see also Yar, 2012).

Measurement issues aside, often only a *perceived* consensus is needed to achieve a particular definition of a problem (or an outsider) (Critcher, 2003). When a definition gains legitimacy, vis-à-vis perceptions that the public are concerned, the conditions for panic are ripe. Whilst panic researchers should not infer public concern from media coverage (as argued above), the media does appear to portray public concern which can then affect political decisions. How? In their study of the mugging phenomenon, Hall et al. (1978) argued that the media work with a 'public idiom' in a panic. This means that the press will speak in terms the readership relate to at the same time as they assume themselves as the 'voice' of the people. Because this voice is then fed back to the elite bodies *as* public opinion (the people are spoken *for*), there is something of a 'magical circle' at work whereby the actual public are surpassed. In this way, the variable of public opinion 'functions rather like the trope of the silent majority; it signifies only insofar as politicians and journalists want it to signify within the context of a given argument' (Stabile, 2001, p. 265).[5] From this position, it is perhaps superfluous to consider whether the public is actually concerned or not. Nevertheless, later panic scholars argued that panic narratives must at least be seen as *capable* of engaging a relation with audiences (to make the case that it was likely that the public was concerned), and in view of that, they sought to understand how an engagement with the public may be achieved. Drawing upon Althusser's (1971) conception of how ideology moves from something abstract or external and into 'being', moral panics are conceived in these assessments as ideologico-discursive formations that *interpellate* through *points of resonance* with lived subjectivities (Hay, 1995, 1996; Hier, 2002a, 2002b; de Young, 2000, 2004).[6] As Hier (2002a) describes, this is a critical interpretation of ideology that assumes that how a person perceives his/her world will have an immediate application to how they act within it. My own work (Wright, 2015) has also employed this understanding. I have proposed that we might view panics as *enacted melodramas* where the boundaries between news producers, claims-makers and news consumers (in cases where those boundaries remain—more on this in Chap. 5) are temporarily dismantled and consumers come to experience the role of the suffering victim. For the most part, however, these scholars (myself included) are making inferences about how panic participants *might* behave rationally at ground level, however 'irrational' or disproportional their collective action can be assessed as. What the public is actually thinking and doing remains as invisible as it was with Hall et al.'s (1978) notion of the public idiom. The spaces of social media may assist us in getting to know what the public actually thinks during a particular episode (Williams & Burnap, 2015; Olsen & Christensen, 2015).

Other commentators question the degree to which public sentiment is required (or symbolically called upon) to move *any* legislation through (see Miller & Kitzinger, 1998; Schlesinger & Tumber, 1994). Jewkes (2011) points out that the public is often indifferent or even resistant to issues we might view as political crusades (anti-smoking and 'safe sex' campaigns are given as examples). Critcher (2003) made the point that the media, politicians and many pressure groups may be seen as permanently oriented towards the moral agenda, and therefore, research should concentrate upon the combined efforts of what he denotes as the powerful 'P's': the press, pressure groups, politicians, the police and the (invoked) public. These groups, he argues, operate within a circuit of communication that is independent of actual public opinion. If enough of them at any given time decide there is something to be concerned about and take action against, then a panic becomes possible. These insights also need to be reconsidered in relation to the contemporary social environment with its agentive folk devils, the media ecosystem and a risk-conscious public.

A related issue to the question of whether the public is needed for a panic to get off the ground is the question of *when* a particular problem assumes the momentum of a panic. This is ultimately a question of *why* a said panic occurs and, I argue, is intimate with the question of *where* a panic occurs in both space and time. As Thompson (1998, p. 20) argues, panic narratives and all their discursive tricks do not 'exist in a vacuum'. Social reactions of any sort occur in and under specific social, cultural and historical (and technical) contexts (Best, 2008; Garland, 2008; see also Hilgartner & Bosk, 1988). I want to devote some space to this question of when and where (and ultimately *why*) a panic occurs. As argued, my central thesis in *Making sense of moral panics* is that the study of situated material reactions can help us to adjust the concept where needed and support us to forge links with social theory which can *then* enable us to consider where its focus is. As I will show in the next chapter, this is my point of departure with at least two of the main scholars in the intellectual project of moral panic, namely, Hier (2002a, 2002b, 2003, 2008, 2011, 2016a, 2016b) and Rohloff (2008, 2011). These scholars argue that analytical insights from *theory* in a first instance can assist us to understand what the concept of panic reveals. Their argument is that theory can tell us where the focus of the concept is (or should be), and that this will enable us to better understand our case studies, whereas mine is for the cases to help us reshape the concept and that links with theory can be made later (once we've collated a number of situated studies) (see Becker, 1998). Their approach is largely deductive, and mine is mostly inductive. This point aside, the why question (why do panics happen?) is intimate with a function question (what do panics achieve?) and an impact question (how do panics affect those who are targeted?). These are important questions in their own right. Panic research and analysis often begins with a suspicion that something has been done that ought not to have been. Innocent people were imprisoned as a direct result of the SRA panic, for example, and should not have been (Garland, 2008; Hill, 2005). In the next section, I look at what the panic sequence is said to achieve and to affect, suggesting as I do that the *why* question of individual material panics needs more careful attention paid to it.

Outside the Machine

> The real Devil, whose shapes the early puritans were trying to establish, was the same devil that the Mods and Rockers represented. (Cohen, 1972, p. 162)

Moral panics are understood to 'work' much like other cultural events (royal weddings, coronations and state funerals) in that they stimulate the sense of an 'imagined community' (Anderson, 1983). Indeed, the practices of a panic fashion an *enemy* to mark the distinction between 'us' (the upstanding citizenship) and them (the wrongdoers). It is through the identification of the outsider that social groups create and recreate themselves, and the sense of who 'us' is, is reconstructed each time a new enemy appears.[7] Cohen (1972) compellingly linked the response to the Mods and Rockers as a declaration about moral boundaries, arguing the period 'can be seen as constituting what Erikson terms a "boundary crisis", a period in which a group's uncertainty about itself is resolved in ritualistic confrontations between the deviant and the community's official agents' (Cohen, 1972, p. 162). This is not to say, however, that the Mods and Rockers were consciously picked out to clarify normative contours, but, rather, that both their behaviour (by nature of its visibility) and their position (as structurally weak) at that particular time provided a sufficient enough forum in which to dramatize and articulate issues previously blurred in ambiguity, more clearly.

Many panic analyses have correlated this 'blurred in ambiguity' variable with the idea of a free-floating anxiety, which is seen to be an all-pervading characteristic of late-modern living (Critcher, 2003; Jenks, 2011; Pratt, 2016; Thompson, 1998). Indeed, the period we live in now, since the late twentieth century, is described as the 'age of anxiety' (Holloway & Jefferson, 1997) where there are a 'culture of fear' (Altheide, 2002; Furedi, 1997; Glassner, 2006) and a 'perpetual state of existential insecurity' (Bauman, 2000; Critcher, 2011; Pratt, 2016). It is a period that has witnessed a continuous state of a sense of change and instability across politics, economies and cultures, the collapse of traditional authorities and identities and the disembedding of time and space (Bauman, 2000; Giddens, 1990, 1991). It is precisely these destabilizing characteristics of modernity, as Jewkes (Jewkes, 2011) argues, that stimulate our need for a sense of community (see also Greer, 2004), which in turn sensitizes us to moral panics. And, as argued in the Introduction, we can now add to the mix of changes other pressures such as the impending threats stemming from climate change, historically significant levels of social inequality and the divisions in social consciousness that both Brexit and the election of Donald Trump have exposed. However, two problems stem from an association between moral panic and the age of anxiety, fear and instability. First, as Critcher (2003) argues, the success of a panic is often used as an indicator of social anxiety or of communities in fear, without other evidence to suggest that anything is actually there. But why are some societies and communities more prone to phenomena like moral panic than others are, when both are as equally subject to the characteristics of the age we inhabit? Care is needed when making seemingly obvious connections between social practices and contextual conditions, and evidence needs to be convincing (see Tonry 2001). Second, attention tends to be directed, where panics do occur, to what effects the panic in question has in terms of restoring a sense of stability, however temporary this might turn out to be (Critcher, 2003, 2006; Jenks, 2011). This is not a wasted exercise, as mentioned above. And, as Goode and Ben-Yehuda (1994b) argue, not only are successive panics built on earlier ones but also in the interval period (panic free), the legacy of prior panics provides the means with which to regulate or condone the behaviour that was deemed harmful or deviant in the first place. Panics tend to leave behind sets of discursive terms to define their problems which may later be used to summon an understanding about another event or trend. The term 'boy racer' is one such example, as are the terms 'rave' and 'video nasty' (Critcher, 2003).

However, Cohen (1972) argued that more moral panics would be generated not because they have an inevitable logic, but because societies regularly make problems for some of their members and then condemn the solutions these members find. Asking *why* they do this at particular spaces and times is critical for understanding why the devil in question takes a particular form, where the lines of power reside and how 'we' are subject to 'manipulation'. Cohen (1972, p. 150) argued that this is where his study of the Mods and Rockers in *Folk Devils* fell short:

> …the reaction itself … is often left unexplained. Models such as deviance amplification deal well enough with what happens in the machine (the feedback and snowballing effects during the reaction sequence) but inadequately with why the initial reaction takes place and even less adequately with why the sequence itself might come to an end. For these problems we have to look outside the machine and outside the theatre.

Though panic studies tend to focus on what panics achieve and whom they affect (and with defensible reasons), there have been some exceptional studies that have looked 'outside the machine' in order to discover why this or that episode came about. Hall et al.'s (1978) analysis of mugging, Jenkin's (1998) study of the construction of sex offenders across twentieth century America and de Young's (2004) assessment of the SRA phenomenon are notable examples. Hall et al. (1978) argued that early 1970s Britain was on the verge of a political 'crisis' as an economic recession threatened to reveal the inequalities inherent in capitalism. The elite, whose interests were under threat, would exploit the Handsworth 'mugging' as evidence to suggest that the 'crisis' felt at the grassroots level was actually one of 'law and order'. A key question for Hall et al. (1978) was how a spectrum of consent for the exercise of a coercive law and order campaign was achieved: why different classes who had become increasingly polarized both economically and politically would, at this injunction, share the same social and moral perspective on crime. They found that the call for tougher measures was articulated through an appeal for 'common sense' at the local level, and that at the basis of this appeal was the sense of *Englishness.* In other words, the 'problem' was to be found in working-class immigrant labour, the absence of a respectable work ethic and the lack of appropriate discipline which posed to threaten the everyday person and his traditionalist, conservative and very *English* values. In this way, power was exercised to reconstruct an imagined community in order for power *to be* exercised, in the form of strong law and order measures primarily targeting black youth, to restore stability in the interests of that power. de Young (2004), on the other hand, located the SRA phenomenon within a union of three culturally significant 'master symbols' of the 1980s: the menacing devil, the vulnerable child and the psychological trauma model. Though each of these symbols could be seen to have its own cultural history and generate its own anxieties, they came together as a trio in the 1980s. The first two symbols operated as 'proxies' for much deeper cultural strains set off with increases in religious fundamentalism and with women's increased involvement in the labour market. The third symbol was propagated by a pseudo-scientific profession eager to legitimate its practice. This trio had come together several times in what might be seen as a set of pre-empting episodes to the SRA panic.[8] Yet, none of these would have quite the same impact as the SRA which was impelled with just the right meta-narrative to resonate with and act as an expression of these deeper tensions. This narrative wove together the ultimate threat to vulnerable children—traumatic sexual abuse within circumstances of satanic malevolence (de Young, 2008). And last, but by no means least, Jenkins (1998), a historian, traces the shift in social responses to adult/child sexual relations in the American social, cultural and political landscape from the late nineteenth century until the 1990s. He identifies three distinct periods of interest group activity (leading to moral panic) which constructed and reconstructed the problem understood as child sexual abuse (CSA). The first panic erupted with a campaign to raise the age of consent with a coalition of feminists, moral crusaders and religious reformers who made claims about widespread venereal disease and the trafficking of young girls. The second panic is described as the 'age of the sex psychopath'. Central to this episode was the image of the crazed sex offender, propagated by sensational media stories of sex-related murders, developing psychological and psychiatric 'expertise' and a body of legislators keen to profit politically. The third manifestation—the most recent—is denoted as the 'child abuse revolution'. Though largely due to a campaign on behalf of feminists calling attention to male oppression in familial settings, a familiar nexus of moral conservatives, the media and legislators (all with their own agendas) created a sense of national urgency to the 'unqualified evil' of CSA (Jenkins, 1998). Like de Young (2004), Jenkins (1998) views each episode's content as a direct reflection of spatial and temporal social, political and ideological 'tensions' which provide the bedrock for (and are crystallized by) the entrepreneurial efforts of campaigners.

The problem of the threat of violent (racialized) 'others' (which was at the heart of the mugging panic) has been seen in other panics, notably those about wilding (Welch et al., 2002), Muslims (Morgan & Poynting, 2012) and asylum seekers (Martin, 2015). The problem of the threat to the innocence of children (at the heart of the SRA and CSA panics) has also been seen in other panics. The panic that erupted in relation to the murder of Jamie Bulger is a case in point (see Furedi, 1997, 2013; Green, 2008; Hay, 1995; Young, 1996). Indeed, Critcher (2003) argues that panics about children and childhood are 'irresistible' insofar as they touch upon 'exceptionally primitive' emotions (Cooper & Whitakker, 2014, p. 260). In Chap. 6, where I examine the case of 'killer kids' as a moral panic, I detail the development of understandings of 'the child' which can assist in an understanding of the salience of threats against them to spark panicked reactions. It is worth noting here that a range of problems have been consistent fodder for moral panics across time and space. Cohen (2002) argues that there are seven 'clusters' of issues about which panics tend to be about: young, working-class men, school shootings, drugs, child abuse, welfare cheats, asylum seekers and the media (or, more to the point, the effects of the media). This last cluster is an interesting set of panics which are often referred to as *media panics* (Drotner, 1999).

Implications

Several key implications stem from the critiques of moral panic discussed in this chapter for those engaging in researching moral panics. First, questions will be asked about whether the measurement of proportionality of the reaction was appropriate. Panic researchers need to take care to be transparent and reflective in their documentation and analysis in order to defend their assessments. Second, research should take heed of the diversity of spaces in which claims and responses are made and make careful consideration of the shape of those claims. Third, it may not be necessary to source and include genuine public sentiment in the study of a moral panic as the legitimacy of a panic can be achieved with only a *sense* that the public is concerned. This is dependent on the panic in question, however. The arrival of social media may enable us to better document what the public is indeed thinking and provide some insight as to how they have come to think this way, as well as challenge the ways by which the traditional news media is able to speak on behalf of the public as Hall et al. (1978) argued they could. In any case, it is critical to understand why a panic narrative takes the shape it does and to examine the ways by which it achieves an imagined legitimacy.

Additionally, an in-depth political, cultural and historical analysis of a material panic, like that which has been conducted by Hall et al. (1978), de Young (2004) and Jenkins (1998), can assist us to understand why a particular panic emerges and then comes to a close. This is pertinent for the inductive approach to material on-the-ground-happening panics, followed by an evaluation of variances across material panics, that I am proposing here. By looking across situated panics, we might trace what was useful about the panic concept for the study of each of them *and* what was not captured. From that assessment, we are better equipped to think about which aspects of the concept we need to keep and discard, whether we need to group panics and/or incorporate new conceptual ideas into the fold. Once we have a renewed and updated concept (or group of concepts), we might then ask more comprehensive questions about where the focus of the concept is (or should be). In the next chapter, I discuss how a group of scholars active in contributing to the intellectual project of moral panic seek answers to this question by drawing on *theory* in a first instance. As indicated, I believe that the first task (renewing the concept of moral panic examining the variances between situated material panics) is much more imperative at this point in time. The objective of the next chapter is to show why.

Notes

1. Jefferson (2008) suggests this is an unfair assessment insofar as the mugging account worked with a commitment to grounded theorising and was critical of a reductive Marxism.

2. Brisman and South (2015) view the panic around climate change differently. They argue that deniers' efforts to demonize climate scientists point to a panic sequence 'in reverse'.
3. The author notes that her mother was one of these young people!
4. Ungar's (2001) argument is considered in more detail in the next chapter, where I explicate the connections being made between moral panic and social theory.
5. Stabile (2001) argues that it is notoriously difficult to capture 'public opinion' without large-scale in-depth research tools. Using formal channels such as polls is problematic as they are often monopolized by elite interests which have no structural homology to informal channels of social communication. Stabile (2001) contends that it would defy the logic of the capitalist media to have opinion 'trickle up' in this way; that one of the functions of crime news (in particular) is to deny a diversity of opinion.
6. Althusser (1971) conceptualized interpellation as the precise operation by which ideology acts to transform individuals as subjects. This can be imagined as a commonplace everyday police 'hailing': 'hey … you there' whereupon the individual recognizes it is he/she being spoken to and by turning to respond becomes a subject.
7. This reflects the 'elasticity of evil' (Cohen, 1974, p. 5). This is the idea that as societies change, so do the terms and conditions upon which inclusion and exclusion depend.
8. These include small-scale panics over heavy metal rock music, the strategy game 'Dungeons and Dragons' and devil-worshipping punk youth in Jamestown, New York.

References

Aldridge, M. (2003). The ties that divide: Regional press campaigns, community and populism. *Media, Culture and Society, 25*(4), 491–509. doi:10.1177/01634437030254004.

Altheide, D. (2002). *Creating fear: News and the construction of crisis.* New York: Aldine de Gruyter.

Althusser, L. (1971). Ideology and the ideological state apparatuses. In B. Brewster (Ed.), *Lenin and philosophy and other essays* (pp. 127–186). London: New Left Books.

Anderson, B. (1983). *Imagined communities: Reflection on the origin and spread of nationalism*. London, UK: Verso.
Bauman, Z. (2000). *Liquid modernity*. Cambridge, UK: Polity Press; Malden, MA: Blackwell.
Beck, U. (1992). *Risk society: Towards a new modernity*. London: Sage.
Becker, H. (1998). *Tricks of the trade: How to think about research while you are doing it*. Chicago: The University of Chicago Press.
Best, J. (1993). But seriously folks: The limitations of the strict constructionist interpretation of social problems. In G. Miller & J. A. Holstein (Eds.), *Constructionist controversies: Issues in social problems theory* (pp. 109–130). New York: Aldine de Gruyter.
Best, J. (2008). *Social problems*. New York: Norton.
Best, J. (2011). Locating moral panics within the sociology of social problems. In S. Hier (Ed.), *Moral panic and the politics of anxiety* (pp. 37–52). Milton Park: Routledge.
Brisman, A., & South, N. (2015). New "Folk Devils", denials and climate change: Applying the work of stanley cohen to green criminology and environmental harm. *Critical Criminology, 23*(4), 449–460. doi:10.1007/s10612-015-9288-1.
Burns, R., & Crawford, C. (1999). School shootings, the media, and public fear. Ingredients for a moral panic. *Crime, Law and Social Change, 32*, 147–168.
Cohen, A. (1974). *The elasticity of evil: Changes in the social definition of deviance*. Oxford: Basil Blackwell.
Cohen, S. (1972). *Folk devils and moral panics*. Herts: Paladin.
Cohen, S. (2002). *Folk devils and moral panics* (3rd ed.). London: Routledge.
Cohen, S. (2011). Whose side were we on? The undeclared politics of moral panic theory. *Crime, Media, Culture, 7*(3), 237–243.
Cooper, A., & Whittaker, A. (2014). History as tragedy, never as farce: Tracing the long cultural narrative of child protection in England. *Journal of Social Work Practice, 28*(3), 251–266.
Critcher, C. (2000). "Still raving": Social reaction to ecstasy. *Leisure Studies, 19*(3), 145–162. doi:10.1080/02614360050023053.
Critcher, C. (2003). *Moral panics and the media*. Buckingham: Open University Press.
Critcher, C. (Ed.). (2006). *Critical readings: Moral panics and the media*. Berkshire: Open University Press.

Critcher, C. (2008). Moral panic analysis: Past, present and future. *Sociology Compass, 2*(4), 1127–1144.

Critcher, C. (2009a). Widening the focus: Moral panics as moral regulation. *British Journal of Criminology, 49,* 17–34.

Critcher, C. (2009b, November). *Onto the highway or up a cul-de-sac? The future destination of moral panic analysis.* Presented at the Special research seminar on moral panics, Department of Sociology and Communications, School of Social Sciences, Brunel University, London, England.

Critcher, C. (2011). For a political economy of moral panics. *Crime, Media, Culture, 7*(3), 259–275.

David, M., Rohloff, A., Petley, J., & Hughes, J. (2011). The idea of moral panic—ten dimensions of dispute. *Crime, Media, Culture, 7*(3), 215–228.

de Young, M. (2000). "The devil goes abroad": The export of the ritual abuse moral panic. In *British criminology conference: Selected proceedings* (Vol. 3).

de Young, M. (2004). *The day care ritual abuse moral panic.* Jefferson, NC: McFarland.

de Young, M. (2008). The day care ritual abuse moral panic: A sociological analysis. *Sociology Compass, 2*(6), 1719–1733.

de Young, M. (2011). Folk devils reconsidered. In S. Hier (Ed.), *Moral panic and the politics of anxiety* (pp. 118–133). London, England: Routledge.

Drotner, K. (1999). Dangerous media? Panic discourses and dilemmas of modernity. *Paedagogica Historica: International Journal of the History of Education, 35*(3), 593–619.

Durkheim, E. (1984). *The division of labour in society* (W. D. Halls, Trans.). London, England: MacMillan.

Erikson, K. (1966). *Wayward puritans.* New York: Macmillan.

Furedi, F. (1997). *The culture of fear: Risking taking and the morality of low expectations.* London, England: Cassell.

Furedi, F. (2013, February 12). The 20th anniversary of James Bulger's death: A tragic episode and its shameful legacy. *The Independent.* United Kingdom. Retrieved from http://www.independent.co.uk/voices/comment.

Garland, D. (2001). *The culture of control.* Oxford: Oxford University Press.

Garland, D. (2008). On the concept of moral panic. *Crime, Media, Culture, 4,* 9–30.

Giddens, A. (1990). *The consequences of modernity.* Cambridge: Polity Press.

Giddens, A. (1991). *Modernity and self-identity. Self and society in the late modern age.* Cambridge: Polity Press.

Glassner, B. (2006). *The culture of fear: Why Americans are afraid of the wrong things; [crime, drugs, minorities, teen moms, killer kids, mutant microbes, plane crashes, road rage, & so much more]*. New York, NY: Basic Books.

Goode, E. (2008). Moral panics and disproportionality: The case of LSD use in the sixties. *Deviant Behaviour, 29*, 533–543.

Goode, E. (2012, November). *The moral panic: Dead or alive?* Seminar presented at the Revisiting moral panics: Moral panics and the family, University of Edinburgh.

Goode, E., & Ben-Yehuda, N. (1994a). *Moral panics: The social construction of deviance*. Oxford, England: Blackwell.

Goode, E., & Ben-Yehuda, N. (1994b). Moral panics: Culture, politics, and social construction. *Annual Review of Sociology, 20*, 149–171.

Green, D. A. (2008). *When children kill children: Penal populism and political culture*. Oxford, England: Oxford University Press.

Greer, C. (2004). Crime, media and community: Grief and virtual engagement in late modernity. *Cultural criminology unleashed* (pp. 109–118). London, England: Cavendish.

Hall, S., Critcher, C., Jefferson, T., Clarke, J., & Roberts, B. (1978). *Policing the crisis: Mugging, the state, and law and order*. London: MacMillan.

Hay, C. (1995). Mobilisation through interpellation. *Social and Legal Studies, 4*, 197–223.

Hay, C. (1996). Narrating crisis: The discursive construction of the "winter of discontent". *Sociology, 30*(2), 253–277.

Healy, G. (2014, January 13). Newtown: The moral panic that wasn't. *Washington Examiner*. Washington. Retrieved from http://www.washingtonexaminer.com/newtown-the-moral-panic-that-wasnt/article/2542105#!

Hier, S. (2002a). Conceptualizing moral panic thought a moral economy of harm. *Critical Sociology, 28*(3), 311–334.

Hier, S. (2002b). Raves, risk, and the ecstasy panic: A case study in the subversive nature of moral regulation. *Canadian Journal of Sociology, 27*(1), 33–59.

Hier, S. (2003). Risk and panic in the late modernity: Implications of the converging sties of social anxiety. *British Journal of Criminology, 54*(1), 2–20.

Hier, S. (2008). Thinking beyond moral panic: Risk, responsibility, and the politics of moralization. *Theoretical Criminology, 12*(1), 73–190.

Hier, S. (2011). Tightening the focus: moral panic, moral regulation and liberal government: Tightening the focus. *The British Journal of Sociology, 62*(3), 523–541. doi:10.1111/j.1468-4446.2011.01377.x.

Hier, S. (2016a). Good moral panics? Normative ambivalence, social reaction, and coexisting responsibilities in everyday life. *Current Sociology*, 001139211665546. doi: 10.1177/0011392116655463.
Hier, S. (2016b). Moral panic, moral regulation, and the civilizing process: Moral panic, moral regulation, and the civilizing process. *The British Journal of Sociology, 67*(3), 414–434. doi:10.1111/1468-4446.12201.
Hilgartner, S., & Bosk, C. L. (1988). The rise and fall of social problems: A public arenas model. *American Journal of Sociology, 94*(1), 53–78.
Hill, M. (2005). The "satanism scare" in New Zealand: The Christchurch Civic Creche case. In A. Kirkman & P. Moloney (Eds.), *Sexulality down under* (pp. 97–113). Dunedin: Otago University Press.
Holloway, W., & Jefferson, T. (1997). The risk society in an age of anxiety. *British Journal of Sociology, 48*, 255–266.
Hunt, A. (2011). Fractious rivals? Moral panics and moral regulation. In S. Hier (Ed.), *Moral panic and the politics of anxiety* (pp. 53–70). Milton Park: Routledge.
Jefferson, T. (2008). Policing the crisis revisited: The state, masculinity, fear of crime, and racism. *Crime, Media, Culture, 4*(1), 113–121.
Jenkins, P. (1992). *Intimate enemies: Moral panics in contemporary Britain*. New York: Aldine de Gruyter.
Jenkins, P. (1998). *Moral panic: Changing concepts of the child molestor in modern America*. New Haven: Yale University Press.
Jenkins, P. (2009). Failure to launch: Why do some social issues fail to detonate moral panics? *British Journal of Criminology, 49*, 35–47.
Jenks, C. (2011). The context of and emergent and enduring concept. *Crime, Media, Culture, 7*(3), 229–236.
Jewkes, Y. (2004). *Media and crime*. London, England: Sage.
Jewkes, Y. (2011). *Media and crime* (2nd ed.). London: Sage.
Jewkes, Y. (2015). *Media and crime* (3rd ed.). Los Angeles: Sage.
Jewkes, Y., & Yar, M. (2010). *Handbook of internet crime*. Collumpton: Willan Publishing.
Jones, P. (1997). Moral panic: The legacy of Stan Cohen and Stuart Hall. *Media International Australia, 85*, 6–16.
Kitzinger, J. (2004). *Framing abuse: Media influence and public understanding of secual violence against children*. London, England: Pluto Press.
Levi, M. (2008). Suite Revenge? The Shaping of Folk Devils and Moral Panics about White-Collar Crimes. *British Journal of Criminology*, *49*, 48–67.

Maratea, R. (2008). The e-rise and fall of social problems: The blogosphere as a public arena. *Social Problems, 55*(1), 139–160.
Martin, G. (2015). Stop the boats! Moral panic in Australia over asylum seekers. *Continuum Journal of Media & Cultural Studies, 29*(3), 304–322.
McLaughlin, E. (2014). See also Young, 1971: Marshall McLuhan, moral panics and moral indignation. *Theoretical Criminology, 18*(4), 422–431.
McRobbie, A. (1994a). Folk devils fight back. *New Left Review, 203,* 107–116.
McRobbie, A. (1994b). *Postmodernism and popular culture.* London, England: Routledge.
McRobbie, A., & Thornton, S. (1995). Rethinking "moral panic" for multi-mediated social worlds. *British Journal of Sociology, 46*(4), 559–574.
Miller, D., & Kitzinger, J. (1998). AIDS, the policy process and moral panics. In *The circuit of mass communication: Media strategies, representation, and audience reception in the AIDS crisis* (pp. 213–241). London, England: Sage.
Miller, T. (2013). Tracking moral panic as a concept. In C. Krinsky (Ed.), *The Ashgate research companion to moral panics* (pp. 37–54). Surrey: Ashgate.
Mitchell, A., & Holcomb, J. (2016). State of the News Media 2016. Retrieved from http://www.journalism.org/2016/06/15/state-of-the-news-media-2016/.
Moore, S. E. H. (2013). The cautionary tale: A new paradigm for studying media coverage of crime. In C. Critcher, J. Hughes, J. Petley, & A. Rohloff (Eds.), *Moral panics in the contemporary world.* New York, NY: Bloomsbury.
Morgan, G., & Poynting, S. (Eds.). (2012). *Global Islamophobia: Muslims and moral panic in the West.* Farnham, Surrey; Burlington, Vt: Ashgate.
Myllylahti, M. (2016). *New Zealand Media Ownership Report 2016* (Academic). Auckland: AUT Centre for Journalism, Media, and Democracy.
Olsen, N., & Christensen, K. (2015). Social media, new digital technologies and their potential application in sensory and consumer research. *Current Opinion in Food Science, 3,* 23–26.
Pratt, J. (2005). Child sexual abuse: Purity and danger in an age of anxiety. *Crime, Law and Social Change, 43,* 263–287.
Pratt, J. (2016). Risk control, rights and legitimacy in the limited liability state. *British Journal of Criminology,* azw065. doi: 10.1093/bjc/azw065.
Pratt, J., & Clarke, M. (2005). Penal populism in New Zealand. *Punishment and Society, 7*(3), 303–322.
Rohloff, A. (2008). Moral panics as decivilising processes: Towards an Eliasian approach. *New Zealand Sociology, 23*(1), 66–76.

Rohloff, A. (2011). Extending the concept of moral panic: Elias, climate change and civilisation. *Sociology, 45*(4), 634–649.
Rohloff, A. (2013). Moral panics over the environment? "Climate crisis" and the moral panics model. In C. Krinsky (Ed.), *The Ashgate research companion to moral panics* (pp. 401–413). Surrey: Ashgate.
Rohloff, A., & Wright, S. (2010). Beyond the heuristic: Moral panic and social theory. *Current Sociology, 58*(3), 403–419.
Schirato, T., Buettner, A., Jutel, T., & Stahl, G. (2010). *Understanding media studies*. Melbourne: Oxford University Press.
Schlesinger, P., & Tumber, H. (1994). *Reporting crime: The media politics of criminal justice*. Oxford, England: Oxford University Press.
Singer, J. B. (2016). Transmission creep: Media effects theories and journalism studies in a digital era. *Journalism Studies*, 1–18. doi: 10.1080/1461670X.2016.1186498.
Stabile, C. A. (2001). Conspiracy or consensus? Reconsidering the moral panic. *Journal of Communication Inquiry, 25*(3), 258–278.
Surette, R. (1988). *Media, crime, and criminal justice: Images and realities* (2nd ed.). Belmont, CA: Wadsworth.
Thompson, K. (1998). *Moral panics*. London, England: Routledge.
Tonry, M. (2001). Symbol, substance and severity in western penal policies. *Punishment and Society, 3*(4), 517–536.
Ungar, S. (2001). Moral panic versus the risk society: The implications of the changing sites of social anxiety. *British Journal of Sociology, 52*(2), 271–292.
Waddington, P. A. J. (1986). Mugging as a moral panic. *British Journal of Sociology, 37*(2), 245–259.
Walsh, J. P. (2016). Moral panics by design: The case of terrorism. *Current Sociology*, 001139211663325. doi: 10.1177/0011392116633257.
Welch, M., Price, E. A., & Yankey, N. (2002). Moral panic over youth violence: Wilding and the manufacture of menace in the media. *Youth and Society, 34*(1), 3–30.
Williams, M. L., & Burnap, P. (2015). Cyberhate on social media in the aftermath of Woolwich: A case study in computational criminology and big data. *British Journal of Criminology*. doi:10.1093/bjc/azv059.
Wright-Monod, S. (2016). *Dolphin "troubles" in New Zealand*. Presented at the ANZSOC Conference.
Wright, S. (2015). Moral panics as enacted melodramas. *British Journal of Criminology, 55*(6), 1245–1262. doi:10.1093/bjc/azv025.

Yar, M. (2012). Crime, media and the will-to-representation: Reconsidering relationships in the new media age. *Crime, Media, Culture, 8*(3), 245–260.
Young, A. (1996). *Imagining crime: Textual outlaws and criminal conversations*. London, England: Sage.
Young, J. (2007). Slipping away … moral panics each side of "the Golden age." In D. Downes, P. Rock, & C. Chinkin (Eds.), *Crime, social control and human rights: From moral panics to states of denial, essays in honour of Stan Cohen* (pp. 53–65). Collumpton, England: Willan.
Young, J. (2009). Moral panic: Its origins in resistance, ressentiment, and the translation of fantasy into reality. *British Journal of Criminology, 49*, 4–16.
Young, J. (2011). Moral panics and the transgressive other. *Crime, Media, Culture, 7*(3), 245–258.

4

Considering the Focus of Moral Panic

In Chap. 1 (Introduction), I suggested that contemporary panic studies will tend to take one of two pathways. They will either employ one of the two moral panic models (Cohen's processual model or Goode and Ben-Yehuda's attributional model) to conduct a case study of a material on-the-ground-happening moral panic, or they will consider where the focus of the concept is (or should be) by taking into account shifts that have occurred across the social and political landscape (notably, the move to a 'risk society') *or* by connecting it with a broader theoretical idea (mainly, the literature on moral regulation). Scholars reflecting back across four decades of moral panic research identify these two groupings of studies in terms of 'projects' that are additional to the 'original project' that established the concept (see Dandoy, 2014). The first of these projects is an empirical project (case studies of material panics) and the second an intellectual one (efforts to consider where the focus of the concept is). My approach to the study of moral panic aims to unite these two projects. It does this by providing a framework that will assist researchers to explore and draw out, by way of an inductive process, the unique features of material on-the-ground-happening episodes; to consider the contexts in which these episodes emerge; and to

S. Wright Monod, *Making Sense of Moral Panics*, Palgrave Studies in Risk, Crime and Society, DOI 10.1007/978-3-319-61821-0_4

think about how, once there is a broad body of inductively studied panics, a given episode challenges the analytical model of panic as it currently stands. This is important for establishing some common ground across the field about the shape of the concept and how it might be used to unpack and understand social reactions as they emerge in contemporary times. In this chapter, I explore the work of a group of scholars active in the intellectual project. This is an important discussion, not only to provide readers with a view of developments within the field of moral panic but also to position why the inductive approach that I propose is a critical one.

As indicated, scholars whose work we can group under the intellectual project of moral panic are concerned with where the focus of the concept is (or should be). Ultimately, their aim is to show how material panics can be understood to be extreme examples of something else, something much broader. To this end, these scholars either locate panic within shifts that have occurred across the global social, political and cultural landscape or connect it with a broader theoretical idea. My position is that each of these exercises is a little premature. My argument is that a panic analysis should explore a material case inductively, and in relation to its specific social, cultural and political environment, *in a first instance.* Once a collation of studies conducted in this way is available, we can review them and look at how the conceptual model of moral panic might be updated. It is my position that considering where the focus of the concept is *begins* from this point. Each of the scholars whose work I discuss in this chapter assumes various configurations of the relationship between material episodes of panic, the contextual conditions in which these episodes emerge, the analytical concept and social theory. By exploring these configurations, I will be able to better make the point that the inductive study of situated material episodes matters.

I must acknowledge at this point that there are many more scholars (other than those whose work I discuss in this chapter) concerned with the study of moral panic and who are active in seeking ways to enhance its value. Some, for example, focus on the legacy of moral panic (see Altheide, 2009; Innes, 2005; Garland, 2008; Miller, 2013; Young, 2009), some are concerned with how to overcome its discontents

(Jenkins, 2009; Klocke & Muschert, 2010; Welch, 2006, 2007) and some draw in key insights from other disciplines (Critcher & Pearce, 2013; Dandoy, 2014; Denham, 2013; Hunt, 2011; Smoczyński, 2016; Thompson, 2013). My choice to discuss only a select group is contingent upon a specific set of the debates that are currently dominating the field.

Abandon Panic: The 'Social Scare'

The first work I discuss is that of Sheldon Ungar (1992, 2001). I should note, as the heading for this section suggests, that Ungar (1992, 2001) rejects the concept of moral panic, and so it would seem out of place to discuss his work in a chapter about considerations of where the focus of it is (or should be). But his argument is important for three reasons. First, he makes a case for revisiting conceptual tools (such as moral panic) as contexts change shape. My proposal to evaluate the concept in relation to a broad body of material cases is in line with this position. Second, his understanding of a shift in the global social, political and cultural landscape is the reasoning behind his rejection of the concept. In this way, his work can be linked with those who locate panic within these broader shifts. And third, this reasoning is directly engaged with by other scholars in the intellectual project (mostly by Sean Hier, as we will see in a moment) who use his work to situate their ideas.

Ungar argues that the concept of moral panic is insufficient for analysing concerns about the problems in a *risk society*. Taking a realist position on risk, Ungar's (1992, 2001) view is that the issues that we largely worry about now *warrant* worrying about. Issues such as global warming, nuclear weaponry and bioterrorism threaten the very existence of human life—they are *actual risks* and not imaginary threats. Risk issues also tend to be unpredictable and incalculable, and possibly irreversible, and so there is no way, as researchers, that we can establish the criterion of disproportionality and claim that a reaction we have observed to a particular issue is out of order. We simply can't make a judgement about a level of concern if the level of threat is unknown and reliable objective measures are not available. But these are not the only reasons for why the concept of panic is now redundant, according to Ungar. He argues that a risk society issue always needs a 'real-world' event to precipitate concern and direct interest group enthusiasm, where a panic need only require the efforts of moral entrepreneurs and other claims-makers (Ungar, 2001). He also contends that the media are more likely to report the 'facts' of risk problems—given the reservations of scientific claims—than they are with *moral* assertions where there is relatively more licence to be creative (and thus sensationalist) (Ungar, 2001). Scholars concerned with the ways by which a variety of environmental harms are communicated by the media would dispute this (see, for example, Boykoff, 2013; Buettner, 2010), but, nevertheless, this was Ungar's position at this time. He also argued that the targets of campaigns (the 'folk devils') in a risk society are not the vulnerable or 'distinguishable social types', but the powerful (political authorities, commercial interests). He describes the change this way:

> …claims-making on risk society issues is, in comparison with conventional moral panic issues, hedged in by more apparent and sticky trajectories, by a more equal balance of power on the part of rival claims-makers, and by a comparative absence of distinguishable types of folk devils that evoke deep-seated hostility and fear. (Ungar, 2001, p. 287)

Because he rejects the concept of moral panic for the study of risk problems, the question of where its focus is (or should be) is not important for Ungar. He is keen, however, to have a conceptual tool that scholars can employ to deconstruct material on-the-ground-happening reactions. He proposes an alternative concept that can better conceptualize anxieties of the risk society: the 'social scare' (Ungar, 1992). Whilst it draws on Cohen's (1972) model of moral panic, for Ungar the social scare is less specific and doesn't require a researcher to make a judgement about the appropriateness of a reaction. It is the response to the reaction (by, say, legislators) that can be judged as disproportionate or inappropriate, rather than the reaction (by the public) itself because that is thought to be a reaction to a real (and incalculable) threat. He explains:

> Social scares entail acute episodes of collective fear that accelerate demands in the political (or related) arena. Accelerated demands urge extraordinary responses – solutions that tend to be costly, often simplify problems to the point of caricature, seek to leap-frog prevailing processes for evolving solutions, and can verge on the draconian.... These demands may or may not be acted upon, depending on factors such as the scare intensity and whether it persists, is renewed, or simply disappears. (Ungar, 1992, p. 485)

It could be said that Ungar (1992, 2001) had considerable foresight with his contention that societies are facing (and becoming anxious about) new kinds of threats, *existential* threats. Indeed, anthropogenic climate change is now understood to be not only real but also the single most urgent crisis facing humanity at this point in time (Pemberton, 2016; White & Kramer, 2015). And US President Trump's denial that climate change exists can be seen as a partisan response given the consensus that exists amongst scientists about the reality of the threat and the public, institutional and political demand for curative action (Dunlap, McCright, & Yarosh 2016; Foran, 2016; see also Brisman & South, 2015). Nevertheless, another scholar who is active in the intellectual project of moral panic, Sean Hier (2003), takes (or took, at the time he was writing) direct issue with Ungar's realist view of risk. Indeed, Hier (2003), drawing on the work of Bauman (2000), Giddens (1990, 1991) and Furedi (1997), challenges the very ontology of risk. Risk, he says, is nothing more than a *concept* which helps us to deal with uncertain situations and conditions.[1] In other words, social actors employ the idea of risk and are 'risk conscious' as it offers a sense of calculation and control in late-modern societies where traditional structures of stability (established religion, full employment and the welfare state) have all but fallen away (see Pratt, 2016). I discuss this challenge in more detail in a later section.

Preserve Panic: Three Dimensions

Critcher (2003, 2006, 2008, 2009a, 2009b, 2011) is keen to preserve the panic concept as an analytical tool, but believes that both Cohen's (1972) processual model and Goode and Ben-Yehuda's (1994a, 1994b) attributional model have been used quite carelessly at times. To evaluate the models, Critcher (2003) re-examines a range of 'case studies'—from Ecstasy to video 'nasties' to paedophilia—via the lenses of each model in order to uncover both 'constancies' (aspects that can be seen to be similar across cases) and 'diversions' (aspects of each case that a model of moral panic cannot account for). This is very much in line with my own proposal for a systematic review of studies in order to capture what moral panics definitely are and definitively are not. However, I propose that this exercise be undertaken after each case has been researched in an inductive way, whereas Critcher is working with cases that have already been scrutinized either using Cohen's prescription of phases or Goode and Ben-Yehuda's formula of criteria, and so many subtleties would already have been lost. Nevertheless, Critcher's (2003, p. 154) conclusion is that we cannot yet do without a model of moral panic:

> Where an issue, in whatever form, emerges as a symbolic threat; where the media as a whole accept a single definition of the problem; where there are organised groups supporting the panic and none disputing it; where expert opinion does—or can be presented to—support the diagnosis of the problem; where the state, however laggardly, does institute repressive measures, then we have the basic requirements of the ideal type fulfilled.

That may be the case, but *all* of the cases that Critcher (2003) reviewed had elements about them that exceeded the boundaries of the models. Indeed, his analysis found that each case had features which moral panic analysis alone was unable to reveal (see also Rocheron & Linne 1989). This supports my argument that each case should be approached inductively. Notably, there were particular discourses in each case that were either informed by or generated by the panicked reaction in question: a discourse of sexuality was important in the AIDS panic, for example; a discourse of hedonism was significant in the panic about raves/Ecstasy; and a discourse about the innocence of children was critical to the panic about child sexual abuse (Critcher, 2003). Critcher (2003) then examined what these moral panics *did*—whether they reaffirmed the moral boundaries of society through the nomination of outsiders (see Erikson, 1966) or indicated that these boundaries were being challenged. His overall conclusion was that moral panics can be understood in terms of three dimensions: as a set of identifiable processes (for which a conceptual model is useful), as sets of discourses (pertaining to the specific issue that is being reacted to) and as expressions of moral values (what they functioned to do or achieve) (Critcher, 2003).

As said above, Critcher undertook a review of case studies, which is just what I propose needs to be done. However, I suggest that such a review be done of studies that have been analysed inductively, whereas Critcher examines studies that have been analysed using phases or criteria (which, as discussed, have been drawn from the analysis of a few select cases). He then *applies* the same phases *and* criteria to each of the cases he reviews, thereby subjecting them to yet another layer of deductive analysis. He also doesn't assess how any of the said cases might challenge or bear upon either of the conceptual models that were used. In fact, he argues that the model—specifically, Cohen's model—should be retained for analysis as it is as a model of processes and processes was one of the dimensions that he observed to be present across all of the cases that he looked at. However, if researchers do as Critcher prescribes and continue to look for processes, they will only be able to capture variations in *issues* and not the differences in how the reactions to various issues unfold. His suggestion that researchers also examine discourses and expressions of moral values in their case studies is more promising, though if these are also features to *look for* and if we are to look for them *in* a panic that we have already established deductively, using a set of pre-established processes, then we can expect the concept of moral panic—as prescribed by Cohen's model—to stay as it is.

Critcher also places emphasis upon how the discourse that emerges as dominant in a panic works as an achievement of moral certainty, and so the emphasis is upon the *function* of the panic. The question of 'why' it occurred in the first place, and how the specific social, cultural and political context can help us to understand a particular panic's appearance, is not attended to in any great depth. In a later paper (Critcher, 2009a), he argues that researchers could ask which wider discourses inform and relate to the dominant discourse in the bounded reaction (explicated by either of the models), and who it is that defines who is 'at risk', but he is still tentative about what this could mean for how the concept—the model of panic—might be modified.

Situate Panic: A Culture of Fear

In a later work again, Critcher (2011) considers shifts that have occurred across the broader social and political landscape and suggests that panic can be located within these. Indeed, modern panics, he argues, must be situated in the context of political economy. Most panics up until this point have been seen to have political but not *economic* dimensions. His argument is drawn from an exploration of the ways by which four scholars have argued the case for a *culture of fear* (Altheide, 2002; Bauman, 2007; Furedi, 2005; Glassner, 2009), as this is the broader context in which panics now emerge.

Critcher (2011) finds seven common themes across the work of the four scholars about the culture of fear, some of which are shared by scholars writing about the 'risk society'. First, a central paradox in the culture of fear is that whilst societies are more secure than ever before, there is a persistent sense that the opposite is true and societies are now *less* secure than ever before. Second, the fear in the culture of fear is free floating and not attached to anything in particular. Third, the fear is culturally made—discourses in the public sphere, especially the mass media, are saturated with talk about risky things, people and situations. Whether the public are actually fearful is not known. Fourth, and this is related to the third theme, the news media plays a formative role in spreading messages of fear. The entertainment media does as well, but not to the same extent as the news media. Fifth, the culture of fear prompts over the top responses to social problems. However, these are not always recognized as being over the top. Sixth, in the culture of fear, those defined as deviants are responded to with exceptional levels of hostility. There is also a sense that no one is to be trusted and that strangers must be approached with caution. Last, the culture of fear is about four to five decades old but has gotten more pervasive and intense in the last two of these.

Critcher (2011) notes that each of these themes has implications for moral panic development (and together they have *profound* implications). However, his main objective is to locate panic within the political economy to demonstrate that panics can be seen to serve the fiscal interests of the political elite. To this end, he finds that only Bauman (2007) is attuned to the state's exploiting of the culture of fear for its own gain. Indeed, Bauman suggests that there are political, economic and cultural interests in maintaining a culture of fear. Critcher proposes that if panics are more likely to occur in a culture of fear, and there are certain interests that are rewarded in ensuring that a culture of fear continues, as Bauman indicates, then it is not a stretch by any manner to suggest that moral panics will inevitably serve those interests. This is exactly what Hall et al. (1978) argued in their analysis of mugging. Critcher was part of that research team, so in many ways, he is returning to his critical roots with this line of argument. He suggests that the time has come, in a culture of fear, for researchers to direct their attention towards the political economy of moral panic (Critcher, 2011).

So, in the end, both Ungar and Critcher can be seen to have considered where the focus of the concept is (or should be) by taking into account shifts that have occurred across the social and political landscape. For Ungar, a shift to a risk society brought with it a change in the nature of social reactions, and so a model designed to explicate 'moral panics' no longer had any utility. For Critcher's emphasis at first was in defence of the concept, but later he suggested that the culture of fear, and the exploitation of this by elite groups, meant that a political economy of moral panics was now required. Next, I consider the arguments put forth by Sean Hier. Hier's aim is to widen the focus of the moral panic concept, and he does this by connecting it with the literature on moral regulation.

Risk and Morality: The Converging Sites of 'Anxiety'

Hier's (2002a, 2002b, 2003, 2008, 2011, 2016a, 2016b) work on moral panics is extensive and complex. First, as argued above, he rejects a realist conception of risk that was central to Ungar's (1992, 2001) assessment (and rejection) of the concept of panic. Indeed, Hier (2003) agrees with cultural theorists who argue that risk *language* is used to secure moral ends. Mary Douglas, for example, contends that 'risk provides the secular terms for rewriting scripture' (that is, of what constitutes *sin*) (Douglas, 1992, p. 26; see also Garland, 2008; Lupton, 1999; Moore and Valverde 2000; Mythen 2007; O'Malley & Mugford, 1991). Critcher (2003) also identified that 'risk talk' was a predominant feature in a number of panics: who was *at risk* of AIDS; the *risk to* party goers; *risk inside* and *outside* familial structures. Garland (2003, p. 64) puts it this way:

> ...as chains of interdependence grow longer, and shared moral codes grow thinner, risk management has become a *necessary* moral technology, operationalizing liberalism's twin concern to maximize freedom of action and to reduce that freedom's harmful consequences. (emphasis added)

Ultimately, for Hier (2003, p.19), if 'post moral techniques and discourses of risk management have ended up doing old moral regulation work', then this would suggest that it is not so much that sites of anxiety are shifting (as Ungar argued), but *converging*. Nevertheless, he is still conscious of the shifts that have occurred across the social and political landscape and the implications this has for the development of moral panic. This can be seen in that like Critcher (2003), Hier (2003) adopts a functional explanation of panic. He suggests that in the context of existential (and ontological) insecurity, a sense of community has an urgency to it as it operates to affirm belonging in a world of generalized strangers and confronts the individuation modernity initiates (see also Jenks, 2011; Jewkes, 2015). This is why we are seeing more moral panics in the contemporary era, as what panics 'do' is identify a threat to the group (which in turn *becomes* a group in the identification of a threat). However, the erection and re-erection of the borders of the community are now done under the guise of 'safety' (i.e. the amelioration of risk). Hence, we no longer have folk devils that may be cast aside, but *dangerous others* that we must be protected from (Hier, 2003).

Hier's (2003) work to this point suggests that the character of material moral panics is changing. This, he contends, can be instructive for understanding why they emerge and where the focus of the concept is (and should be). Indeed, Hier (2002b, 2008, 2011) argues that researchers can uncover the foundations of a particular panic by examining the discursive tactics that are used by moral entrepreneurs to stimulate concern and to demonize a target in that panic (see also de Young, 2004, 2008). They will then be able to draw inferences from this knowledge about *why* panics happen. In other words, the unique features of material cases, examined inductively, will enable researchers to figure out what the concept of moral panic reveals and where its focus is (and should be). I, too, propose for the inductive study of situated material reactions. However, I suggest that the study of situated material reactions is a first step towards updating and informing a revision of the *concept* of moral panic. Hier, on the other hand, is not primarily concerned with the shape of the analytical concept as such. He is more concerned with understanding the emergence of material panics and achieving this understanding by connecting material panics with developments in social theory. Further, by imagining material on-the-ground-happening panics not as extraordinary events but as routine episodes, and looking at what they *do* (their function), we are able to explain why they appear without making a normative assessment. If we put at the centre of our research the understanding that material panics contribute to the reproduction of security, we can overcome the critique that moral panic is a loaded concept that tends to be employed by Left-wing scholars in order to challenge cultural politics and expose elite interests. Pertaining to these twin aims, Hier (2002a, 2008, 2011) argues that the proxies of risk, harm and personal responsibility that are characteristic of contemporary panics are also visible in more routine practices of moral regulation under neo-liberalism. Thus, he argues, material moral panics can be seen as volatile manifestations of the more routine project of everyday moral regulation.

Volatile Episodes: Moral Panic and Moral Regulation

Hier (2002b) describes moral behaviours as dispositions and habits of individuals that are constituted and naturalized through a process of a 'calling' to engage in particular practices of 'care for the self' in the contemporary, neo-liberal political era. That is to say, individuals are asked under neo-liberal conditions to take on responsible forms of personal risk management, and, if they do so, they will become moral individuals.[2] Hier (2008) argues that discourses work to make this happen by presenting two figures: the responsible individual and a 'harmful other'. The responsible individual is the subjectivity that the discourse invites a person to enter. The harmful other is an abstract subjectivity that represents the potential threat that risky behaviours pose and the potential harm that could entail from that threat. Hier (2008) offers the example of the discourses which call us (individually) to drink responsibly and how these sit in tension with (and yet rely on) the discourse which represents the collective harm of the drunk driver. We are told that we should manage our drinking practices for two reasons: (i) to avoid becoming the risky other who is harmful to the wider group (i.e. the drunk driver), and (ii) to avoid becoming subject to such harm (i.e. from a drunk driver). However, moral callings in this way are not always heeded (or seen not to be heeded). At such conjunctions, the abstract subjectivity is filled by an identifiable person or persons (a particular person does get drunk and then gets behind the wheel). The threat then becomes more specific. Moreover, it may not be possible for morally responsible individuals undertaking risk-averse practices to prevent all harms that the harmful other enacts (as the drunk driver may crash into other, non-suspecting drivers and pedestrians). When this happens, a *collective* discourse of risk management (erected by concerned citizens) moves into take action against the harmful subject (who can now be recognized as a particular individual or set of individuals). Put simply, when everyday discourses of regulation in which subjects are asked to act responsibly fail to direct the behaviour of one or more individuals, and he, she or they then act in a way that presents a threat, they will be identified as 'dangerous others'. Concerned citizens then place limitations upon his, her or their agency. For Hier (2002b, 2008, 2011), these are the moments of moral panic.

Hier's linking of material moral panics with moral regulation is an astute one, and it certainly neutralizes the claim that the concept of moral panic is a normative tool used by politically invested scholars. But does that mean that all panic reactions are instances of moral regulation, and that the concept will only reveal such instances? The concept was designed to capture the processes by which events, objects and persons (events and objects that are often mindlessly trivial, and persons who present no shred of any threat) are reacted to in extraordinary ways. For example, in response to Hier's work, Critcher (2008, p. 9) suggests that Hier risks 'encompassing potentially *any* topic within its remit' (emphasis added) by connecting moral panic with moral regulation. Rohloff (2011) also observes that he draws his conclusions on only a select number of case studies (see Hier, 2002b, 2008; Hier, Lett, Walby, & Smith, 2011). Hier's focus on discourse *inside* a panic may also be problematic, at least in terms of a notion that the discourse will 'reveal' foundational truths. What is missing from Hier's ideas is a consideration of the specific social, cultural and political context of a panic. Though he acknowledges that contextual shifts have seen changes in how panic discourse appears, his tendency to over-rely on 'insecurity' as a way to explain why we are seeing more moral panics emerge exposes this gap. Critcher (2008, 2009b) goes on to argue that better specification of the scope of moral regulation is needed so that researchers might clarify the boundaries between those issues that are merely dissenters of regulatory discourses and those that are more likely to erupt into panics. He suggests that we work with a dimensional categorization (separate to his own three-dimensional framework for the study of individual cases of moral panic) based upon how an issue is discursively constructed: as a threat to basic values (the moral order dimension); the extent to which there is a proposed solution (the social order dimension); and the regulation of others insofar as it requires the ethical formation of the self (the governmentality dimension) (Critcher, 2008, 2009b). It is those issues that score high on the first two (child sexual abuse, violent crime and asylum seeking) that are potential panics. Issues such as smoking, obesity and sexually transmitted diseases score high only on the third, and so they are not likely to erupt into panics. Critcher (2009b) suggests that it would be difficult to imagine the language of 'evil', which tends to be central in moral panics, being present in discourses about smokers, foodies and careless lovers. Indeed, whilst many groups have labelled Big Tobacco and the sugar industry 'evil', the potential harm that might stem from their products can be avoided if one doesn't buy cigarettes or eat too much sugar.[3] Moreover, these are powerful industries that have the resources to 'fight back' (see Brulle, 2014; McRobbie & Thornton, 1995). On the other hand, if an 'outbreak' of a particular STD could be linked to the practice of casually hooking up with someone found on the dating app Tinder, which has at least two 'panic-stimulating' ingredients already (new sexual relations amongst young people and new media), a panic could erupt.

Critcher (2008) also questions whether the moral regulation literature shares the agenda of critical research, observing Hunt's (1999) outright rejection of any potential relationship (between panic and moral regulation) and a similar hesitancy on behalf of Moore and Valverde (2000).[4] Hier (2008) is quite clear that his intentions for rethinking panic in terms of regulatory processes are about moving beyond what he terms the 'revisionist works' (in particular, de Young, 2004; McRobbie, 1994; McRobbie & Thornton, 1995) which still rely upon 'cognitive, behavioural, and normative measurement criteria' (Hier, 2008, p. 180). Hier seeks, in other words, to understand panic as a rational response, however 'irrational' its appearance seems to the researcher. His urgency to address this concern of the critics might also account for his haste to make links with social theory. However, as argued in Chap. 3, it is generally the *whole* reaction that is denoted by panic researchers as 'irrational', after it has been subject to processes of inflammation and amplification independent of any one party's control. As Critcher (2009a, p. 32) also contends:

> If there is no disparity to identify between the reality of the social problem and its representation—if perhaps the distinction between reality and representation is denied—then the whole political point, the urge to social justice, has been lost.

My own position is similar to Critcher's one. I consider Hier to have made a constructive link which can explain *some* volatile social reactions to *some* events, objects and persons, but I don't accept that it offers a full and final conclusion about where the focus of the concept of moral panic is (or should be). It might be, as he claims, the most defended extension so far (Hier, 2016a), but more contributions to the intellectual project will probably change that. Hier himself now acknowledges that there are shortcomings in the panic-moral regulation connection in a recent work, arguing that it was 'never presented under the guise of a definitive statement on how contemporary moral panics are expressed' (Hier, 2015, p. 371). In another assessment, where he presents a case for a 'good panic', he notes that the notion of moral panic as a volatile moment of moral regulation remains tied to a panic as a negative assessment of a social reaction which is problematic. Panics can be good, he argues, if we imagine them as 'normatively ambivalent operations of power' (Hier, 2016a). I discussed this idea in more detail in Chap. 3.

Decivilizing Episodes: An Eliasian Approach

The work of another scholar, Amanda Rohloff (2008, 2011), connects panic with quite a different idea. Drawing on Norbert Elias's work on civilizing processes, she proposes that moral panic can be seen as short-term decivilizing episodes. The argument begins with Elias's (2000) developmental idea of civilization as a *process* entailing an increase in interdependencies at the local level and the growth of state authorities at the structural level.[5] That is, as populations grow, the division of labour increases so societies become more complex, differentiated and increasingly dependent on each other. This corresponds with an increasing state monopolization over the control of violence and taxation on behalf of the state. Fundamentally, individuals are compelled towards increasing self-restraint as the state moves into a more executive role which is seen as a long-term process that also generates increased mutual identification and a corresponding decrease in cruelty (Rohloff, 2011, see also Mennell, 1990). However, these kinds of civilizing processes were not conceived of by Elias (2000) as linear and unproblematic. Indeed, he argued that 'several types of change, even in opposite directions, can be observed simultaneously' (Elias, 2000, p. 450). Elias (2000) termed these 'opposite' changes '*de*civilizing processes', and others have since proposed that we can identify these through 'symptoms' and criteria (see Mennell, 1990; Fletcher, 1997). However, as Rohloff (2011) argues, whilst decivilizing *symptoms* may appear to be the reverse of civilizing symptoms, it does not follow that decivilizing *processes* are civilizing processes in reverse. In fact, the long chains of interdependencies and the advances in technology that are characteristic of civilizing processes may, in fact, enable decivilizing processes to materialize. One key example where civilizing processes have given rise to decivilizing trends is the rise of the Nazi regime (Elias, 1996).

Rohloff's (2008, 2011) argument is that moral panics can be seen as short-term decivilizing episodes that arise, in part, from civilizing processes. There are three main characteristics to the Eliasian concept of decivilizing processes, as observed by Pratt (2005, p. 259):

> …a shift away from self-restraint towards restraint imposed by external authorities; the development of behaviour and sensibilities that generate the emergence of less even, stable, and differentiated patterns of restraint; and a contraction in the scope of mutual identification between constituent groups and individuals. When these occur they are likely to be accompanied by a decrease in the state monopoly of violence, a shortening of interdependencies, and a concomitant rise of fear, danger, and incalculability.

For Rohloff (2008, 2011), the similarities with this account and moral panic are striking when we consider that panics have the following components: (i) the attribute of concern (rise in fear), (ii) the impetus that 'something must be done' (a shift towards external constraint) and (iii) hostility towards a 'folk devil' (mutual identification decreases). But to avoid merely applying decivilizing symptoms to a moral panic and determining that panics are indeed decivilizing episodes (much the same way as one might apply a moral panic model and pronounce that this or that phenomena qualify as a moral panic), Rohloff (2008, 2011) wants more empirical research to be undertaken on the interplay between civilizing *offensives* (deliberate attempts by a person or group to initiate changes in behaviour of another person or group—to 'civilize' them) and long-term processes (both decivilizing and civilizing). Rohloff (2008, 2011) argues that if it can be firmly established that that offensives may contain decivilizing symptoms, researchers would have a new lens to examine campaigns undertaken by 'moral entrepreneurs' (Becker, 1963) during moral panics, and they would also be able to connect those panics with longer-term historical trends.

She demonstrates this with an example. Using Elias's figurational approach, Rohloff's (2008, 2011) research focuses first on the content of the documentary *An Inconvenient Truth* presented by former US presidential candidate Al Gore. She identifies Gore as a 'moral entrepreneur' and she locates several themes in the campaign to be akin to those that are often seen in moral panics. In the Mods and Rockers case, for example, the media reported statements from local tradesmen, councillors and police about what they would do 'next time' (Cohen, 2002). The event of Hurricane Katrina, along with other disasters, was similarly depicted in *An Inconvenient Truth* as a prediction of things to come. The imagery of Katrina also served to symbolize the dangers of global warming in the same way that Clacton became a code word for clashes between the Mods and Rockers (and the labels 'Mods' and 'Rockers' themselves became terms evoking images of delinquent youth) (Cohen, 2002). Rohloff (2011) then assesses the campaign for signs of either civilizing *or* decivilizing symptoms. She suggests that the campaign might facilitate changes in consumption patterns (presented by Gore to be responsible for the development of climate change), but it may also, for some at least, bring about a sense that those who do not monitor their consumption patterns are deviants, irresponsible others, perhaps even *dangerous others*. In this way, the campaign, or others like it, could, in fact, stimulate moral panics about eco-deviants. Her conclusion is that we might view moral panics as decivilizing episodes which both *further* and *counter* civilizing processes. The call for increased self-restraint with regard to the consumption of consumer goods in *An Inconvenient Truth*, for example, may be seen as reflective of longer-term processes of increasing mutual identification. That is, there are/were *already* trends evident of increased foresight and recognition of the interdependencies of human beings with nature; *already* movements towards consumer restraint. Gore's campaign and its prophecies of doom attempt to accelerate this pattern.

Rohloff's (2008, 2011) focus is very similar to Hier's insofar as she examines the nature of panic discourses in order to make inferences about why material panics emerge and where the focus of the concept is (and should be). Her analysis is similar to Hier's again, in that there doesn't appear to be a concern with how a material panic challenges the shape of the concept of moral panic. It is clear in Rohloff's writings that she doesn't make a clear distinction between moral panics that emerge and play out in real social situations and the concept of moral panic, though it is implied through a consideration of where the focus of the concept is. The same might be said of Hier's work.

Rohloff (2008, 2011) is also keen to dispute the notion that moral panics can be seen in terms of the irrational behaviour of misguided social actors, yet another similarity to Hier. Her argument is that the goal of establishing disproportionality relies on an involved analysis (from an invested position), and therefore closes research to the possibility that a social reaction may not be an irrational peculiarity. The figurational approach for social analysis that Elias uses is attractive in this sense. The approach argues for a 'relative detachment principle' (where the sociologist is neither completely involved nor completely detached from the subject matter), which is viewed as being more conducive to increasing the 'reality congruence' (and decreasing the 'fantasy content') of knowledge (see Bloyce, 2004; Dunning, 1992; Elias, 1978; Maguire, 1988). Rohloff's position is that questions such as 'how do *particular* social problems lend themselves to panic construction?' and 'how do *particular* people become subject to disidentification?' are still conceivable, but that they must come *after* the reaction in question has been subject to inquiry so as to lessen the bias of the researcher intruding into the research (see Rohloff & Wright, 2010). This raises a question of whether the research upon which to make such an assessment be undertaken in the first place, however. Surely, there would be some degree of suspicion about the nature of a reaction that had prompted the researcher's interest and concern? Rohloff tends to assume that researchers will set about studying a moral panic even if they don't necessarily think a panic has occurred! Hier (2016b) also disputes Rohloff's position that she eliminates the criteria of disproportionality from the panic study. He argues that what follows from Rohloff's contention that knowledge might be distorted by experts who make claims (say, by playing up the level of threat) or by the media in translating the technical language is a reaction that is based on a sense that there is an exaggerated threat. Therefore, the criterion of disproportionality is reproduced in Rohloff's accounts, albeit perhaps inadvertently. I should reiterate here that my position, which I share with many others, including Critcher (2009a, 2011), Cohen (1972, 2002), Garland (2008) and Young (2011), is that a moral panic *is* a disproportionate reaction to a perceived problem.

Implications

So, it would seem that the answer to where the focus of the concept of moral panic is (or should be) remains elusive, or at least a consensus about what that answer could be does. I suggest that this is because different scholars observed different relationships between material panics, the concept of panic, the specific social, cultural and political contexts in which panics have occurred, and social theory. Ungar (1992, 2001) placed his focus upon the relationship between material panics and late-modern contextual conditions, which he argued rendered the concept of moral panic problematic. Critcher (2003, 2006, 2008, 2009a, 2009b, 2011) focused upon how the concept might be renewed for application across material cases, but left alone how these cases might initiate changes to the shape of the concept. At first, he also demonstrated a tentativeness about whether *contexts* mattered. Later, he indicated that social, cultural and political contexts were important with his call for a political economy of moral panic. Hier (2002a, 2002b, 2003, 2008, 2011, 2016a, 2016b) focused on how the discourse inside a material panic revealed where the focus of the concept is (and should be). He concluded that moral panics were volatile manifestations that happen alongside more routine processes of moral regulation. Rohloff (2008, 2011) also forged a relationship between material panics and social theory, using the figurational sociology of Elias. She did not overtly conceive of the concept of panic as something analytically distinct from a material panic, and so did not encourage researchers to draw on material reactions to suggest changes to the shape of the concept of panic. Both Hier and Rohloff were additionally concerned to place some distance between moral panic and the criterion of disproportionality, and demonstrate material panics as rational reactions.

It is useful, however, that each of these scholars identifies a configuration of relationships between material events, contextual conditions, analytical models and social theory, though each assembles this configuration differently. This alone indicates that the leap to make connections between moral panic and theory is premature, even though the objectives of their studies are defensible, and the levels of sophistication in their accounts are often outstanding. My position is that connections between moral panic and social theory will be more effectively made after we have made significant headway towards updating the concept of moral panic in a way that is responsive to inductive case study analysis in complex contemporary social contexts. To make sure that any such headway is made, there first needs to be a clear, systemic and transparent approach for the study of material on-the-ground-happening reactions (that are suspected to be moral panics).

In the next chapter, I examine the relationship between the news media and moral panic, outline the practices of making *crime* news and discuss the significance of digital, social and mobile media in panic development, with a particular focus on social media.

Notes

1. Hunt (2003) also challenged the ontology of risk at the same time as Hier. He argued that despite the greater potential impact of today's risks, there appears no qualitative distinction to justify an epochal change.
2. The 'calling' is on behalf of spatially and temporally situated bodies such as the church, professional organizations and interest groups. For Hier (2008), the state only comes into the equation by responding to limit the agency of those who do not heed 'calls'.

3. Lupton (2015) notes that in health discourses, risk is tied to notions of disgust and revulsion, which can lead to the dehumanization of some groups and resulting in the unjust treatment of them. She draws on the example of smokers, whose 'disgusting' habit can result in them being seen to be less deserving of medical attention.
4. This may reflect the tendencies of analyses informed by Foucault's 'governmentality' to view concerns as conceptually and epistemologically incompatible with sociological approaches (see Garland, 1997).
5. Elias (1984) uses the terms 'civilized' in a detached (non-normative) sense to represent the configuration of state processes, social interdependencies and the internalization of constraint among individuals.

References

Altheide, D. (2002). *Creating fear: News and the construction of crisis.* New York: Aldine de Gruyter.

Altheide, D. (2009). *Terror post 9/11 and the media* (Vol. 4). New York: Peter Long Publishing.

Bauman, Z. (2000). *Liquid modernity.* Cambridge, UK: Malden.

Bauman, Z. (2007). *Liquid times: Living in an age of uncertainty.* Cambridge: Polity Press.

Becker, H. (1963). *Outsiders: Studies in the sociology of deviance.* New York: The Free Press.

Bloyce, D. (2004). Research is a messy process: A case study of a figurational approach to conventional issues in social science research. *Graduate Journal of Social Science, 1*(1), 144–166.

Boykoff, M. T. (2013). Public enemy no. 1?: Understanding media representations of outlier views on climate change. *American Behavioral Scientist, 57*(6), 796–817. doi:10.1177/0002764213476846.

Brisman, A., & South, N. (2015). New "Folk Devils", denials and climate change: Applying the work of Stanley Cohen to green criminology and environmental harm. *Critical Criminology, 23*(4), 449–460. doi:10.1007/s10612-015-9288-1.

Brulle, R. J. (2014). Institutionalizing delay: Foundation funding and the creation of U.S. climate change counter-movement organizations. *Climatic Change, 122*(4), 681–694. doi:10.1007/s10584-013-1018-7.

Buettner, A. (2010). Climate change in the media: Climate denial, Ian Plimer, and the staging of public debate. *MEDIANZ: Media Studies Journal of Aotearoa New Zealand, 9*(1), 79–97. doi:10.11157/medianz-vol12iss1id48.
Cohen, S. (1972). *Folk devils and moral panics*. Herts, England: Paladin.
Cohen, S. (2002). *Folk devils and moral panics* (3rd ed.). London: Routledge.
Critcher, C. (2003). *Moral panics and the media*. Buckingham, England: Open University Press.
Critcher, C. (Ed.). (2006). *Critical readings: Moral panics and the media*. Berkshire: Open University Press.
Critcher, C. (2008). Moral panic analysis: Past, present and future. *Sociology Compass, 2*(4), 1127–1144.
Critcher, C. (2009a). Widening the focus: Moral panics as moral regulation. *British Journal of Criminology, 49*, 17–34.
Critcher, C. (2009b, November). *Onto the highway or up a cul-de-sac? The future destination of moral panic analysis*. Presented at the Special research seminar on moral panics, Department of Sociology and Communications, School of Social Sciences. London, England: Brunel University.
Critcher, C. (2011). For a political economy of moral panics. *Crime, Media, Culture, 7*(3), 259–275.
Critcher, C., & Pearce, J. M. (2013). A missing dimension: The social psychology of moral panics. In C. Krinsky (Ed.), *The Ashgate research companion to moral panics* (pp. 371–386).
Dandoy, A. (2014). Towards a Bourdieusian frame of moral panic analysis: The history of a moral panic inside the field of humanitarian aid. *Theoretical Criminology*. doi:10.1177/1362480614553522.
de Young, M. (2004). *The day care ritual abuse moral panic*. Jefferson, NC: McFarland and Company.
de Young, M. (2008). The day care ritual abuse moral panic: A sociological analysis. *Sociology Compass, 2*(6), 1719–1733.
Denhem, B. E. (2013). Intermedia agenda setting and the construction of moral panics: On the media and policy influence of Steven Soderbergh's Traffic. In *The Ashgate research companion to moral panics* (pp. 319–333). Surrey: Ashgate.
Douglas, M. (1992). *Risk and blame: Essays in cultural theory*. London: Routledge.
Dunlap, R. E., McCright, A. M., & Yarosh, J. H. (2016). The political divide on climate change: Partisan polarization widens in the U.S. *Environment:*

Science and Policy for Sustainable Development, 58(5), 4–23. doi:10.1080/00139157.2016.1208995.

Dunning, E. (1992). Figurational sociology and the sociology of sport: Some concluding remarks. In E. Dunning & C. Rojek (Eds.), *Sport and leisure in the civilising process: Critique and counter-critique* (pp. 221–284). Basingstoke: Macmillan.

Elias, N. (1978). *What is sociology?* New York: Columbia University Press.

Elias, N. (1984). *What is sociology?*. Columbia University Press.

Elias, N. (1996). *The Germans: Power struggles and the development of habitus in the nineteenth and twentieth centuries*. Oxford, England: Polity Press.

Elias, N. (2000). *The civilising process: Sociogenetic and psychogenetic investigations* (Revised). Oxford: Blackwell.

Erikson, K. (1966). *Wayward puritans*. New York: Macmillan.

Fletcher, J. (1997). *Violence and civilization: An introduction to the work of Norbert Elias*. Cambridge, England.

Foran, C. (2016, December 25). Donald Trump and the triumph of climate-change denial. *The Atlantic*. Retrieved from https://www.theatlantic.com/politics/archive/2016/12/donald-trump-climate-change-skeptic-denial/510359/.

Furedi, F. (1997). *The culture of fear: Risking taking and the morality of low expectations*. London, England: Cassell.

Furedi, F. (2005). *Politics of fear*. London: Continuum.

Garland, D. (1997). Governmentality and the problem of crime. *Theoretical Criminology, 1*(2), 173–214.

Garland, D. (2003). The risk of risk. In *Risk and morality*, 48–86. Toronto, Canada: University of Toronto Press.

Garland, D. (2008). On the concept of moral panic. *Crime, Media, Culture, 4*, 9–30.

Giddens, A. (1990). *The consequences of modernity*. Cambridge: Polity Press.

Giddens, A. (1991). *Modernity and self-identity. Self and society in the late modern age*. Cambridge: Polity Press.

Glassner, B. (2009). *The culture of fear: Why Americans are afraid of the wrong things; [crime, drugs, minorities, teen moms, killer kids, mutant microbes, plane crashes, road rage, & so much more]*. New York, NY: Basic Books.

Goode, E., & Ben-Yehuda, N. (1994a). *Moral panics: The social construction of deviance*. Oxford, England: Blackwell.

Goode, E., & Ben-Yehuda, N. (1994b). Moral panics: Culture, politics, and social construction. *Annual Review of Sociology, 20*, 149–171.

Hall, S, Critcher, C., Jefferson, T., Clarke, J., & Roberts, B. (1978). *Policing the crisis: Mugging, the state, and law and order*. London: Macmillan.

Hier, S. (2002a). Conceptualizing moral panic thought a moral economy of harm. *Critical Sociology, 28*(3), 311–334.

Hier, S. (2002b). Raves, risk, and the ecstasy panic: A case study in the subversive nature of moral regulation. *Canadian Journal of Sociology, 27*(1), 33–59.

Hier, S. (2003). Risk and panic in the late modernity: Implications of the converging sties of social anxiety. *British Journal of Criminology, 54*(1), 2–20.

Hier, S. (2008). Thinking beyond moral panic: Risk, responsibility, and the politics of moralization. *Theoretical Criminology, 12*(1), 73–190.

Hier, S. (2011). Tightening the focus: Moral panic, moral regulation and liberal government: Tightening the focus. *The British Journal of Sociology, 62*(3), 523–541. doi:10.1111/j.1468-4446.2011.01377.x.

Hier, S. (2015). The cultural politics of contemporary moral panic studies: Reflections on a changing research agenda. *Czech Sociological Review, 51*(3), 362. doi:10.13060/00380288.2015.51.3.181.

Hier, S. (2016a). Good moral panics? Normative ambivalence, social reaction, and coexisting responsibilities in everyday life. *Current Sociology*. doi:10.1177/0011392116655463.

Hier, S. (2016b). Moral panic, moral regulation, and the civilizing process: Moral panic, moral regulation, and the civilizing process. *The British Journal of Sociology, 67*(3), 414–434. doi:10.1111/1468-4446.12201.

Hier, S. P., Lett, D., Walby, K., & Smith, A. (2011). Beyond folk devil resistance: Linking moral panic and moral regulation. *Criminology and Criminal Justice, 11*(3), 259–276. doi:10.1177/1748895811401977.

Hunt, A. (2003). Risk and moralization in everyday life. *Morality and risk* (pp. 165–192). Toronto, Canada: University of Toronto Press.

Hunt, A. (2011). Fractious rivals? Moral panics and moral regulation. *Moral panic and the politics of anxiety* (pp. 53–70). Milton Park, England: Routledge.

Hunt, A. (1999). Anxiety and social explanation: Some anxieties about anxiety. *Journal of Social History, 32*(3), 509–528.

Innes, M. (2005). A short history of the idea of moral panic. *Crime, Media, Culture, 1*(1), 106–111.

Jenkins, P. (2009). Failure to launch: Why do some social issues fail to detonate moral panics? *British Journal of Criminology, 49*, 35–47.

Jenks, C. (2011). The context of and emergent and enduring concept. *Crime, Media, Culture, 7*(3), 229–236.

Jewkes, Y. (2015). *Media and crime* (3rd ed.). Los Angeles: Sage.

Klocke, B. V., & Muschert, G. W. (2010). A hybrid model of moral panics: Synthesizing the theory and practice of moral panic research. *Sociology Compass, 4*(5), 295–309.

Lupton, D. (1999). *Risk and sociocultural theory: New directions and perspectives*. Cambridge: Cambridge University Press.

Lupton, D. (2015). The pedagogy of disgust: the ethical, moral and political implications of using disgust in public health campaigns. *Critical Public Health, 25*(1), 4–14. https://doi.org/10.1080/09581596.2014.885115

Maguire, J. (1988). Doing figurational sociology: Some preliminary observations on methodological issues sensitizing concepts. *Leisure Studies, 7*, 187–193.

McRobbie, A., & Thornton, S. (1995). Rethinking "moral panic" for multimediated social worlds. *British Journal of Sociology, 46*(4), 559–574.

McRobbie, Angela. (1994). Folk devils fight back. *New Left Review, 203*, 107–116.

Mennell, S. (1990). Decivilising processes: Theoretical significance and some lines of research. *International Sociology, 5*(2), 205–223.

Miller, T. (2013). Tracking moral panic as a concept. In *The Ashgate research companion to moral panics* (pp. 37–54). Surrey: Ashgate.

Moore, D., & Valverde, M. (2000). Maidens at risk: "Date rape drugs" and the formation of hybrid risk knowledges. *Economy and Society, 29*(4), 514–531.

Mythen, G. (2007). Reappraising the risk society thesis: Telescopic insight or myopic vision? *Current Sociology, 55*(6), 793–813.

O'Malley, P., & Mugford, S. (1991). Moral technology: The political agenda of random drug testing. *Social Justice, 18*(4), 122–227.

Pemberton, A. (2016). Environmental victims and criminal justice: Proceed with caution. In T. Spapens, R. White, & M. Kluin (Eds.), *Environmental crime and its victims: Perspectives within green criminology* (pp. 63–86). London: Routledge.

Pratt, J. (2005). Child sexual abuse: Purity and danger in an age of anxiety. *Crime, Law and Social Change, 43*, 263–287.

Pratt, J. (2016). Risk control, rights and legitimacy in the limited liability state. *British Journal of Criminology*. doi:10.1093/bjc/azw065.

Rocheron, Y., & Linne, O. (1989). Aids, moral panic and opinion polls. *European Journal of Communication, 4*(4), 409–434.

Rohloff, A. (2008). Moral panics as decivilising processes: Towards an Elisian approach. *New Zealand Sociology, 23*(1), 66–76.
Rohloff, A. (2011). Extending the concept of moral panic: Elias, climate change and civilization. *Sociology, 45*(4), 634–649.
Rohloff, A., & Wright, S. (2010). Beyond the heursitic: Moral panic and social theory. *Current Sociology, 58*(3), 403–419.
Smoczynski, R. (2016). Mapping new research directions in the sociology of moral panic. *Studia Socjologiczne, 3*(222), 9–29.
Thompson, K. (2013). Cultural trauma and moral panic: 9/11 and the mosque at ground zero affair. In *The Ashgate research companion to moral panics* (pp. 387–400). Surrey: Ashgate.
Ungar, S. (1992). The rise and (relative) decline of global warming as a social problem. *The Sociological Quarterly, 33*(4), 483–501.
Ungar, S. (2001). Moral panic versus the risk society: The implications of the changing sites of social anxiety. *British Journal of Sociology, 52*(2), 271–292.
Welch, M. (2006). *Scapegoats of September 11th: Hate crimes and state crimes in the war on terror*. Piscataway: Rutgers University Press.
Welch, M. (2007). Moral panic, denial and human rights: Scanning the spectrum from overreaction to underreaction. In D. Downes, P. Rock, C. Chinkin, & C. Gearty (Eds.), *Crime, social control and human rights: From moral panics to states of denial. Essays in honour of Stanley Cohen* (pp. 92–106). Collumpton: Willan Publishing.
White, R., & Kramer, R. C. (2015). Critical criminology and the struggle against climate change ecocide. *Critical Criminology, 23*(4), 383–399. doi:10.1007/s10612-015-9292-5.
Young, J. (2009). Moral panic: Its origins in resistance, ressentiment, and the translation of fantasy into reality. *British Journal of Criminology*, 49, 4–16.
Young, J. (2011). Moral panics and the transgressive other. *Crime, Media, Culture, 7*(3), 245–258.

5

Media in a Moral Panic

The news media is integral to moral panic construction, although, as Reed (2015) demonstrates, the Salem witch trials succeeded without it. As argued in Chap. 2, Cohen (1972) observed that the practices of news-making were instrumental in the initial stages of the reaction to the Mods and Rockers and remained central as the panic developed. Hall, Critcher, Jefferson, Clarke, and Roberts (1978) found that the news media was dependent on information from the police and the judiciary, and that an analysis of this relationship could help to explain how the panic about mugging got underway. Goode and Ben-Yehuda (1994) didn't place quite as much importance on the media in their analyses as did Cohen and Hall et al. As argued in Chap. 2, panics in the USA (where Goode and Ben-Yehuda were focused) are more dependent on the rhetorical activities of interest groups than they are on media practices. McRobbie (1994) argued that the emergence of new media platforms in the 1990s meant that there were many more vehicles for 'right-thinking' people and other interested parties to voice their claims than there had been before. She also suggested that a crowded media marketplace would mean that some media would routinely sensationalize ordinary events in order to be competitive. These changes

S. Wright Monod, *Making Sense of Moral Panics*, Palgrave Studies in Risk, Crime and Society, DOI 10.1007/978-3-319-61821-0_5

meant that panics would develop quite differently than they had done before, and that folk devils would be able to 'fight back'. So far, only a handful of scholars have attempted to consider how panics emerge in complex media 'ecosystems' of multiple sites, platforms and tools, where content is co-created and shared amongst 'networked publics'.

In this chapter, I do three things. First, I explore in detail the relationship between the news media and moral panic, drawing primarily from understandings developed in both Cohen's (1972) and Hall et al.'s (1978) analyses. Whilst contemporary media ecosystems have altered practices of communication, most people still engage with the mainstream news media (Mitchell & Holcomb, 2016) and prefer to do so when consuming 'the news' (Costera Meijer & Kormelink, 2015), so it (the mainstream news media) still matters for understanding how panics develop, and the insights about how and why it matters from the original project of moral panic remain valuable. Indeed, it was these insights that were critical to the construction of the *concept* of moral panic that is still very much used by scholars to make sense of social reactions that appear to be out of proportion to an objective reality.

Second, I outline the practices of making *crime* news. Moral panic became important in criminology for its capacity to demonstrate the practices by which the media define and distort the images of those who have deviated, which can then lead to unjust practices of exclusion. In turn, whilst it is not the case that news about a deviant act or person will always develop into a moral panic, or that every moral panic is one about a deviant act or person (certainly, as indicated, there have been moral panics documented about all manner of events, objects and persons—see Chap. 1), insights from media criminology, particularly those about the processes of making outsiders and legitimizing action against them in the media, should remain critical to an understanding of the relationship between the news media and moral panics, as well as to any extensions of the panic concept (see Maneri, 2013; Wright, 2015). Again, whilst the practices of communicating about crime have changed, and we now have media ecosystems, as Jewkes (2015) notes, the messages remain the same, and the core understandings about the ways in which these messages are delivered are still relevant.

Third, I discuss the significance of digital, social and mobile media in panic development, with a particular focus on social media. In lieu of a broad body of empirical work into how moral panics play out in contemporary media ecosystems, I draw insights from media and communication studies, politics, youth culture and marketing. Research into media within these disciplines can tell us much about what social media is, does and enables that are of particular bearing to panic research.

Media and Making Panics

An examination of Cohen's (1972) inventory stage and one of Hall et al.'s (1978) understanding of the structural relationships between the news media and institutional elites illustrates that the media are involved in a panic in three key ways: *amplifying a problem*, *shaping up a folk devil* and *setting an agenda*. As I will discuss in more detail further below, the news media will engage in these practices for a number of reasons, not least of which is a vested interest in meeting commercial ends. Panics attract readers and viewers who in turn attract advertising dollars.

An event or happening is *amplified* and made to appear bigger and of more significance than it actually is or was by way of several practices. Cohen (1972) observed that in the reports about the Mods and Rockers, their actions and behaviours were exaggerated and distorted, more incidences were predicted and a set of key markers were drawn upon in such a way that they came to symbolize the episode. As discussed in Chap. 2, headlines and article text used sensational phrases and words such as 'riot', 'battle', 'orgy of destruction' and 'screaming mob' to describe the events and the people who were involved. The numbers of young people involved in the incidents on the beaches at Clacton and other nearby towns were inflated, the nature of the violence was overemphasized and the extent of the damage was overstated. Plural words were used to describe something that happened once (reporting that boats were overturned, when only one actually had, for example), repeatedly reporting one event several times and reporting rumours as though they were cold hard facts all served to further distort the image of what was really going on (Cohen, 1972).

There were also suggestions that further clashes were inevitable and that the damage would be far worse than in the initial confrontations between the Mods and Rockers. What is particularly important about this *predictive* feature for Cohen (1972) is that it not only alerted the potential Mods and Rockers to the places where excitement could be found (consequently triggering a predicted event) but it also attracted the attention of the local community *and* offered a justification for increased control by the authorities. If seemingly small or benign events could be interpreted as precursors of something larger and more damaging, they could be quickly 'nipped in the bud' with retaliatory action. There were also reports of non-events (where a predicted incident *failed* to occur) which emphasized elements that might have occurred whilst downplaying the elements that did not. Cohen (1972) argues that referring back to predictions in this way amassed a sense of truth about them, despite the ways in which actual events transpired completely contradicted this truth.

Particular words and images were used to communicate 'the facts' about the confrontations between the Mods and Rockers, and these came to *symbolize* the episode as a whole. The name of the town in which the first incident had occurred, Clacton, was used as a way to refer to what could possibly happen in other towns: 'we don't want another Clacton'. Styles of dress and how individuals wore their hair became key identifiers by which the police, the media and members of the general public could locate a Mod or a Rocker and be vigilant towards their actions. The Mods and Rockers themselves each learnt about what they *should* wear and about what kind of things they were *expected* to do when they found the beaches where all the excitement was. They would subsequently pose for press photographers in ways they thought a Mod or a Rocker might do, having read about these characters in the news. In turn, these images taken of the Mods and Rockers crystallized the understandings of them by others (Cohen, 1972). As a result, the labels 'Mods' and 'Rockers' used to describe these individuals became symbolic terms for understanding the events that seemed to continue to unfold and the negative emotions experienced by audiences about them (shock, horror, despair, concern, fear, threat and foreboding).

Hall et al.'s (1978) study emphasized the significance of discursive linking or 'convergence' of two issues by the media. This occurs where new events and practices are talked about in terms of other events and practices already well understood so as to suggest that they are alike in their nature. If the old and known about event or practice is understood to be threatening, so too will the new event or practice be understood to be as well. Hall et al. (1978, p. 223) use the example of 'student hooliganism' to illustrate this practice:

> Convergence occurs when two or more activities are linked in the process of signification as to implicitly or explicitly draw parallels between them. Thus the image of 'student hooliganism' links student protest to the separate problem of hooliganism—whose stereotypical characteristics are already part of socially available knowledge.... In both cases the net effect is amplification, not in the real events being described, but in their threat potential for society.

Each of these practices that the media undertake when there appears to be a problem to report about—predicting, symbolizing and converging—contributes to amplifying that problem and making it appear bigger than it is.

Locating and *shaping up a folk devil* serve to refine the nature of the threat and allow audiences to assess the suitability of proposed remedies. In Cohen's (1972) account, much of the legwork for this practice was achieved with the practices of symbolization as just described. Four decades of panic analysis shows us, however, that the process of shaping up the folk devil is unique in each individual case and is dependent upon the nature of the precipitating event or events, the interests of the moral entrepreneurs, and whether the proposed devil has access to social or economic capital and can resist the label. de Young (2004) demonstrated, for example, that child care workers in the satanic ritual abuse panic were able to resist their demonization in part by drawing on their established esteem as professional nurturers. If a proposed devil is something like an inanimate object (say, a series of comic books) or a disease (say, Ebola), then it depends upon whether the corporate owner (the comic book producer or distributor) or caretaker (the health authority) is able to swiftly turn things around. Sometimes, the threat does not become clear until quite some time into an episode. At other times, its nature changes shape and might seem quite removed from the initial precipitator event. Nevertheless, the folk devil, in whatever guise it appears in, must come to be seen in negative terms in a way that is explicit, stereotypical and 'sharper than reality'. Cohen (1972) argues that the media achieves this by constantly making negative references to the said folk devil, which serves to strip away any former positive or neutral connotations they (or it) may have had. He describes how during this process, identifiers that were associated with the Mods and Rockers (style of clothing, way of wearing their hair and their vehicles) came to be seen as 'badges of delinquency'. Cohen (1972) observed that the media also drew on dramatic interviews that journalists had conducted with 'representative' individuals from both groups. He argues that whilst these interviews were likely to be genuine, reporters probably chose to interview those they imagined to be most like a thuggish-type 'hooligan'. Hall et al.'s (1978) study drew attention to the ways by which the application of a new label—mugging—prohibited audiences from understanding a regular crime in a familiar run-of-the-mill way. The new label gave regular crimes a sense of novelty, which the press then emphasized by claiming that mugging was a 'frightening new strain of crime' (Hall et al., 1978). In this way, the shaping up of the folk devil was intertwined with the process of amplifying a problem.

Setting an agenda is achieved by defining what the nature of the threat is and by 'calling for action', often a particular action. In Cohen's account, the amplification of the problem and shaping up of a folk devil that had taken place in the inventory was later extended and sharpened up via a range of opinion pieces that were either of the media (editorials, letters to the editor) or in the media (excerpts from speeches, sermons and political statements). These opinions explained why the problem was developing (orientation); the nature of who the Mods and the Rockers were and what kind of antics they were up to (images); and why they behaved like they did (causation). This set of opinions offered a sense that 'something should be done' before things got 'out of control'. Thereafter, Cohen (1972) recorded a variety of solutions proposed by many different reactors (ranging from banning all Mods and all Rockers from beachside towns to practices of public shaming). All reactors were in agreement that whatever action was taken, it needed to be drastic and implemented immediately. What eventuated, after several parliamentary readings, was the Malicious Damage Act of 1964. This act was written to strengthen and widen existing laws relating to vandalism, but ultimately, as Cohen (1972) described, it had few real teeth and was more of a gesture designed to dampen down the emotion relating to the events. He noted that the first reading of the bill, one month following the events at Clacton, drew on the images that were developing in the media inventory about the clashes (but didn't yet use the terminology of the Mods and Rockers, which Cohen attributed to the symbolization not yet having taken full affect). In the second reading, another two months later, 12 of the 16 members in the debate mentioned the clashes on the beaches and seven members specifically referred to 'the Mods and Rockers' by name. By this stage, the inventory phase was well underway.

Hall et al. (1978) saw a different trajectory. They argued that the professional demands of impartiality, balance and objectivity mean that the media routinely engage with 'accredited experts' and 'opinions of the powerful'. These experts provide an initial definition for a given issue (and so are *primary* definers). This initial definition is then interpreted by the media and reworked into language that the respective media audience will be familiar with (in this way, the media are *secondary* definers). Whilst some original meaning will invariably be lost via the process, Hall et al. (1978) argued that in this way, the media consciously or unconsciously reproduce the definitions of the powerful. In turn, these groups are afforded the ability to frame events and limit the ways by which they can be thought about.

Both Cohen and Hall et al. were anxious to demonstrate how the routine practices of news-making can lend themselves to the construction of a moral panic. Additionally, it was the practices of reporting about *crime* and *deviance* that was seen to be central to the panic about the Mods and Rockers and about the panic over mugging. Particularly important to both Cohen and Hall et al. were the ritualized ways by which deviants are publically labelled and symbolically cast aside by the media as moral boundaries were redrawn (see Innes, 2005). This intimate and important connection has not always made its way into panic studies of a more general sort (i.e. those not about crimes) (Maneri, 2013). In the next section, I look in detail at the routine practices of news-making *about crime* to show what is particular about them and why they are able to grasp a hold on the ways in which audiences think.

Making Crime News

The media are recognized as being a particularly powerful agent in informing public discourses on issues of crime and justice (Altheide, 2002; Peelo, 2006; Reiner, 2002). As a result, a great deal of energy has been devoted to understanding the relationship between crime reporting and media audiences. Some scholars argue that because most people do not experience crime first-hand, but learn of it through the media, the media is a key influencer (Barak, 1994; Burns & Crawford, 1999; Hans & Dee, 1991; Surette, 1988, 2015). Others, such as Katz (1988), argue that audiences are drawn to the media depictions of crime for their 'daily moral workout' via which the boundaries of a community become known (see also Peelo, 2005). What Katz meant by this was that when we read or hear about what other people got caught for and got punished for, we are reminded of what *not* to do. Crime news also produces a sense of collective consensus amongst audiences. Katz (1988, p. 64) asserts:

> The reading of crime is a collective, ritual experience. Read daily by a large portion of the population, crime news generates emotional experiences in individual readers, experiences which each reader can assume are shared by many others. Although each may read in isolation, phenomenologically the experience may be a collective, emotional 'effervescence' of moral indignation.

There have also been questions in this body of work asked about whether the media can cause deviant behaviour by unjustly stereotyping some groups and individuals leading to self-fulfilling prophecies, as well as questions about how crime entertains us but also leaves us fearful (see Garland, 2001; Reiner, 2002; Greer & Reiner, 2012).

News about crime is constructed within a context of institutional codes and corporate demands, as is all news (Jewkes, 2015). As audiences, we understand 'the news' to provide a social good of sorts, and we hold that principles of objectivity and transparency underlie news-making practices. Whilst there may be some truth to this, it is also a fact that all news organizations are corporate organizations that need to make a profit. As identified earlier, news stories are essentially consumer products, something we (the public) will purchase and engage with if we are inclined to do so, for whatever reason (Cohen & Young, 1981). The more attractive this product is to us, the more inclined we will be to purchase it.

Two processes are involved in the assembly of this consumer product in order to make it more attractive. The first of these is a process of *selection* which is guided by a set of *news values.* Many events take place and all sorts and scales of incidents happen in daily life, yet only a handful of them will make the news. News values are 'qualities of events' that when present 'recommends them for inclusion in the news product' (Golding & Elliot, 1979, p. 114). News values determine what is *newsworthy* or not and what events and happenings *should* make the news. Nowhere are these news values written down, but news professionals will admit to having a sense of what is newsworthy and will make 'good copy' (Greer, 2013). Galtung and Ruge (1965) produced a typology of news values, identifying 12 general news values that continue to remain relevant for many newsrooms and different kinds of news reports. This was updated by Harcup and O'Neill (2001), and updated again to account for the role of social media in news-making practices by Harcup and O'Neill (2016). Criminologists examining the ways in which news is produced about crime argue that deviance and crime are significant news values in themselves. As Ericson et al. (1987, p. 4) observe: 'deviance is *the* defining characteristic of what journalists regard as newsworthy' (see also Ericson, Baranek, & Chan, 1991; Greer, 2013). This aside, a set of specific news values to guide the selection of events and happenings that become crime news have been observed (Greer, 2013; Jewkes, 2015; see also Chibnall, 1977; Ericson et al., 1987; Reiner, 2002). Whilst Greer (2013) notes six news values and Jewkes (2015) lists 12, I suggest the following nine are the most important for investigating the relationship between the media and crime in the contemporary era.

The first of these is *violence.* The salience of violence in news reports is observed by Hall et al. (1978, p. 68):

> Violence represents a basic violation of the person; the greatest personal crime is 'murder', bettered only by the murder of a law-enforcement agent, a policeman. Violence is also the ultimate crime against property and against the State. It thus represents a fundamental rupture in the social order. The use of violence marks the distinction between those who are *of* society and those who are *outside* it. (original emphases)

Indeed, violence is such a staple of crime news that most reports about crime in Western contexts are about violent crime (Ericson et al., 1991; Reiner, 2002; Jewkes, 2015; Greer & Reiner, 2012; Greer, 2013). A study conducted in Britain, for example, found that up to 65% of crime news was about interpersonal violence, when at the same time, police statistics had recorded only about 6% of crime as interpersonal violence (Williams & Dickinson cited in Reiner, 2002).

The second crime news value is *proximity*, or how nearby or relevant to one's own life an event can be shown to be to the audience. Proximity can be by way of location or by way of culture (Jewkes, 2015). Audiences are more likely to be disturbed by something that happens in their own neighbourhood than they are by the same event happening across town. Equally, people living in Western countries are more likely to be disturbed by events in other Western nations, even those that are far away, more so than they might be by similar events happening in places that are relatively close, but within another culture.

The third crime news value is *risk.* News items are valuable if they suggest that danger is about and that the reader is a potential victim. As Stanko and Lee (2003) observe, violence is often presented in the media in a way that lifts it out of its context to suggest that it can occur anytime, to anyone and anywhere. Moore (2013) argues that the media also construct 'cautionary tales' when reporting about criminal events. Cautionary tales are stories which highlight threats to the self by placing emphasis on the actions of the victim. Moore (2013) argues that close analysis of stories about rape (in taxis, at festivals on campuses), for example, finds that they are stories warning about the risk of *catching* a taxi and about *going to* a music festival. They are stories about careless women (not predatory men) that function to alert women to take precautions.

A sense of the *extraordinary* is the fourth crime news value. The more unusual qualities a crime has, the more it offers itself as 'good copy'. A crime journalist in New Zealand noted the newsworthiness of a murder of a fireman whose handless body washed up on a Wellington beach in July 2006:

> It was classic … body on the beach, hands cut off. You know—what it's all about. (*Respondent A*, cited in Wright, 2010, p. 119)

The fifth news value is *personification* or reporting on individuals. 'Fall from grace' situations, where people in positions of power of high social status can be revealed to have engaged in deviant sexual activity, are particularly attractive for these purposes, as are their involvement in drug offences or abuses of their status. Greer and McLaughlin (2013) refer to this as 'taking scalps'. They argue that the more important the individual or institutional scalp, the more acclaim it offers the publication that reports upon it. Sir Jimmy Savile was 'scalped' by the UK media with the revelations that he had sexually abused hundreds of teenage girls (Greer & McLaughlin, 2013). In the American context, Bill Clinton could be said to have been 'scalped' for his relationship with Monica Lewinsky.

The sixth crime news value is *emotion*, particularly if an emotional scene can be *seen*, rather than read about or heard. Indeed, the seventh crime news value is *spectacle*. It is said that in television news, there has always been a bias towards a good picture as opposed to a catchy story (see Chermak, 1995; McGregor, 2002), and television news has in turn been afforded more validity and authenticity with its facility to present events visually (Jewkes, 2015). In our digitalized and hyper-mediatized era, images are now critically important for all news media platforms (see Ayres & Jewkes, 2012; Greer, 2013; Greer, Ferrell, & Jewkes, 2007; Greer & Jewkes, 2005; Harcup & O'Neill, 2016; Jewkes, 2015). In crime news, the grislier, the more personal and the more emotional the spectacle, the better. In fact, emotional spectacles have become significant for 'news' in general. The ability to make the audience 'feel something' is also important. A New Zealand journalist, reflecting on his craft, recently said this:

> I can't be the only journalist who has felt a perverse glow of pride when a reader says a story I've written made them cry, or more venal still, given a quite inward cheer when an interview subject is moved to tears. (Dudding, 2015, p. 12)

The eighth crime news value is *children.* News reports about children as victims of crime (especially violent crime) provoke particularly emotional responses in audiences (Gekoski, Gray, & Adler, 2012). On the other hand, reports about children as perpetrators are particularly extraordinary (Jewkes, 2015). This is because we understand children to be inherently innocent and allocate childhood to be a time of innate defenselessness. The best example to illustrate the salience of both sides of this news value is the James Bulger murder in Britain, in the early 1990s. The case was intrinsically newsworthy as it was a murder of a toddler (the quintessential innocent) by two 10-year-olds (who nobody imagined would be capable) (see Jewkes, 2015). I go into more detail about the events of the crime, as well as the media treatment of them, in more detail in Chap. 6.

The ninth crime news value is *shareability*, which refers to the likelihood that this or that story will be shared by audience members on their social media pages, such as Twitter and Facebook. Shareability is determined by 'stuff that makes you laugh and stuff that makes you cry' (former Guardian website editor Janine Gibson cited in Harcup & O'Neill, 2016, p. 11).

News values interact and add value to each other (Gekoski et al., 2012; Soothill, Peelo, Francis, Pearson, & Ackerley, 2002). A crime story will be more newsworthy if it has a visual of, say, a victim of a violent crime who is demonstrably upset. It is likely to be shareable as a result. In this way, the newsworthiness of some elements of a story can lift and make more salient the lesser newsworthy aspects. Katz (1987) also argues that an event or happening is newsworthy if its story can be seen to offend a moral universe or tell a moral tale, one that is relevant to the community it is being told to.

The crime news product is also subject to a process of *construction* (see Altheide, 2002; Epstein, 2000; Hall, 1980; Jacobs, 1996; Jewkes, 2004; Johnson-Cartee, 2005; Schlesinger & Tumber, 1994). One of the tasks of the media is to make raw events comprehensible and to construct order upon and draw meaning out of random, chaotic scenes (Hall et al., 1978). Media criminologists have signaled a number of important ways by which journalists achieve this undertaking. Framing refers to the ways by which the communication about events, objects and persons is organized to suggest that those events, objects and persons should be thought about in a particular way (Entman, 1993). Many scholars have illustrated the ways in which criminal events, objects and persons have been framed for an audience (Ayres & Jewkes, 2012; Barak, 2007; Moore, 2014; Peelo, 2006; Reiner, Livingstone, & Allen, 2003). Hall et al. (1978) argued the media inserts raw events into 'maps of meaning' to make them communicable. Maps of meaning are inferential structures that an audience will be familiar with (see also Critcher, 2003). The media also impose order on raw material with narratives (Jewkes, 2014; Reiner et al., 2000; Rowe, 2013; Wright, 2016). Indeed, the construction of a narrative is an efficient way to cast out an outsider and legitimize action that can be taken against them (Anker, 2005; Hall et al., 1978; Wright, 2015, 2016). As argued, one of the functions of crime news is to mark the moral boundaries of a society and to warn of what sanctions might apply should one be tempted to transgress (Box, 1971; Katz, 1988; see also Cromer, 1978; Erikson, 1966; Foucault, 1991). And it may be that narratives are an increasingly important format by which crime news is presented. As Rowe (2013) argues, in contemporary crowded media ecosystems, where there are many news producers, a familiar narrative works to attract and hook a reader in (see also Jewkes, 2015). And it may be that issues of all origin and nature are being presented like crime stories routinely are. Altheide (2002, 2009) suggests that news production has become permanently oriented to a 'problem' frame, whereby social complexities are presented as simple problems requiring basic solutions (see also Braun, 2007).

The focus of this chapter thus far has been upon the practices of the news media in a moral panic and how these are related to ordinary and routine practices of crime news-making. We know that a great deal of what we see in the news is news about crime; that news values such as violence, risk and emotion guide the selection of raw events for crime news; that these events are then communicated via frames, in maps of meanings, and as narratives. This illustrates that the media, when reporting on deviance and crime, inadvertently engages in practices that have the potential to develop into those that we see in a panic (amplifying a problem, shaping up a folk devil and setting an agenda). A panic will involve, however, additional actors (moral entrepreneurs, interest groups and politicians), whose practices both appear in the news media and interact with those of the news media. Cohen (1972, 2002), drawing from Wilkins (1964), described a 'feedback loop' whereby understandings are received, interpreted and then acted upon or towards (and then received, interpreted and then acted upon or towards once more). Feedback loops augment and crystallize meanings. Practices by other actors in a panic may be seen by the media to potentially increase sales or fit with an ongoing narrative already in the news. Therefore, practices in the media (those *of* other actors) are also of the media. Moreover, most panics will be able to be traced *via* the news media (Cohen, 2002).

Today's news, however, comes to us via multiple digital, social and mobile media platforms. As discussed, we now have media *ecosystems*, in which content is *co*-created by producers and consumers, and shared amongst 'networked publics' (Boyd, 2014; Jewkes, 2015; Yar, 2012). And, as argued, only a handful of panic scholars have considered the role of new forms of mediated communication, namely, social media, in their case studies. Hier (2016) analysed Twitter data in his analysis of two 'good' panics, for example. Richey (2016) analysed the role of Tinder and Facebook in a panic about the representation of images of humanitarian acts. In the next section, I draw on research from media and communication studies, politics, youth culture and marketing to understand what social media is, does and enables. I consider how the intersections between legacy media (traditional forms of news media such as newspapers, television, radio, etc.) and 'new' media have affected the content of news. I then suggest how the contemporary media ecosystem might affect the practices of amplifying a problem, shaping up a folk devil and setting an agenda.

Digital, Social and Mobile Media

Digital media is any written or visual material that can be created, seen, preserved and distributed electronically, and includes computer software, video, online games, web pages as well as social networking sites like Facebook and Instagram. Social media, as a separate term, usually refers to social networking sites (Facebook, Google+, Instagram and Pinterest), video sharing sites (YouTube and Vine), and blogging (WordPress and Blogger) and microblogging platforms (Twitter and Tumblr). Mobile media are the tools that enable users to create, upload and share content (mobile phones, tablets and apps). The distinctions between digital, social and mobile media are unavoidably blurry as people engage with all three simultaneously (sharing an article from an online news site to Facebook using a mobile phone), and some scholars therefore view them as a whole. Boyd (2014), for instance, whose research looks at social media use amongst young people, includes mobile media in her definition of social media. Marketing scholars use the acronym DSMM (digital, social media and mobile) when referring to the use of these in marketing practices. Boyd (2014) also describes the phenomenon of 'networked publics' as communities that are structured by networked technologies (social media and mobile phones). Networked technologies facilitate the construction of spaces in which imagined communities emerge via the intersections of people, technology and practice. People belong to many publics which may overlap with each other, and these publics can be political, cultural or commercial, depending on who is addressing them or to what they aspire. Networked publics are both spatial communities (in that they exist in social media sites and platforms) and imagined communities (in that people participating in them envision themselves belonging to a wider assembly of others).

The emergence of digital, social and mobile media, and networked publics, has created some seismic shifts across the social, cultural and political landscape. For some, this shift—particularly the rise of social media—provides opportunities for political emancipation. As such, it will be social media (as defined above) that I will focus on from this point onwards. Breuer, Landman, and Farquhar (2015), for example, found that in the Tunisian revolution in 2010 and 2011, social media enabled users to break an imposed media blackout by providing material for legacy media to use; recruit protesters through emotional mobilization practices; and connect otherwise disparate groups of protesters. Tufekci and Wilson (2012), who surveyed participants in Egypt's Tahrir Square protest, also found that Facebook provided information that could not be controlled by authorities and that this information was critical in helping individuals to make decisions about taking part in the protest. For these scholars, social media plays a key role in a new system of political communication (Tufekci & Wilson, 2012). Gies (2016), who interviewed participants in the campaign to overturn the conviction of Amanda Knox and Raffaele Sollecito for the murder of Meredith Kercher in Perugia, 2007, found that social media allowed campaigners to challenge the understandings that were being promoted by criminal justice agencies which suggested the two accused were guilty. This is another example of social media's capacity to mobilize and connect people, and operate as an agent to organize them towards honourable ends. Gerbaudo (2012), who conducted 80 interviews with activists in Egypt, Spain and the USA, describes this capacity of social media as a *choreography*.[1]

Other scholars have argued that social media enables other practices, leading to negative ends. Boyd's (2014) research is about young people, and she makes the point that whilst practices amongst teenagers remain largely the same as they have always been, the technological properties of social media—which she terms 'affordances'—mean that certain types of practices are made possible. She argues that there are four of these affordances: persistence (of content); visibility (for audiences); spreadability (capability to share content); and searchability (ability to find content). These affordances help to create new social dynamics, which can result in harmful effects. Boyd (2014) notes that young people 'stalk' each other by searching for visible, persistent content. Spreading or 'sharing' content augments the visibility of it and may lead to conflict or 'drama' between groups of young people. Young people also seek out attention by searching and spreading material. This can be problematic if they don't (and they tend not to) have the skills to consider or respond to any consequences that may follow (Boyd, 2014).

Research looking at online firestorms (also known as 'shitstorms' and 'Twitterstorms') is also pessimistic about what social media enables. A firestorm is defined as 'a sudden discharge of large quantities of messages containing negative WOM (word of mouth) and complaint behavior against a person, company, or group in social media networks' (Pfeffer, Zorbach, & Carley, 2014, p. 118). Pfeffer et al. (2014) argue that the dynamics of firestorms are very like how rumours develop and circulate, but firestorms can be either rumour-based *or* fact-based. There are seven factors of social media that facilitate online firestorms. The first factor is *speed*, accompanied by *volume* (see also Maratea, 2008). Where traditional media sources (newspapers, etc.) take a day to react to events, reactions in social media communities may occur in hours or even minutes. And of all social media platforms, the microblogging site Twitter is the fastest. Speed, however, comes at a cost. The number of celebrities that have been falsely reported dead via Twitter illustrates this well. Jeff Goldblum, Robert Redford, Carlos Santana, Paul McCartney and Jackie Chan have all been pronounced dead in a tweet whilst very much still alive.

The second factor is the *absence of discursive interactions*. Twitter, for example, encourages fast 'either-or' choices to share (or retweet). It also limits messages to 140 characters. An in-depth discussion about an act or event between tweeters is therefore difficult. The third factor is *network clusters*. Pfeffer et al. (2014) explain that if Amy is connected to Sam and Sam is connected to Joe, then Amy is also connected to Joe. Anything Amy posts is likely to be seen by Joe. The information then 'echoes' from different directions, giving the impression that everyone is talking about the same thing or has the same opinion about something. Local clusters can also facilitate the spread of opinions through other clusters and beyond. Joe might share the post from Amy, and then someone in his network might also share the post. Pfeffer et al. (2014) describe that the process is very similar to what happens in an echo chamber. An echo chamber describes a situation in which information, ideas or beliefs are amplified or reinforced through being shared and repeated inside a 'bounded' system (Jamieson & Cappella, 2010). Different or competing views tend to be under-represented (or even disallowed or censored) in an echo chamber.

Pfeffer et al. (2014) point out that whilst interpersonal communication between people (on the phone, in face-to-face conversations and via email) tends to form patterns that give rise to network clusters, online clusters are larger and communication happens between users more often. One might have hundreds of 'friends' on Facebook and thousands of 'followers' on Twitter. They may also *be* a friend and follower of hundreds and thousands more. Moreover, *every* connection in social media gets the same amount of attention. There is no discrepancy between strong and weak ties (which would help to buffer or filter information being shared) nor any impact from emotion or sense of reciprocity between those connected. What results is an *unrestrained information flow*. This is the fourth factor of social media that contributes to online firestorms (Pfeffer et al., 2014).

The fifth factor is a *lack of diversity*. People connect with people who are like them and have similar interests and opinions, creating a filter bubble (Maratea, 2008; Pariser, 2011). This happens both offline and online. However, online communication, via social media, is additionally affected by the technology that supports it. Posts are rated as more interesting for you if your friends were interested in it or you were interested in something very similar in the past. What stems from this is that the information available to a single user is not only limited but also heavily biased (Pfeffer et al., 2014; see also Bro & Wallberg, 2014).

The sixth factor is *cross media dynamics*, which is understood by media practitioners as *media convergence* (Du Fresne, 2016). This describes how social media is an information source for legacy news, sometimes *leading* the news (see O'Connor, 2012). I discuss this further and in more detail below.

The seventh factor is *networked-triggered decision processes*. This is a combination of factors, but it can be seen in stand-alone terms. Pfeffer and Carley (2013) propose that offline decision-making processes unfold in this way: a person receives information about an opinion (they now have *knowledge* of it); they take up a positive or negative stance in relation to that opinion (they are *persuaded*); they then talk to others about their decision and in doing so influence others' decisions in relation to that opinion (this is called *propagation*); opinions are stabilized as people meet others with the same opinion (*affirmation* occurs). Negative feedback will destabilize an opinion formed. However, in social media, these processes unfold differently. The online filter bubble limits the information a user can receive, so affecting their knowledge. The echo chamber ensures persuasion and affirmation. What results is that a user is offered the impression that *the majority of* people hold a particular opinion or think in a particular way. Pfeffer et al. (2014) argue that the consequences are dramatic. Indeed, they suggest that: 'cognitive processes can be replaced by network effects in social media opinion spreading' (Pfeffer et al., 2014, p. 123). I will return to this point further below. What I want to turn to now is a consideration of how the arrival of digital, social and mobile media has changed the ways that *news* is both produced and consumed.

Bastos (2015), a scholar of journalism studies, traces the gradual shift in news production practices, from the introduction of online editions to accompany print editions during the 2000s to a 'pivotal turn' towards digital editions *instead of* print editions from about 2012. Similarly, Lamberton and Stephen (2016) observe three 'eras' of 'new' media developments: the era of digital media (2000–2004), the era of online networking (2005–2010) and the era of social media (2011–2014). More recent shifts have seen social media sites like Snapchat, Facebook and Google designing and providing systems for journalists to share their work via their respective sites (Bell, 2016).[2]

Audiences have also changed the ways in which they engage with news. Researchers at the Pew Research Centre have found that in 2016, 81% of Americans got their news online, and about 62% got their news via social media (Mitchell & Holcomb, 2016). Young adults (under 30 years) were more likely to get their news from social media sites such as Facebook and Twitter. However, the data also show that most Americans still prefer to get their news from news organizations and are hesitant about what they read that has been shared with them by family and friends.[3] In another study by the Centre, it was found that news consumers were more likely to go directly to a news organization for news about business and finance, and more likely to discover news about the community on social media (Mitchell et al., 2017). So, there are qualitative differences between news sources, at least in terms of how audiences engage with them.

These changes are a response to the new media ecosystem, and they have, in turn, affected the *content* of news. Bastos (2015) notes that the interactive component of online editions served to shift editorial decisions towards producing more compact, visually appealing news. The advent of social media then altered it again. Paulussen and Harder (2014) document that journalists use social media in a variety of ways: (i) as a platform for dissemination (see also Bell, 2016); (ii) to monitor and identify issues that may be missed on regular news outlets; and (iii) as a *source* of news. Paulussen and Harder (2014) found that the news media will cite tweets and Twitter users in their reports and often over and above the opinions of other, more traditional voices, such as politicians, police or community leaders. They argue that Twitter has the potential to increase the diversity of voices in the media as a result. Maratea (2008) also found that journalists looking for an 'opinion' or an angle to direct their story, and politicians searching for a sense of the significance of current events, will often look at what's happening in the blogosphere. However, Maratea (2008) found that there was a hierarchy of blogs and only some blogs—those with lots of incoming links—would be looked at in turn, these blogs, by being looked at and used by journalists and politicians, could be seen as 'elite blogs' (Maratea, 2008).[4]

Nevertheless, because journalists are using Twitter as a source, tweeters can 'break stories' and become gatekeepers of information. Elite persons who use Twitter understand this and do so with a view to set agendas (Adi, Erickson, & Lilleker, 2014). Whether elites *can* set agendas via Twitter is a topic of some debate. Studies have found that consistency across tweets tweeted by elites is important in setting a coherent agenda (Adi et al., 2014; Skogerbø & Krumsvik, 2015). In turn, media reporting of events unfolding on Twitter can lead to increased Twitter traffic about those events. Most news sites have buttons for users to click so they can tweet a story or share on Facebook (illustrating the salience of shareability as a news value).

Bastos (2015) argues that in order for news organizations to remain competitive, their news content may need to better reflect audiences' preferences in the near future. Sharing of content by users and attention to this sharing by legacy media is *cross media dynamics* at work. What can result is an echo chamber *between* social media and legacy media (Pfeffer et al., 2014). Another key issue, as Bell (2016) argues, is that Facebook also has algorithms that track what users do whilst in the site. Facebook then directs tailored material towards users using that information. It *sorts* news, resulting in a filter bubble.

The affordances of social media have also shifted the content of news in other ways. Journalists have argued that the race to be first, a long-standing journalistic norm, has become ever more intense with the advent of sites like Twitter where information is instantaneous (Singer, 2016). Investigative reporting on significant events is often left wayside as haste takes precedence over depth (Du Fresne, 2016). Other industry norms have also been affected. 'Clickbait', a term used to describe online stories designed to capture the attention of a casual new-site browser or to trigger an emotional response, generates more traffic and so now takes priority over more serious content (Blom & Hansen, 2015; see also Jewkes, 2015). This is an institutional response to practices of *news seeking* (Stephens & Jarvis, 2016) and *way finding* (Pearson & Kosicki, 2016) by news consumers. Du Fresne (2016) calls the combination of haste and clickbait the 'race to the bottom'.

Another study, by Beckers and Harder (2016), found that the media uses social media, Twitter especially, as a tool by which to measure public opinion. Of their sample of stories mentioning Twitter, 67% of items referred to tweeters in common terms such as 'people' and 'fans' thereby implying unanimity not only amongst tweeters but also the public (Beckers & Harder, 2016). Beckers and Harder (2016) concluded that the media uses Twitter to make inferences about 'what *everybody* thinks' in the same ways that they would previously use 'vox pops' or the 'man on the street'. Of particular interest to panic researchers, over 25% of items also used a hyperbolic marker to indicate a heightened level of concern (commotion; fuss; a Twitter storm; 'the whole thing exploded'). Further, over 30% of items also mentioned the tweeter's emotions (and 75% of *these* mention negative emotions) (Beckers & Harder, 2016), illustrating that pejorative assessments of issues carry some newsworthiness. Academic researchers have also used social media data as evidence of 'the public mood' (see Williams & Burnap, 2015). Beckers and Harder's (2016) study offers some cautions about doing so.

Implications

In the end, there are two features of the contemporary media ecosystem that researchers of moral panics need to be mindful of. First, moral entrepreneurs and interest groups may, and in fact are likely, to make and disseminate their claims via social media sites. This is because the affordances of social media expand the visibility of claims as well as speed up the diffusion of them. Folk devils can also use social media to 'fight back'. Social media may also choreograph action on the ground or it might allow for the drama to unfold amongst some groups of networked publics. Because social media can limit the information users receive, resulting in filter bubbles, claims made by moral entrepreneurs may be more readily accepted by some networked publics than they may have been previously. Social media also allows information, ideas or beliefs to be amplified or reinforced through being shared and repeated inside echo chambers, which ensures persuasion and affirmation. Indeed, social media supports the development of panics by *enabling* the efforts of moral entrepreneurs and expanding their claims.

Second, the intersections between social media and legacy media mean that feedback loops, which are central to moral panics, are now part and parcel of the production of news. Legacy media competes with social media; employs social media to both disseminate news and find news; and draws on social media as a tool to make inferences about what everybody thinks. The recognition, by media scholars, that news organizations now take account of what is likely to be shared (and the inclusion of shareability as a news value), also means that news organizations are more responsive to audience desires than they were previously. What is understood to be newsworthy is likely to shift and change in relation to these desires, and we may see some very peculiar events, objects and persons emerge as the subjects of moral panics as a result. What can be gathered, overall, is that the processes of amplifying a problem, shaping up a folk devil and setting an agenda in the new media ecosystem are likely to unfold in highly dynamic ways, at unprecedented speeds, and with many twists and turns. Empirical cases, studied inductively, are critical to our understanding of the ways in which they do, and how these ways might alter the shape of the concept of moral panic.

That said, researchers should be aware that these two features may not be of significance in a specific case. Moral entrepreneurs may or may not make their claims on social media platforms, and legacy media may or may not need to compete with social media in coverage of a certain event, object or person that has been seen to be a problem. Whether they are of significance is *wholly dependent* on the panic in question, yet another indicator that inductive research is important. Over the next two chapters, I employ the framework I outlined in Chap. 1 to examine two on-the-ground-happening material panics. In the first panic, about killer kids, social media did not feature at all, but this is only because the episode emerged in 2002, long before the era of social media. In the second panic, Twitter and Facebook were present, but it was a series of elite bloggers and their commenters who played the most significant role in the ways by which the panic unfolded and the 'problem' was sustained.

With that disclaimer, I now turn to my examination of killer kids, a case of panic that emerged in relation to a lethal attack on a pizza delivery man in Auckland, New Zealand, in 2002. This case had all the ingredients of a typical moral panic: a horrible crime committed by a group of young people; sensationalist media coverage; a range of opinions diagnoses and remedies proposed by a number of moral entrepreneurs; and a proposal for a knee-jerk law change. However, a study of the case via the framework outlined in Chap. 1 reveals a far more complex picture than the conceptual model of moral panic, in its current shape, would have been able to expose.

Notes

1. Activism still requires people who are willing to *act*, however.
2. Facebook, for example, has a concept called Instant Articles. Journalists can link an RSS feed of their work into Instant Article and their article will appear on a Facebook page. Journalists using the tool have found that their articles are reaching up to four times as many people, simply because audiences can remain in Facebook and no longer have to click out and into a news organizations' site for access (Bell, 2016).
3. Social campaigners using social media understand that the legacy media remains important. In the efforts to overturn the conviction of Knox and Sollieto, campaigners knew they needed to also be 'in the mainstream media' (Geis, 2016).
4. Whether there are 'elite tweeters' has not yet been established to my knowledge. Several studies have examined tweets made by elite actors (see Adi et al., 2014; Bennett, 2016) but I imagine 'elite tweeters' to be everyday citizens whose tweets regularly make the news. President Trump might be seen as an elite actor who tweets *and* an elite tweeter in that his tweets make the news daily (albeit in a satirical way).

References

Adi, A., Erickson, K., & Lilleker, D. G. (2014). Elite Tweets: Analyzing the Twitter communication patterns of Labour Party peers in the House of Lords: Elite Tweets. *Policy & Internet, 6*(1), 1–27. doi:10.1002/1944-2866.POI350.

Altheide, D. (2002). *Creating fear: News and the construction of crisis*. New York: Aldine de Gruyter.

Altheide, D. (2009). *Terror post 9/11 and the media* (Vol. 4). New York: Peter Long Publishing.

Anker, E. (2005). Villains, victims and heroes: Melodrama, media and September 11. *Journal of Communication*, (55).

Ayres, T. C., & Jewkes, Y. (2012). The haunting spectacle of crystal meth: A media-created mythology? *Crime, Media, Culture, 8*(3), 315–332. doi:10.1177/1741659012443234.

Barak, G. (2007). Mediatizing law and order: Applying Cottle's architecture of communicative frames to the social construction of crime and justice. *Crime, Media, Culture, 3*(1), 101–109.

Bastos, M. T. (2015). Shares, Pins, and Tweets: News readership from daily papers to social media. *Journalism Studies, 16*(3), 305–325. 10.1080/1461670X.2014.891857.

Beckers, K., & Harder, R. A. (2016). "Twitter Just Exploded": Social media as alternative vox pop. *Digital Journalism, 4*(7), 910–920. doi:10.1080/21670811.2016.1161493.

Bell, E. (2016, March). *The end of news as we know it: How Facebook swallowed journalism.* Lecture, University of Cambridge. Retrieved from https://medium.com/tow-center/the-end-of-the-news-as-we-know-it-how-facebook-swallowed-journalism-60344fa50962#.q0bsrc1al.

Bennett, S. (2016). New "Crises," Old habits: Online interdiscursivity and intertextuality in UK Migration Policy Discourses. *Journal of Immigrant & Refugee Studies*, 1–21. 10.1080/15562948.2016.1257753.

Blom, J. N., & Hansen, K. R. (2015). Click bait: Forward-reference as lure in online news headlines. *Journal of Pragmatics, 76*, 87–100. doi:10.1016/j.pragma.2014.11.010.

Box, S. (1971). *Deviance, reality and society.* London, England: Reinhart and Winston.

Boyd, D. (2014). *It's complicated: The social life of networked teens.* New Haven, CT: Yale University Press.

Braun, J. A. (2007). The imperatives of narrative: Health interest groups and morality in the network news. *The American Journal of Bioethics, 7*(8), 6–14.

Breuer, A., Landman, T., & Farquhar, D. (2015). Social media and protest mobilization: Evidence from the Tunisian revolution. *Democratization, 22*(4), 764–792. doi:10.1080/13510347.2014.885505.

Bro, P., & Wallberg, F. (2014). Digital gatekeeping: News media versus social media. *Digital Journalism, 2*(3), 446–454. doi:10.1080/21670811.2014.895507.

Burns, R., & Crawford, C. (1999). School shootings, the media, and public fear. Ingredients for a moral panic. *Crime Law and Social Change, 32*, 147–168.

Chermak, S. M. (1995). *Victims in the news: Crime and the American news media*. Boulder: Westview Press.
Chibnall, S. (1977). *Law and order news: An analysis of crime reporting in the British Press*. London: Tavistock Publications Limited.
Cohen, S. (1972). *Folk devils and moral panics*. Herts, England: Paladin.
Cohen, S. (2002). *Folk devils and moral panics (3rd Edition)*. London: Routledge.
Cohen, S., & Young, J. (Eds.). (1981). *The manufacture of news: Deviance, social problems and the mass media* (2nd ed.). London: Sage.
Costera Meijer, I., & Groot Kormelink, T. (2015). Checking, Sharing, Clicking and Linking: Changing patterns of news use between 2004 and 2014. *Digital Journalism, 3*(5), 664–679. https://doi.org/10.1080/21670811.2014.937149
Critcher, C. (2003). *Moral panics and the media*. Buckingham, England: Open University Press.
Cromer, G. (1978). Character assassination in the press. In C. Winick (Ed.), *Deviance and mass media* (pp. 225–241). Beverly Hills: Sage.
de Young, M. (2004). *The day care ritual abuse moral panic*. Jefferson, NC: McFarland and Company.
Du Fresne, K. (2016, March 4). Changing media landscape sometimes hard to understand. *Dominion Post*. Wellington, New Zealand. Retrieved from http://www.stuff.co.nz/dominion-post/comment/columnists/77448066/changing-media-landscape-sometimes-hard-to-understand.
Dudding, A. (2015, July 12). Sob story. *Sunday*, 8–12.
Entman, R. M. (1993). Framing: Toward clarification of a fractured paradigm. *Journal of communication, 43*(4), 51–58.
Epstein, E. J. (2000). *News from nowhere: Television and the news* (2nd ed.). New York: Random House.
Erikson, K. (1966). *Wayward puritans*. New York: Macmillan.
Ericson, R., Baranek, P. N., & Chan, J. B. L. (1987). *Visualizing deviance: A study of news organisation*. Toronto: University of Toronto Press.
Ericson, R., Baranek, P. N., & Chan, J. B. L. (1991). *Representing order: Crime, law and justice in the news media*. Toronto: University of Toronto Press.
Foucault, M. (1991). *Discipline and punish* (3rd ed.). London: Penguin Books.
Galtung, J., & Ruge, H. (1965). The structure of foreign news: The presentation of the Congo, Cuba and Cyprus crises in four Norwegian newspapers. *Journal of Peace Research, 2*(1), 64–91.
Garland, D. (2001). *The culture of control*. Oxford: Oxford University Press.

Gekoski, A., Gray, J. M., & Adler, J. R. (2012). What makes a homicide newsworthy? UK national tabloid newspaper journalists tell all. *British Journal of Criminology, 52,* 1212–1232.

Gerbaudo, P. (2012). *Tweets and the streets: Social media and contemporary activism*. London, England: Pluto Press.

Gies, L. (2016). Miscarriages of justice in the age of social media: The Amanda Knox and Raffaele Sollecito Innocence Campaign. *British Journal of Criminology, 57*(3), 723–740. doi:10.1093/bjc/azw017.

Golding, P., & Elliot, P. (1979). *Making the news*. London: Longman.

Goode, E., & Ben-Yehuda, N. (1994). *Moral panics: The social construction of deviance*. Cambridge, MA: Blackwell.

Greer, C. (2013). Crime and the media: Understanding the connections. In C. Hale, K. J. Hayward, A. Wahidin, & E. Wincup (Eds.), *Criminology* (3rd ed., pp. 143–163). Oxford: Oxford University Press.

Greer, C., & Jewkes, Y. (2005). Extremes of otherness: Media images of social exclusion. *Social Justice, 32*(1), 20–31.

Greer, C., Ferrell, J., & Jewkes, Y. (2007). It's the style that matters: Style, substance and critical scholarship. *Crime, Media, Culture, 3*(1), 5–10.

Greer, C., & McLaughlin, E. (2013). The Sir Jimmy Savile scandal: Child sexual abuse and institutional denial at the BBC. *Crime, Media, Culture, 9*(3), 243–263.

Greer, C., & Reiner, R. (2012). Mediated Mayhem: Media, crime, criminal justice. In M. Maguire, R. Morgan, & R. Reiner (Eds.), *The Oxford handbook of criminology* (pp. 245–278). Oxford, England: Oxford University Press.

Hall, S. (1980). Encoding/decoding. In *Culture, media, language: Working papers in cultural studies* (pp. 128–138). London, England: Hutchinson and Co.

Hall, S., Critcher, C., Jefferson, T., Clarke, J., & Roberts, B. (1978). *Policing the crisis: Mugging, the state, and law and order*. London: MacMillan.

Hans, V. P., & Dee, J. L. (1991). Media coverage of law: Its impact on juries and the public. *The American Behavioral Scientist, 35*(2), 136–149.

Harcup, T., & O'Neill, D. (2001). What is news? Galtung and Ruge revisited. *Journalism Studies, 2*(2), 261–280. doi:10.1080/14616700118449.

Harcup, T., & O'Neill, D. (2016). What is news? News values revisited (again). *Journalism Studies*, 1–19. 10.1080/1461670X.2016.1150193.

Hier, S. (2016). Good moral panics? Normative ambivalence, social reaction, and coexisting responsibilities in everyday life. *Current Sociology*. 10.1177/0011392116655463.

Innes, M. (2005). A short history of the idea of moral panic. *Crime, Media Culture, 1*(1), 106–111.

Jacobs, R. N. (1996). Producing the news, producing the crisis: Narrativity, television and news work. *Media, Culture and Society, 18*(3), 373–397.

Jamieson, K. H., & Cappella, J. N. (2010). *Echo chamber: Rush Limbaugh and the conservative media establishment*. Oxford: Oxford University Press.

Jewkes, Y. (2004). *Media and crime*. London, England: Sage.

Jewkes, Y. (2014). Punishment in black and white: Penal "Hell-Holes", popular media, and mass incarceration. *Atlantic Journal of Communication, 22*(1), 42–60. doi:10.1080/15456870.2014.860144.

Jewkes, Y. (2015). *Media and crime* (3rd ed.). Los Angeles: Sage.

Johnson-Cartee, K. S. (2005). *News narratives and news framing: Constructing political reality*. Lanham: Rowman & Littlefield Publishers.

Katz, J. (1987). What makes crime "news"? *Media, Culture and Society, 9*, 47–75.

Katz, J. (1988). *Seductions of crime: Moral and sensual attractions in doing evil*. New York: Basic Books.

Lamberton, C., & Stephen, A. T. (2016). A thematic exploration of digital, social media, and mobile marketing: Research evolution from 2000 to 2015 and an agenda for future inquiry. *Journal of Marketing, 80*(6), 146–172. doi:10.1509/jm.15.0415.

Maneri, M. (2013). From media hypes to moral panics: Theoretical and methodological tools. In C. Critcher, J. Hughes, J. Petley, & A. Rohloff (Eds.), *Moral panics in the contemporary world* (pp. 171–192). New York: Bloomsbury.

Maratea, R. (2008). The e-rise and fall of social problems: The blogosphere as a public arena. *Social Problems, 55*(1), 139–160.

McGregor, J. (2002). Terrorism, war, lions and sex symbols: Restating news values. In *What's news? Reclaiming journalism in New Zealand* (pp. 81–95). Palmerston North, New Zealand: Dunmore Press.

McRobbie, A. (1994). *Postmodernism and popular culture*. London, England: Routledge.

Meijer, I. C., & Kormelink, T. G. (2014). Checking, sharing, clicking and linking: Changing patterns of news use between 2004 and 2014. *Digital Journalism, 3*(5), 664–679.

Mitchell, A., Gottfried, J., Shearer, E., & Lu, K. (2017). *How Americans encounter, recall and act upon digital news*. Pew Research Centre.

Mitchell, A., & Holcomb, J. (2016). *State of the News Media 2016*. Retrieved from http://www.journalism.org/2016/06/15/state-of-the-news-media-2016/.

Moore, S. E. H. (2013). The cautionary tale: A new paradigm for studying media coverage of crime. In C. Critcher, J. Hughes, J. Petley, & A. Rohloff (Eds.), *Moral panics in the contemporary world*. New York: Bloomsbury.

Moore, S. E. H. (2014). *Crime and the media*. New York: Palgrave Macmillan.

O'Connor, R. (2012). *Friends, followers, and the future: How social media are changing politics, threatening big brands, and killing traditional media*. San Francisco: City Lights Books.

Pariser, E. (2011). *The filter bubble: What the internet is hiding from you*. London, England: Viking/Penguin Books.

Paulussen, S., & Harder, R. A. (2014). Social media references in newspapers: Facebook, Twitter and YouTube as sources in newspaper journalism. *Journalism Practice, 8*(5), 542–551. doi:10.1080/17512786.2014.894327.

Pearson, G. D. H., & Kosicki, G. M. (2016). How way-finding is challenging gatekeeping in the digital age. *Journalism Studies*, 1–19.

Peelo, M. (2005). Crime and the media: public narratives and private consumption. *Questioning crime and criminology*, 20–36.

Peelo, M. (2006). Framing homicide narratives in newspapers: Mediated witness and the construction of virtual victimhood. *Crime, Media, Culture, 2*(2), 159–175.

Pfeffer, J., & Carley, K. M. (2013). The importance of local clusters for the diffusion of opinions and beliefs in interpersonal communication networks. *International Journal of Innovation and Technology Management, 10*(05), 1340022. 10.1142/S0219877013400221.

Pfeffer, J., Zorbach, T., & Carley, K. M. (2014). Understanding online firestorms: Negative word-of-mouth dynamics in social media networks. *Journal of Marketing Communications, 20*(1–2), 117–128. doi:10.1080/13527266.2013.797778.

Reed, I. A. (2015). Deep culture in action: Resignification, synecdoche, and metanarrative in the moral panic of the Salem Witch Trials. *Theory and Society, 44*(1), 65–94. doi:10.1007/s11186-014-9241-4.

Reiner, R. (2002). Media made criminology: The representation of crime in the mass media. In M. Maguire, R. Morgan, & R. Reiner (Eds.), *Oxford handbook of criminology* (3rd ed., pp. 376–416). Oxford: Oxford University Press.

Reiner, R., Livingstone, S., & Allen, J. (2000). No more happy endings? The media and popular concern about crime since the Second World War. In T. Hope & R. Sparks (Eds.), *Crime, risk and insecurity: Law and order in everyday life and political discourse* (pp. 107–126). London, England: Routledge.
Reiner, R., Livingstone, S., & Allen, J. (2003). From law and order to lynch mobs: Crime news since the Second World War. In P. Mason (Ed.), *Criminal visions: Media representations of crime and justice* (pp. 13–32). London: Routledge.
Richey, L. A. (2016). "Tinder Humanitarians": The moral panic around representations of old relationships in new media. *Javnost—The Public, 23*(4), 398–414. doi:10.1080/13183222.2016.1248323.
Rowe, M. (2013). Just like a TV show: Public criminology and the media coverage of 'hunt for Britain's most wanted man'. *Crime, Media, Culture, 9*(1), 23–38. doi:10.1177/1741659012438298.
Schlesinger, P., & Tumber, H. (1994). *Reporting crime: The media politics of criminal justice*. Oxford, England: Oxford University Press.
Singer, J. B. (2016). Transmission Creep: Media effects theories and journalism studies in a digital era. *Journalism Studies*, 1–18.
Skogerbø, E., & Krumsvik, A. H. (2015). Newspapers, Facebook and Twitter: Intermedial agenda setting in local election campaigns. *Journalism Practice, 9*(3), 350–366. doi:10.1080/17512786.2014.950471.
Soothill, K., Peelo, M., Francis, B., Pearson, J., & Ackerley, E. (2002). Homicide and the media: Identifying the top cases in The Times. *The Howard Journal, 41,* 401–421.
Stanko, E. A., & Lee, R. M. (2003). Introduction: Methodological reflections. In *Researching violence: Essays on methodology and measurement*. London: Routledge.
Stephens, M., & Jarvis, S. E. (2016). The Partisan affect of News Seekers vs. Gatekeepers: Linguistic differences in Online vs. Front-Page News in Campaign 2012. *Communication Research Reports, 33*(3), 275–280. doi:10.1080/08824096.2016.1186626.
Surette, R. (1988). *Media, crime, and criminal justice: Images and realities* (2nd ed.). Belmont, CA: Wadsworth.
Surette, R. (2015). *Media, crime, and criminal justice: Images, realities, and policies* (5th ed.). Stamford, CT: Cengage Learning.
Tufekci, Z., & Wilson, C. (2012). Social media and the decision to participate in political protest: Observations from Tahrir Square. *Journal of Communication, 62*(2), 363–379. doi:10.1111/j.1460-2466.2012.01629.x.

Wilkins, L. T. (1964). *Social deviance: Social policy, action and research.* London: Tavistock.
Williams, M. L., & Burnap, P. (2015). Cyberhate on social media in the aftermath of Woolwich: A case study in computational criminology and big data. *British Journal of Criminology, 56*(2), 211–238. doi:10.1093/bjc/azv059.
Wright, S. (2010). *Angel faces, killer kids and appetites for excess: Reapproaching moral panic* (Ph.D.). Victoria University of Wellington, Wellington, New Zealand.
Wright, S. (2015). Moral panics as enacted melodramas. *British Journal of Criminology, 55*(6), 1245–1262. doi:10.1093/bjc/azv025v2.
Wright, S. (2016). "Ah … the power of mothers": Bereaved mothers as victim-heroes in media enacted crusades for justice. *Crime, Media, Culture, 12*(3), 327–343. doi:10.1177/1741659015623597.
Yar, M. (2012). Crime, media and the will-to-representation: Reconsidering relationships in the new media age. *Crime, Media, Culture, 8*(3), 245–260.
Young, J. (1974). Mass media, drugs and deviance. In P. Rock & M. Mackintosh (Eds.), *Deviance and social control* (pp. 229–259). London, England: Tavistock.

6
Killer Kids—A Case Study

The material case of moral panic that is the focus of this chapter illustrates the depth and breadth of concern that often emerges when a child is involved in a horrible event. As discussed in Chap. 3, childhood has become an important theme that threads through many contemporary panics (Critcher, 2003). In the first section of this chapter, I explore how our cultural understandings of children and of childhood developed, and I do this to provide a broader backdrop for understanding why the case of killer kids emerged. Why it emerged in the specific ways in which it did will be attended to after the inductive analysis of the material on-the-ground-happening episode.

Mini-monsters

Jenks (1996) identifies two images of children that underpin our understandings of children (see also de Young, 2004; Hill, 2005). These images coexist but are diametrically opposed to each other. The first image is of the Apollonian child who is innocent and naive, vulnerable and dependent. The second image is of the Dionysian child: the impish

S. Wright Monod, *Making Sense of Moral Panics*, Palgrave Studies in Risk, Crime and Society, DOI 10.1007/978-3-319-61821-0_6

demanding child who is oriented towards self-gratification and is susceptible to corruption. Western societies invest heavily in the first image by assigning its features as *natural* characteristics of children, inherent to *all* children (Davies, 1997; Hockey & James, 1993). This investment is conducted with a 'knowing', not an entirely conscious knowing, that this preferred idea of 'the child' is a social construction and that the Dionysian image could appear at any time.

Indeed, historical accounts demonstrate that 'the child' is a slippery concept, a product of culture rather than a set of definitive and innate qualities of a particular time in the lifespan of a human being (Holland, 2004; Jenks, 1996; Jewkes, 2004). In Western societies, this product is marked by its relation to adulthood and denoted by its special, Apollonian qualities. These are qualities that were gradually bestowed upon children in the shift from agricultural societies to industry and the formation of the nuclear family. Smaller families mean children have become rare commodities. Children have moved from being conceived of as 'chattels' to having immeasurable or 'priceless' emotional value (Jenks, 1996). Their value also stems from a host of social, legal and institutional developments that have ensured children's physical distance from adulthood and emphasized their unique differences. Alongside the introduction of compulsory schooling, the outlawing of child labour and the development of welfare agencies, paediatrics and psychological theories and practices of child development and care have emerged to ensure the well-being of the young (Best, 1990; Davies, 1997; Hacking, 1991; James & James, 2004). We deny this history of childhood but our knowing of its truth is revealed through our *practice* of childhood: as we socialize real children into the norms of childhood and as we regulate our own relations with them (James & James, 2004). Part of this practice is to reproduce not just an understanding of 'childhood' but of society itself, as the idea of the child often symbolizes all that is stable and all that is possible (Jackson & Scott, 1999; Jenks, 1996).

Some scholars argue that contemporary anxieties about children are manifestations of our attempts to manage new risks. That is, as adults become more risk aware and more preoccupied with preventing risk, the need to protect children—who are thought to be innately vulnerable—becomes ever more imperative (Critcher, 2003;

Macdonald, 2003). Others argue that anxieties about risky children are quite routine. As Scraton (1997, p. 166) contends, every ageing generation 'wrings its hands at the declining moral fibre of its children'. Nevertheless, children who commit *impossible* acts, those thought to be so far removed from the scripts of idealized childhood, generate fear and alarm, and *panic* (Cohen, 1972; Cromer, 2004). They reveal that the image of the Dionysian child is omnipresent, despite all our intentions to ensure that real children emulate its opposite. Jewkes (2004) argues that the way we cognitively manage and reconstruct the quintessential child figure is by locating ideal children and those who deviate from this preferred image in stark division to the other: in terms of 'tragic victims' (those who are *at* risk—the Apollonian children) and 'mini-monsters' (those who *pose* a risk—the Dionysian children) (see also Valentine, 1996).

The most well-known example where each of these images can be seen in relation to each other is in the aftermath of the murder of toddler James Bulger in Britain in 1992 (see Davis & Bourhill, 1997; Green, 2008; Hay, 1995; James & Jenks, 1996; Jenks, 1996; Muncie, 2004; Valentine, 1996). James had been with his mother at a Liverpool mall when he was led away by two 10-year-olds. His body was found two days later on a railway line, several kilometres away. The two offenders, Robert Thompson and Jon Venables, were tried and found guilty in November 1993. What followed was an unprecedented social reaction. The press was saturated with details of the event, and public attitudes turned 'unrelentingly retributivist and punitive' (Franklin & Petley, 1996, p. 134). Terrified parents clung to their own children's hands whilst experts and politicians scrambled to lay blame upon someone or some*thing* (Hay, 1995). Young (1996) claims that at the heart of the reaction was the disturbance between semblance and substance—that is, the appearance of innocence children (that images of Thompson and Venables exhibited) with the knowledge of evil deeds committed by those children. The real violence of the crime, as Brown (2005) argues, was the violence enacted against adult notions of child*hood.* Adults' understanding of who children were and what they might do became undone. Furedi (2013) describes it this way:

> It was as if suddenly adults did not quite know what made their children tick. What this reaction signalled was not that parents feared that their children were murderers in the making. What it reflected was a sense of estrangement—do we really know them?

It is this uncertainty about childhood which lends itself to the development of moral panics about children. The next sections report on the case of 'killer kids' which emerged in New Zealand in 2002 and continued through to 2008. The similarities between the panic about James Bulger's murder and the case of killer kids are striking, almost parallel at many junctures, despite the two emerging almost a decade and half a globe apart. Killer kids still carved its own course, however, and the ways by which it did reveal much about why an inductive approach to the study of panic is important. I begin by addressing the questions of the first phase of panic research outlined in the last chapter. Why did I believe there was a case of moral panic before me? What happened? Was there a folk devil? Was there evidence of disproportionality?

The Murder of Michael Choy

On 25 August 2002, a photograph of 13-year-old Bailey Junior Kurariki was splashed across two-thirds of front page space of New Zealand national newspaper the *Sunday Star Times*. It was a striking photograph of a beautiful, wide-eyed and smiling child of Polynesian heritage. The table that he was seated behind reached up to his mid-chest area, illustrating how small he was. Situated *within* the image, adjacent to and parallel in size to Bailey's face and in bold font was the headline 'Our youngest killer' (Wellwood, 2002). For copyright reasons, I am unable to reproduce this image here. However, readers can find it in a Google image search using Bailey's given name and surname as keywords.[1]

Bailey had been part of a group of six youths who had fatally attacked pizza delivery person Michael Choy with a baseball bat a year earlier. The image was taken inside a courtroom after the group had been found responsible for the murder. Bailey, the youngest of the group, who had played the role of 'lookout' in the crime, was convicted of manslaughter. Two of the older offenders, 16-year-old Alexander Peihopa, who had carried out the physical attack on Mr. Choy, and 17-year-old Whatarangi Rawiri, were convicted of murder. The media had paid little attention to the murder at the time that it had occurred, however, despite that it was riddled with newsworthy elements (see Chap. 4). This is most likely because these events occurred *on the same day* as the attacks on the World Trade Centre in New York—11 September 2001,[2] and the New Zealand media were understandably preoccupied with events that were unfolding on the world stage. More attention was paid to the case during the trial. The media at this time covered the crown's argument and gave details of the fatal attack on Michael Choy. The extraordinary sight of a 13-year-old boy in the dock was also often mentioned. After the image appeared, however, coverage of the case *saturated* the press, with the focus now almost entirely on Bailey's involvement in the crime. And the media set about actively demonizing him. It was said that he was a nasty piece of work and pivotal in the death of Michael Choy (Wellwood, 2002). He was cold-blooded and heartless ('Who is responsible?', 2002); the most troubling of the group of young offenders ('Young and bad', 2002); 'extremely difficult' (Wall, 2002b); and he couldn't control himself (Wall, 2002a). Reports also featured an array of statements from significant public figures about why the murder had occurred and who could be held responsible, with many also offering dire predictions if something was not done *now*. Then Commissioner for Children Roger McClay called for an immediate governmental inquiry into the issue of 'killer kids', whilst politicians across the political spectrum urged for an investigation into the inadequacy of welfare organizations. Lobby groups and 'expert' individuals argued New Zealand's youth justice system, which is often considered innovative and 'world-leading' for its particular blend of justice and welfare objectives, was a failed experiment.

A Moral Panic?

The above paragraphs describe what could initially be observed of the matter of 'killer kids'. As one development gave way to another I suspected that I was witnessing a moral panic unfold. There had been a trigger event (the display of the image), the inventory of a 'threat' by the media (Bailey/killer kids), a reaction by 'right-thinking people' and sets of diagnoses and solutions proposed by experts. The six responsible for Michael Choy's death were sentenced on 16 September 2002. From this point, reports about the case grew further apart and less evocative in their tone. However, a sense of momentum would regather about six weeks later as reports started to include questions about the efficacy of the justice system to deliver 'justice' for Michael Choy's family and to manage the risk that Bailey, and other young offenders, posed. These questions would simmer away for the next six years. In response to them, Member of Parliament Ron Mark introduced The Young Offenders (Serious Crimes) Bill, which sought to reduce the age of criminal liability from 14 years to 12, in 2006. If accepted into law, the actions of young offenders could be 'nipped in the bud' swiftly and sharply, before they could cause any further harm.[3] The Bill, then, in panic terms, was a proposal for 'a way of coping'.

My initial observations of the episode were made in 2002, in the immediate aftermath of the trial for Michael Choy's murder. However, I did not undertake an analysis into the case until 2007, after the introduction of Young Offenders (Serious Crimes) Bill. By that time, I was confident that I had a panic to investigate in that there was clear evidence of disproportionality. The focus on Bailey and the representation of him as a 'killer', when he had been part of a group and had been convicted of manslaughter, not murder, immediately suggested that the 'threat' was being misrepresented. Bailey also received a sentence of 7 years, of which he served 6½ years incarcerated in a criminal justice facility. The United Nations Convention for the Rights of the Child (UNCRoC) stipulates in Article 37(b) states that:

> No child shall be deprived of his or her liberty unlawfully or arbitrarily. The arrest, detention or imprisonment of a child shall be in conformity with the law and shall be used only as a measure of last resort and for the shortest appropriate period of time.

Bailey's sentence was described by the defence team at the time of the sentencing as 'adult sized ... manifestly excessive and inappropriate' (Hogan cited in 'Boy did not plan', 2003), suggesting that it was out of step with the UNCRoC's principle in Article 37. Statistical data would also later show that the predicted battalion of violent youth offenders, that the Young Offenders (Serious Crimes) Bill purported to address, never appeared.[4] And, both at the time and much later, media professionals reflected on the treatment of Bailey by the press, determining it to be excessive and pejorative (see Wright Monod, 2016). It hence became clear that a measure by which a panic can be claimed could be satisfied, and that the case required further investigation.

The primary data sample used to examine 'killer kids' was made up of 'hard news' reports, articles, editorials and features relating to the event of the murder of Michael Choy, the trial and incarceration of the youths convicted and the formulation of the Young Offenders (Serious Crimes) Bill from the period of the time of the event (September 2001) until the period immediately after Bailey Kurariki was released from prison in April 2008. The sample was drawn from four broadsheet newspapers that are published daily in each of the four main cities of New Zealand: *The New Zealand Herald* (Auckland), *The Dominion Post* (Wellington), *The Press* (Christchurch) and *The Otago Daily Times* (Dunedin). Also included in the sample were three associated websites that are the online editions of these publications: www.nzherald.co.nz (*The New Zealand Herald*), www.odt.co.nz (*The Otago Daily Times*) and www.stuff.co.nz (which is the website of Fairfax Media, the press organization that owns the remaining publications used in this sample). Additionally, I assessed the two parliamentary debates about the Young Offenders (Serious Crimes) Bill: the first on 29 March 2006 and the second on 21 May 2008. At the time that the case first emerged, the need to consider the role of social media and of networked publics was not as pertinent as it would be to the analysis of a panic emerging today. Though there was evidence of commentary about the case on blogs and interest groups websites towards the end of the sampled period, I chose not to include these because their impact on the ways in which the episode unfolded was minimal when compared with the mainstream (legacy) media coverage.

Media data were located using the newspaper database *Australia and New Zealand Reference Centre* and employing the search terms 'Michael Choy' or 'Kurariki'. Articles within the period August 2001–May 2008 were downloaded in digital form ($n = 334$). A mixed sample of visually and verbally dominant bulletins (both hard news and commentary) was also purchased from the publicly owned television channel Television New Zealand (TVNZ) ($n = 32$). I organized the sample into a chronological order and then took 'a long soak' in the data (Hall, 1975), repeatedly reading it and rereading it to identify and confirm patterns of meaning. To assist me in this, I followed the set of questions in the second phase of researching a material moral panic: What is the panic about? What meanings are developing and across what spaces? How are they developing? Who are the claims-makers and what are their interests? What action is made possible from the emerging meanings?

Three Discourses, Two Phases, One Episode

The material episode of killer kids was marked by the presence of three separate discourses: (1) a discourse of moral reprisal, (2) a discourse of social rescue and (3) a discourse of criminal risk. The episode also played out over two phases: (1) a short feverish outburst, from the time of the appearance of the image on 25 August 2002 until the sentencing almost 4 weeks later, and (2) a lengthy simmering campaign, which emerged during the outburst phase but then got off ground in a fuller manner in November 2002 and lasted until May 2008. The next sections explore each of the three discourses more closely in relation to these two phases.

Moral Reprisal

The discourse of *moral reprisal* was sparked into being at the very moment the image of Bailey appeared in the *Sunday Star Times*. In every respect, this was a *panic* discourse, and the image's appearance was the trigger event. The discourse defined the 'problem' in terms of malevolent children, social disorder at the hands of dysfunctional families and moral decay in the move towards a more permissive society. It was a discourse initially *of* the media, and each of the things that the media is said to do in a moral panic can be seen in action: amplifying a problem, shaping up a folk devil and setting an agenda.

It was claimed by editors that the nation was horrified and in a collective sense of shock about the fact that a group of young people had committed a murder, one only 12 years old at the time. New Zealanders were said to be 'reeling' (Robson, 2002), 'angry' ('Young killer is no star', 2002), 'shocked and horrified' ('Don't blame', 2002), and 'outraged' (O'Conner, 2002). The emphasis at the time of the crime had been placed on the fact that it took place in South Auckland, an area known as 'the badlands' with 'packs of young children' roaming the streets (Purdy, 2001). It meant, also, that Bailey's dangerousness had a context, and that others from the same context might be similarly dangerous. Some journalists looked past context and attributed Bailey's dangerousness to his age with suggestions that youth had become more threatening than at any time in the past. Young offenders were becoming 'more sophisticated' ('Sorting out children', 2002) and 'potentially lethal, capable of casual violence of the worst sort' ('Young and bad', 2002). Additionally, there were suddenly more *of* them. Headlines such as 'Children Who Kill: Stand By For More' (Mirams, 2002) followed the conviction of the six teens. We were to be bombarded with 'an ugly rash of young killers' (Dekker, 2002) with no sense of boundaries or responsibilities (Mirams, 2002). Boys like Bailey were 'no longer rouge aberrations' ('Young killer is no star', 2002), and there was a 'saga of youth crime sweeping the country' ('Time to act', 2002). Bailey's actions in the crime were said to serve 'as a clear warning' ('Lining up to kill', 2002). The very same disruption to childhood that had occurred in the Bulger case was happening in New Zealand. Commentators put it in these ways:

> If such an innocent-looking child can take part in planning and executing such a senseless slaying, what hope is there for retaining the trust of others? ('Benefits disappear', 2002)
>
> Are our children worse than they used to be? Is this the onset of a wave of hideous child crime, payback for some creeping national deficiency? (Dekker, 2002)

Media reports also shaped the devil by singling out Bailey from the group of which he was a part and repeatedly referring to him as *New Zealand's Youngest Killer*. A count revealed that there were 54 references to Bailey as 'New Zealand's youngest killer' in the outburst phase in the print media alone. It was also implied that he had long been 'a killer' in the making. It was reported that he was feared by children across South Auckland and had been 'running riot for years … terrorizing, beating and robbing other children, encouraging friends to truant from school, shoplifting, tagging, sniffing glue and smoking cannabis' (Wall, 2002a). He was a ringleader and an experienced criminal who was 'fated to go off the rails' (Rudman, 2002).

Much was also made of Bailey's appearance. He was described as 'angelic' ('Lining up', 2002), 'cherub-faced' (Bingham, 2002), 'baby-faced' (Collins, 2002) and 'peach skinned' (Dekker, 2002). Many claimed that his appearance seemed at odds with a 'killer' character. Editors exclaimed that he had '…the face of an angel, but the mind of a cold-blooded killer' (Collins, 2002), and that the 'angelic face of Bailey Kurariki … disguises the terrible reality' ('Young and bad', 2002). Indeed, it was this disturbance *between semblance and substance*, which was also a feature of the Bulger case (Young, 1996) that was thought to be the defining aspect of the case. It was 'the most chilling aspect of a horrific story' ('Time to act', 2002), and New Zealanders were asked to think about 'how that face of innocence turned into a killer' ('Benefits disappear', 2002).

The press set an agenda, by calling for *something to be done.* Dealing with the issues that had led to the crime was 'urgently needed' ('Why no inquiry on BJ', 2002) and the country's 'highest priority' ('Children who turn to killing', 2002). As one editor expressed:

> Not too long ago, a story such as Kurariki's would have been considered monstrous and unthinkable in New Zealand, an aberration. Now it is becoming a regular jolt to our senses. We cannot allow ourselves to become inured to it … it is essential *something is done.* ('Time to act', 2002, emphasis added)

The discourse of *moral reprisal* was also a discourse of Right-wing leaning commentators and politicians. Their statements sharpened up the media's early achievements in amplifying a problem. It was claimed that Bailey was not unique 'by any stretch of the imagination' (Lashlie cited in Mirams, 2002), and that there were 'hundreds of others out there' (Latta cited in 'Interview with Paul Holmes', 2002). The folk devil was also confirmed. Bailey was described as 'a dangerous little boy' (Newbold cited in Andrew, 2002) by one commentator and as 'a thoroughly evil little snot' (Clarke, 2002) by another.

Responding to the media's call for *something to be done*, commentators set an agenda with suggestions for a number of solutions, each of which rested on a specific diagnosis about the problem. Some called for a return to conservative family values:

> Liberal politicians, academics and social engineers have presided over the destruction of the sanctity of marriage, the institution of the family and the mystery of sex, the denigration of manhood and fatherhood and have sanctioned the wholesale slaughter of the most defenseless among us, the unborn child … yet we wonder why the likes of 13-year-old Bailey Junior Kurariki turns out to be the evil, twisted, cruel little psychopath he is. (George, 2002)

Others took aim at New Zealand's hybrid welfare/justice approach to youth justice. Whilst this approach has been considered as 'world-leading' by academics and justice officials worldwide for its emphasis on restorative practices,[5] commentators active in the discourse of *moral reprisal* argued that these had failed to teach some young offenders 'a lesson'. Bailey was a 'frightening example' of what could happen when the system didn't stamp down early ('Sorting out the children', 2002).

This discourse of *moral reprisal* dominated the outburst phase of the episode, from the time of the appearance of the image of Bailey Kurariki until just after the sentencing of the offenders four weeks later. Its arguments did not go unchallenged, however. The discourse of *moral reprisal* had to work against the claims of a discourse that was significantly concerned with the welfare of young offenders, both prior to their offending and thereafter.

Social Rescue

The discourse of *social rescue* argued for perspective in relation to the claims that were being made, for 'the system' to be held accountable and for the crime to be seen as an incident arising from modern conditions and the social consequences of the free market. This was a discourse of child welfare experts and Left-leaning politicians (and some editors), and was largely a discourse that emerged in response to the arguments put forth by the discourse of *moral reprisal.* The crime, it was argued, was not a symptom of social ruin, but simply a horrible outcome of a pathetic prank:

> This was not a 'highly organized unit' carrying out the robbery with military precision ... it was a ragbag bunch of neighbourhood kids ... [and] a harebrained scheme to get some food and some small change. (Mansfield cited in 'Alleged murder decoy', 2002)

One editor made the point that children, on a whole, remained far more offended against (by adults) than they did offend (Dekker, 2002). New Zealanders were also reminded of the enduring nature of anxiety about youth crime:

> "Complaints about the younger generation go right back to Pliny in Ancient Rome" (Dekker, 2002).

The discourse of *social rescue* blamed the murder on modern, social conditions. It was argued that modern children faced a number of unique life hurdles, one of which was an unprecedented exposure to vivid violent and sexual messages via the media. The logic of the free market and the dramatic economic restructuring that began in 1984 and almost overnight turned New Zealand from being one of the most regulated welfare states into one of the most deregulated were also to blame. It was these developments that had propagated 'the conditions that breed children who kill' (Gordon, 2002). Solutions could be found in a multi-agency approach and 'multi-systemic therapy' to untangle the psychological and emotional damage suffered by individual 'hardcore' children like Bailey (Boyd, 2005). One commentator noted with some irony that jail would offer Bailey the type of opportunities that should have been available to him as a matter of course:

> If we had 'no tolerance' for illiteracy, 'no tolerance' for school expulsion, 'no tolerance' for school failure, and 'no tolerance' for neglecting our most vulnerable children, then the youth crime rate would fall dramatically.... It's a shame, is it not, that he [Bailey] had to commit such a terrible crime to get some decent opportunities? (Gordon, 2002)

The discourse of *social rescue* was also relatively self-aware of itself in relation to its nemesis. The discourse of *moral reprisal*, it was argued, was a 'cacophony of hate, anger, resentment, pain and bewilderment' by the 'swelling tide of the lock 'em up and throw away the key brigade' (O'Conner, 2002).

Both discourses subsided after the sentencing of the offenders and the outburst phase came to a close. That the sentences were interpreted to be 'excessive' suggests that the discourse of moral reprisal commanded the interpretative terrain. This is not to suggest that the punitive mood of the discourse of moral reprisal would have affected the sentencing Judge in his decision-making, but to say that the outcome of that decision tempered that mood. The third discourse, the discourse of *criminal risk*, was also punitive in its tone, but it was focused less on reasons for why Bailey was a dangerous child and more the on the efficacy of the criminal justice system to control him. This discourse argued that New Zealand's justice system was far too lenient (picking up on one of the arguments of the discourse of moral reprisal), that 'justice' needed to be served and that community safety needed to be assured.

Criminal Risk

Elements of the character of the discourse of *criminal risk* emerged immediately after the trial in the outburst phase and in threads of the discourse of moral reprisal. However, it was not until November 2002, after the sentencing and sometime after the outburst had settled, that the discourse of *criminal risk* would form a definitive shape. Whilst some editors and commentators were intermittently active in this discourse, it was mostly steered by a particular subset of 'Right-thinking' moral entrepreneurs: the law and order lobby group, the Sensible Sentencing Trust (SST) and Michael Choy's mother, Rita Croskery. The SST had formed in 2001 with the objective to place pressure on the government to respond to everyday New Zealanders' concerns and use 'common sense' when making decisions to do with violent offenders. Rita Croskery joined the SST after her son had died, and in November of 2002, she became the group's ambassador for victims of violent crimes, the very point at which the discourse of *criminal risk* would take on a definitive shape. Together, the SST and Rita Croskery would argue that New Zealand's 'world-leading' youth justice system and its emphasis upon restorative practices were effectively aiding and abetting the development of a burgeoning bunch of 'seasoned criminals'. Bailey Kurariki would become their poster boy.

The discourse of *criminal risk* was initially focused upon a specific set of questions about whether the justice system could deliver a sense of 'justice' for Rita and her family. Despite the 7-year term handed down to Bailey, it was argued that he would 'probably be out of jail' ('Doubtful the Choy quest', 2002) after serving only one-third of his sentence. This meant that he would become part of a trend of offenders 'leaving prison early for the living room sofa' ('Doubtful the Choy quest', 2002),[6] and this was seen as offensive, and to 'anyone's sense of justice' ('Dilemma over what', 2002). Rehabilitative practices were also interpreted as 'special attention', i.e. people who committed the most serious crimes were perceived to get more help than those who didn't (Bingham, 2002). A visit to Bailey by two All Blacks (New Zealand's national rugby team) in an effort to provide positive role models for him was fervently condemned by McVicar, for example, who argued that not only would Bailey think he was a hero, but that the visit sent the wrong message to other young offenders (Gamble, 2002).

Questions about justice for Rita and her family gave way to questions about safety for the wider community as Bailey's first parole bid approached almost a year later. Rita planned to attend the hearing and was particularly vocal in the press with her view that Bailey was a 'shrewd and cunning criminal' who would be a 'real menace' if released early (Rita Croskery cited in Crean, 2003). McVicar also stated:

> Until this young killer learns some rules, he should stay where he is… if he comes out and goes back into the environment from which he came, and starts reoffending, then we've got a criminal for life. (McVicar cited in Kay, 2003)

Incidentally, the parole board would reject his bid, firm in a view that he still posed an 'undue risk to the community' ('Parole board got it', 2004).

The discourse of *criminal risk* would simmer across the next six years. Stephen Franks, the justice spokesperson for the far-Right-leaning political party ACT, argued that the justice system needed to send a consistent message to young offenders, and not hand out second and third chances on a regular basis (Franks cited in Claridge, 2003). Frontline police wanted more powers to intervene with young offenders (Watt, 2007). Editors would periodically reflect on the case and wonder what could be done to prevent young people from committing horrible crimes. One argued that holding them for long periods might do the trick ('Parole board got it', 2004). Another advocated early screening ('Let's Screen Early', 2008). The criminal case also remained inherently newsworthy, providing a backdrop for other news stories. The following excerpt from a news story illustrates this well:

> When Bailey Kurariki became one of New Zealand's youngest convicted killers in September 2001, the country sat up and asked why and how a 12-year-old child could have taken part in such a brutal killing.... Seven years on since the brutal murder of Mr Choy, New Zealand remains in the grip of teenage attackers. This time, their fingers are wrapped firmly around jagged rocks and handles of knives. (McDonald, 2008)

However, the discourse of *criminal risk* would mostly surface in the campaign against parole led by Rita, which she argued was a 'dangerous experiment' (Croskery cited in Davis, 2007). Her experience was evident of that, she argued: 'we do not want another tragedy such as ours... public safety is paramount' (Croskery cited in 'NZ's youngest killer fails', 2007). Those who attacked her son were *not* on parole at the time, however. Rita would attend all parole hearings of each of the youths involved in the murder of her son and regularly make statements to the media about these, and especially about her attendance at Bailey's hearings. She found these hearings harrowing and would often express so in an emotional way, lending another newsworthy component to the story (see Wright, 2016). Moreover, she would frequently draw attention to the contradictions inherent in the image of Bailey, and of the risk of taking him, and others like him, at face value:

> He is a real con-man ... he has got such an angelic face and knows how to talk to people and behave. (Croskery cited in 'Young Killer Applies', 2003)

> He has got a brilliant smile. You wouldn't think he was dangerous. He doesn't look dangerous but those are the worst kind, with all the cunning. (Croskery cited in 'NZ's youngest killer fails', 2007)

Indeed, over the course of the episode, Rita's campaign against parole became her legacy to achieve justice on behalf of her dead son. This is best illustrated with her pledge to continue campaigning after Bailey had been granted home detention in an article poignantly headlined 'Mum's marathon mission stretches on' (Binning, 2008):

> I'm doing it for Michael, because that's what I said to him [when he died]—that I would do what I could to keep these people behind bars for as long as possible.... People think just because that little brat [Kurariki] is out now that is the end of it but it's not. (Rita Croskery cited in Binning, 2008)

The arguments of the discourse of *criminal risk*, in particular the idea that getting young offenders *into* court, and early, would mitigate against the risk they posed, would become a formal proposal with the introduction of the Young Offenders (Serious Crimes) Bill. The Bill proposed to lower the age of criminal liability from 14 years of age to 12.[7] Significantly, it appeared to have been the Choy case that was the driving force behind the Bill's formulation:

> It is those crimes that, left unchecked, create the long-term adult criminal. We believe we will stop some young people graduating to serious crime and ending up like Bailey Kurariki in jail. (Mark cited in 'Bill urges jail', 2006)

The Bill would pass its first reading but remain in the select committee stage for two years. This afforded time for a number of challenges to its foundational assumptions from those with the expertise to appear. Youth court judges, the Children's Commissioner, the New Zealand Law Society and the Human Rights Commission all made submissions to the select committee fundamentally opposing the Bill's proposed changes (see Lynch, 2010).[8] Principal Youth Court Judge Andrew Becroft publically described the Bill as an 'abysmally drafted' document that had been put together in response to a problem that simply was not there—'where is the statistical evidence to suggest offending by 10 to 13-year-olds is spiraling out of control?' (Becroft cited in 'If it's not broken', 2007). The Law and Order select committee would recommend to parliament that it reject the Bill on the basis that its proposed changes would not only seriously undermine the jurisdiction of the Youth Court in New Zealand, but that its implementation would also contravene the UNCROC and the International Covenant on Civil and Political Rights, both of which New Zealand had ratified (Law and Order Committee, 2007). And, as indicated, the Bill would be subsequently thrown out of parliament on 21 May 2008, and only a short time after Bailey had been released from jail.

Just as each of these discourses could be seen to be quite different in their character, the effect of each on the episode as a whole would also be quite different. The discourse of *moral reprisal* amplified the problem, shaped the folk devil, set an agenda and proposed solutions. It was, in all respects, a panic discourse. The discourse of *social rescue* attempted to interrupt the course of the episode with its counterclaims. The outburst would subside once the sentences for the youths involved in the murder of Michael Choy had been handed down. These were described as excessive sentences, and they appeared to soothe the punitive temper of the discourse of *moral reprisal.* The episode would re-emerge in November of 2002 with the entry of the discourse of *criminal risk*, which kept the events of the murder of Michael Choy firmly in the public eye for the next six years. This discourse was focused on achieving justice and enduring safety, and was largely driven by the SST and Michael Choy's mother, Rita Croskery. This phase of the reaction resembled a *moral campaign* (see Goode & Ben-Yehuda, 1994) though ultimately the episode can still be seen as one entity, one panic. Bailey remained at the centre of dialogue and the problem remained to be one about kids who kill.

What explains the unique shape of this episode, a short-range outburst followed by a more lengthy campaign? What, in this place, supports the development of the meanings that give rise to this shape? What, at this time, supports the development of these meanings? These are the questions of the third phase of panic research, and they are addressed in the next section.

Truths, Fantasies and Punitive Tempers

The events of the murder of Michael Choy and the trial for the six accused a year later touched on a set of truths assumed of news images and of crime images, a plethora of racialized fantasies about 'criminal others' and a punitive sensibility amongst ordinary folk which was gaining a good deal of political influence at that time.

News Images and Crime Images

News images are understood to be 'truthful'. Scholars have argued that photographs are unique in that they appear to simply stand in for what is seen by the human eye, thus denying that they hold any connotative qualities (Hall, 1981; Holland, 2004; Lister & Wells, 2001). That is a little more difficult to say in an era of Photoshop and routine practices of digital manipulation. However, *news* photographs, like news itself, are underwritten with notions of neutrality and objectivity; indeed, even more so by virtue of the capacity to 'show' (Hall, 1981; Holland, 2004; Pogliano, 2015). This understanding masks the work involved in the construction of a news photograph at its site (setting, lighting, arrangement, author and subject) as well as dismisses the professional knowledge of the 'decisive moment' in which the photographer seeks to 'capture' his or her subject/s at a moment that conveys the essence of the scene (Holland, 2004; Pogliano, 2015). It also conceals the techniques of image construction, juxtaposition and manipulation and the complex ways in which these things intersect across multiple news platforms (Jones & Wardle, 2010).

Crimes images are also understood to be truthful. The law, for example, 'looks at photographs as if there were nothing impeding its capacity to see' (Biber, 2007, p. 5). Indeed, we consider images of crime to be the most truthful of all genres of photographs: they are *evidential* (Carrabine, 2015; Tagg, 1988). This is despite that images of criminal events and bodies have always been 'staged', partly as criminal acts tend to take place outside of public view (and thus, our witnessing of them takes place after the fact and via mediated representations), and partly as the construction of 'real' crime is deeply entangled with constructions of fictional crime (Ferrell & Websdale, 1999).

The image of Bailey Kurariki was one taken by a press photographer inside a courtroom, shortly after the trial for the murder of Michael Choy had come to close. Therefore, it was concurrently a news image *and* an image of a convicted criminal. The headline 'Our Youngest Killer' that captioned Bailey's imagery suggested that this was *not* a child, at least in the sense that most readers would have understood a child to be (innocent, naïve and vulnerable). Indeed, this was *no longer* an image of a child. The anchorage of the image as one of a criminal suggested that there was a profound deception inherent in what was seen. The headlines 'Freaks of Nature' which appeared in the Daily Mirror and 'How Do You Feel Now You Little Bastards' which the Daily Star ran in relation to the 10-year-old murderers in the Bulger case in the UK (see Franklin & Petley, 1996) would also have prohibited a denotative reading of a child. In both cases, therefore, the children concerned were 'conceptually evicted' from the category of the child (Jenks, 1996). The fact that Bailey looked like a quintessential Apollonian child was a deliciously newsworthy component of the case, as illustrated by the commentary about the 'chilling' disturbance between Bailey's angelic appearance and the knowledge of the crime he had been part of. There was another element in the image of Bailey, however, which ensured that Bailey would ultimately come to be understood as a mini-monster.

Criminal Brown Others

In the New Zealand context, Polynesian children with brown faces are subject, like all children are, to the social and historical constructions of 'the child', but, unlike other children (those with pale faces), they are additionally vulnerable to understandings of them as the deficient ethnic 'other'. New Zealand, like Canada, the USA and Australia, is a settler society with a history of systemic dispossession of the economic, cultural, social and spiritual foundation of the indigenous Maori. The legacy of this dispossession is stark. As Hogg and Carrington (2016) state, day-to-day life for most indigenous people around the world is one experienced in poverty, with all of the associated ills such as high levels of poor heath and familial violence, coupled with disproportionate contact with criminal justice systems. Pacific peoples in New Zealand have had a different history, but suffer, as a population group, many of the same social ills as Maori do. Groups of Pacific peoples migrated to New Zealand after WW2 to fulfil a shortage in the low and semi-skilled labour force. By the 1970s, in a time of economic downturn, they were seen as free-riders taking the jobs from ordinary (European) New Zealanders. Some unjust practices were enacted under the banner of this fiction. Police conducted 'dawn raids', in which they would forcibly enter a house at dawn in Pacific communities to locate 'illegal immigrants' and deport them, for example (Hill, 2010; Grainger, 2009). Both populations (the indigenous Maori and Pacific people) can be seen therefore as 'southern others': marginalized and excluded, and often *criminalized* others (Carrington, Hogg, & Sozzo, 2016). And both populations are subject to a racialized regime of representation whereby they are talked about and depicted as 'mad, bad and sad' across multiple public arenas (Beddoe, 2014; Came & McCreanor, 2015; Loto et al., 2006). Maori and Pacific children are often presented as underachievers with behavioural problems, and as tragic victims of violent 'brown' parents (Beddoe, 2014; Phillips & Mitchell, 2010; Smith, 1996), all of which are known risk factors for early engagement in a criminal activity (Farrington, 2007). Each time a brown-faced child is displayed in these terms, a racialized regime of the Polynesian 'other' child emerges, one that reinforces for the observer that these children do not quite fit the mould of the imagined, idealized child. Therefore, the image of Bailey was not an exposé of innocence corrupted nor could it be seen to be a deceptive image. Indeed, the image of Bailey provided *proof* that brown children were criminogenic. And this was *in spite of* his angelic appearance.

Penal Populism

New Zealand has the second highest incarceration rate amongst English-speaking countries in the OECD. At the end of 2012, for example, 192 per 100,000 persons were imprisoned. Comparatively, the USA imprisoned 710 per 100,000 persons, and the UK imprisoned 147 per 100,000 persons. Australia, New Zealand's closest geographic neighbour and a nation it has much in common with socially and culturally, imprisoned 130 per 100,000 persons in 2012 (Statista, 2017). New Zealand's notably high incarceration rate is not an indicator of abnormally high rates of serious crime, however. Instead, it has been attributed to New Zealand being a society in which *penal populism* has flourished, particularly over the last two decades (Pratt, 2006). Penal populism refers to a political discourse which champions the voice of the 'common man' in penal affairs, which leads to political parties competing with each other to be 'tough on crime'. Though democratic in principle, in *practice* it consists of the pursuit of policies that have little to do with reducing crime and promoting justice, and more to do with gaining an electoral advantage (see Bottoms, 1995; Roberts et al., 2003). However, Pratt (2008) argues it represents more than 'tapping in' to populist concerns at intermittent times. It is, rather, a product of a realignment of power which now extends across much of the modern social landscape. What characterizes this new axis of power is a stronger resonance between governments and extra-establishment individuals, groups and organizations who claim to represent 'the people'. In effect, this has often meant that rational argument is put aside in favour of public sentiment where issues of crime and punishment are concerned. Indeed, the central paradox that characterizes a trend, particularly in English-speaking countries, towards punitive penal reform is that it bears little relationship to *actual* crime rates. New Zealand is often seen as a case in point to demonstrate the influence of penal populism as it has enjoyed something of a 'full house' with respect to factors that cause the phenomena (see Pratt, 2008).

Pratt and Clarke (2005) discuss how penal populism gained momentum in New Zealand beginning with a general shift towards longer sentences and stricter parole requirements in the 1990s. Then in 1999, a Citizens Initiated Referendum (CIR) endorsing greater emphasis upon the needs of victims alongside harsher penalties for violent offenders won a 91.75% public vote. This would become, as Pratt and Clarke argue (2005, p. 305), a 'regular referent' against which the subsequent Sentencing, Parole, and Victims' Rights Acts of 2002 could be judged. Together, these Acts increased penalties, restricted parole and extended the rights of victims. Though developed amidst a law and order theme of the general election of 2002, which was not an unusual theme (a similar one was prevalent in the election of 1987), two factors would guarantee the Acts' materialization. First, most major political parties had taken a stance to be 'tough' on crime, and so in effect, there was a political consensus to address the law and order issue in such a manner.[9] Second, the SST was gaining authority as a lobby group aiming to bring about tougher sentences for prisoners. Pratt and Clarke (2005, p. 306) contend that the law and order component of the 2002 general election campaign was effectively led by the SST with 'politicians running to catch up with their demands'. Indeed, in November 2002, it was observed by a reporter that the SST's founder, Garth McVicar, had become 'an almost automatic media destination' (Gamble, 2002) about matters to do with law and order. This can account in part for why the SST (and Rita Croskery) was a dominant actor in the discourse of *criminal risk* and why this discourse then unfolded in terms of an anti-expert, emotional dialogue about the efficacy of the criminal justice system to deliver justice and manage risk. Indeed, the Choy case had all the ingredients that could illustrate the SST's forebodings about the fallout from an increasingly permissive society and the failings of the criminal justice system: a violent crime committed against a man who was going about his daily business, a set of plans to commit a callous offence that was made by young people who were seemingly unperturbed by any consequences that may stem from this act, and a bereaved mother who was ready to speak publically about the loss of her son and her perceptions of being wronged by the criminal justice system. In time, the SST would be accused of parading Rita's pain and exploiting her to meet its own institutional objectives ('Victim's mum exploited', 2008). And later, Rita's anguish and her mission to continue campaigning against parole, as well as her refusal to accept that the offenders involved in her son's murder were remorseful, came to be interpreted as 'bitter' and 'tragic' (Church, 2012). These reflections arguably challenged the legitimacy of the SST as a 'victim-centred' lobby group and Rita's voice as a spokesperson for victims of crime, which may in turn have played a part in the demise of the panic.

Implications

I have argued that context matters for understanding why a said panic occurs and for making connections between the concept of moral panic and social theory, which in turn can broaden the explanatory power of moral panic. In this chapter, I argued that the shape of the episode—a short-range outburst followed by a lengthy campaign—could be attributed to the events of the murder of Michael Choy touching on a set of truths assumed of news images and of crime images, racialized fantasies about 'criminal others' and a punitive sensibility amongst ordinary folk which was gaining a good deal of political influence in 2002. It was these contextual features that would support the meanings in the discourses that gave rise to the panicked reaction about killer kids. To illustrate this, I want to draw on another very similar case that unfolded in the same context, but at a different time. In June 2014, Arun Kumar was killed whilst tending his grocery shop in the west Auckland suburb of Henderson. A 14-year-old was subsequently charged with murder, and a 12-year-old was accused of manslaughter. The pair had planned to rob the shop and had taken a knife and a metal pole with them to carry out the deed. A year later the older boy was found guilty of the lesser charge of manslaughter, and the younger boy was found not guilty of the charge against him. Media coverage of the case was similar to that of the Choy murder during the trial in that it focused upon who was in court and what was said and so forth. The reaction afterwards, however, was far more subdued. Whilst the slain man's bereaved family questioned the verdicts, as one might expect they would, the media focused predominantly upon the defence teams' explanation that the crime was a direct result of the deprived background of each of the youths.

Reports also cited clinical experts who explained that bad choices came from 'significant emotional deregulation', which stemmed from lives of trauma (Boyer & Dennett, 2015). This dialogue is akin to the discourse of *social rescue* which unsuccessfully challenged the discourse of *moral reprisal* in the case of killer kids. So which contextual feature was missing? Though the interval between the two cases has seen some questions about the efficacy of the 'get tough' on crime agenda and some emphasis to reduce criminal justice spending (see Workman, 2008), New Zealand remains a relatively punitive country, sporting a high incarceration rate when compared to other English-speaking OECD countries, as indicated earlier. In addition, youth criminality is still a highly politicized topic, and there have been some questionable changes to youth justice legislation in the recent past. From 1974 until 2010, the age of criminal liability in New Zealand was 14 years. Young people aged 12 and 13 could be prosecuted for murder and manslaughter only. In 2010, however, amendments were made to the Child, Youth and the Families Act 1989, whereby young people aged 12 and 13 can have criminal charges brought against them in two further circumstances: (i) where the alleged offence carries a maximum penalty of at least 14 years, and (ii) where the maximum penalty is 10 years and the child can be proved to be a 'previous offender'. Commentators have argued that these changes illustrate that New Zealand's youth justice system is 'catching up' with the more punitive adult system in this country (Lynch, 2012). Moreover, a new punitive penal practice has been identified: the security sanction. The security sanction serves to manage 'risk' and protect the public from the possibility of offences against them by way of the use of measures such as prolonged sentences and restrictions of public space (see Pratt & Anderson, 2016). Therefore, the most significant difference between the two cases is that no pictures of the two involved in the Kumar murder have been published by the media or released in any public arena to date. Thus, the truth of news images and crime's images did not play a part in the responses to the Kumar murder. Incidentally, one of the clinical experts cited by the media shortly after the trial for the Kumar murder had completed argued for lessons to be drawn from the Choy case, in particular the negative impacts upon Bailey Kurariki's future that stemmed from the way he was depicted by the press (Lambie cited in Boyer & Dennett, 2015). Nevertheless, the differences between the two cases illustrate that whilst context matters, it is the *interaction* between the material panic and the context in which it emerges that matters most. Without imagery, the truth of news images and crimes images didn't have a focus. On the other hand, without this contextual feature that imagery would not have been meaningful.

In Chap. 8, I consider how these contextual features might lend themselves to a more abstract idea. In Chap. 7, I once again employ the framework to examine a case of moral panic about 'gangster guns'.

Notes

1. The *Sunday Star Times* shares copyright with the photographer, but they couldn't give me permission to use the image as it was taken inside a courtroom. No explanation for why was forthcoming. Jones and Wardle (2010) came across a similar embargo.
2. New Zealand is 17 hours ahead of New York.
3. The Bill was considered by parliament but would eventually be rejected as a law in May 2008, just weeks after Bailey Kurariki—by this point aged 18 years—was released from prison.
4. The biggest increase in recorded offences between 1998 and 2008 is for the age group 31–50 years. Recorded offences by youths 13 years and under across the same period show the lowest increase (www.stats.govt.nz).
5. For a clear assessment of this claim, and a formative review of the principles underpinning the model employed, see Becroft (2003) and Lynch (2012).
6. As noted, Bailey would serve 6½ years of his 7-year term incarcerated in a justice facility.
7. In New Zealand at that time, those aged between 10 and 13 years could only be charged for murder or manslaughter and were protected by the principle of 'doli incapax' if so charged.
8. The Children's Commissioner by this time was Dr. Cindy Kiro.
9. The Green party was not part of this consensus (Pratt & Clarke, 2005).

References

Alleged murder decoy "streetwise" beyond years court told. (2002, August 21). *The New Zealand Herald*. Retrieved from http://www.nzherald.co.nz.

Andrew, K. (2002, September 4). It's too tough—Killer. *The Press*, p. 1.

Becroft, A. (2003, December). *Youth justice—the New Zealand experience: Past lessons and future challenges*. Presented at the "Juvenile Justice: From Lessons of the Past to a Road for the Future" conference, Sydney, Australia. December 1–2.

Beddoe, L. (2014). Feral families, troubled families: The spectre of the underclass in New Zealand. *New Zealand Sociology, 29*(3), 51–68.

Benefits disappear in uproar over rugby icons' visit. (2002, November 13). *Taranaki Daily News*, p. 8.

Best, J. (1990). *Threatened children: Rhetoric and concern about child-victims*. Chicago: Chicago University Press.

Biber, K. (2007). *Captive images: Race, crime, photography*. Oxon: Routledge-Cavendish.

Bill urges jail for 12-year-olds. (2006, March 17). *The Dominion Post*, p. 3.

Bingham, E. (2002, August 31). Boy killer a special case. *The New Zealand Herald*. Retrieved from http://www.nzherald.co.nz.

Binning, E. (2008, April 26). Mum's marathon mission stretches on. *The New Zealand Herald*. Retrieved from http://www.nzherald.co.nz.

Bottoms, A. E. (1995). The philosophy and politics of punishment and sentencing. In C. Clarkson & E. Morgan (Eds.), *The politics of sentencing reform* (pp. 17–49). Oxford: Clarendon.

Boy did not plan Choy killing court told. (2003, June 12). *Dominion Post*, p. A5.

Boyd, S. (2005, March 26). Nicked in the bud. *Dominion Post*, p. WM2.

Boyer, S., & Dennett, K. (2015, July 26). Our youngest killers. *Sunday Star Times*, p. A12. Auckland, New Zealand.

Brown, S. (2005). *Understanding youth and crime: Listening to youth?* (2nd ed.). Berkshire: Open University Press.

Came, H. A., & McCreanor, T. (2015). Pathways to transform institutional (and everyday) racism in New Zealand. *Sites: A Journal of Social Anthropology and Cultural Studies, 12*(2), 24. doi:10.11157/sites-vol12iss2id290.

Carrabine, E. (2015). Visual criminology: History, theory, method. In H. Copes & J. M. Miller (Eds.), *Routledge handbook of qualitative criminology* (pp. 103–121). Florence, KY: Routledge.
Carrington, K., Hogg, R., & Sozzo, M. (2016). Southern criminology. *British Journal of Criminology, 56*(1), 1–20. doi:10.1093/bjc/azv083.
Children who turn to killing. (2002, September 19). *Waikato Times*, p. 6.
Church, P. (2012, January 16). Sensible sentencing. Retrieved from http://www.laidlaw.ac.nz/_blog/Our_Blog/post/Sensible_Sentencing/.
Claridge, A. (2003, September 15). Surge in violence by teens. *The Press*, p. A1.
Clarke, A. (2002, September 3). Who will take the rap for BJ? *The Nelson Mail*, p. 7.
Cohen, S. (1972). *Folk devils and moral panics*. Herts, England: Paladin.
Collins, A. (2002, September 1). Loss of innocence. *Sunday News*, p. 7.
Crean, M. (2003, October 6). Home detention possible for killer. *The Press*, p. A2.
Critcher, C. (2003). *Moral panics and the media*. Buckingham, England: Open University Press.
Cromer, G. (2004). "Children from good homes": Moral panics about middle-class delinquency. *British Journal of Criminology, 44*(3), 391–400.
Davies, S. (1997). A sight to behold: Media and the visualisation of youth, evil and innocence. In J. Bessant & R. Hil (Eds.), *Youth, crime and the media* (pp. 55–63). Hobart, Australia: National Clearinghouse for Youth Studies.
Davis, H., & Bourhill, M. (1997). "Crisis": The demonisation of children and young people. In P. Scraton (Ed.), *"Childhood" in "crisis"?* (pp. 28–57). London: UCL Press Limited.
Davis, J. (2007, January 22). Parole hearing for young killer. *The Press*, p. A1.
de Young, M. (2004). *The day care ritual abuse moral panic*. Jefferson, NC: McFarland and Company.
Dekker, D. (2002, September 7). Are we failing our children? *The Southland Times*, p. 31.
Dilemma over what to do with BJ. (2002). *The Nelson Mail*, p. 7.
Don't blame social workers. (2002, September 9). *Waikato Times*, p. 6.
Doubtful the Choy quest for justice served by appeals. (2002, September 18). *Taranaki Daily News*, p. 8.
Farrington, D. P. (2007). Childhood risk factors and risk focused prevention. In M. Maguire, R. Morgan, & R. Reiner (Eds.), *The Oxford handbook of criminology* (4th ed., pp. 602–640). Oxford, England: Oxford University Press.

Ferrell, J., & Websdale, N. (1999). Materials for making trouble. *Making trouble: Cultural constructions of crime, deviance, and control* (pp. 3–21). New York: Aldine de Gruyter.

Franklin, B., & Petley, J. (1996). Killing at the age of innocence: Newspaper reporting of the death of James Bulger. *Thatcher's children: Politics, childhood and society in the 1980s and 1990s* (pp. 134–154). Falmer: London, England.

Furedi, F. (2013, February 12). The 20th anniversary of James Bulger's death: A tragic episode and its shameful legacy. *The Independent.* United Kingdom. Retrieved from http://www.independent.co.uk/voices/comment.

Gamble, W. (2002, November 15). Justice campaigners in it for the long term. *The New Zealand Herald.* Retrieved from http://www.nzherald.co.nz.

George, G. (2002, August 29). How we managed to turn some of our kids into killers. *The New Zealand Herald.* Retrieved from http://www.nzherald.co.nz.

Goode, E., & Ben-Yehuda, N. (1994). *Moral panics: The social construction of deviance.* Cambridge, MA: Blackwell.

Gordon, L. (2002, September 4). Reclaiming our lost youth. *The Press,* p. A15.

Grainger, A. (2009). Rugby, Pacific peoples, and the cultural politics of national identity in New Zealand. *The International Journal of the History of Sport, 26*(16), 2335–2357. doi:10.1080/09523360903466776.

Green, D. A. (2008). *When children kill children: Penal populism and political culture.* Oxford, England: Oxford University Press.

Hacking, I. (1991). The making and molding of child abuse. *Critical Inquiry, 17*(2), 253–288.

Hall, S. (1975). Introduction. In A. Charles, H. Smith, E. Immirizi, & T. Blackwell (Eds.), *Paper voices: The popular press and social change, 1935–1965* (pp. 9–24). London, England: Chatto and Windus.

Hall, S. (1981). The determinations of news photographs. *The manufacture of news: Social problems, deviance, and the mass media* (pp. 226–243). London, England: Constable.

Hay, C. (1995). Mobilisation through interpellation. *Social and Legal Studies, 4,* 197–223.

Hill, M. (2005). The "satanism scare" in New Zealand: The Christchurch Civic Creche case. In A. Kirkman & P. Moloney (Eds.), *Sexuality down under* (pp. 97–113). Dunedin, New Zealand: Otago University Press.

Hill, R. S. (2010). Fitting multiculturalism into biculturalism: Maori-Pasifika relations in New Zealand from the 1960s. *Ethnohistory, 57*(2), 291–319. doi:10.1215/00141801-2009-064.
Hockey, J., & James, A. (1993). *Growing up and growing old: Ageing and dependency in the life course.* London: Sage.
Hogg, R., & Carrington, K. (2016). Crime and violence outside the metropole: An Australian case study. In J. F. Donnemeyer (Ed.), *The Routledge international handbook of rural criminology* (pp. 181–191). Oxon: Routledge.
Holland, P. (2004). *Picturing childhood: The myth of the child in popular imagery*. New York: I. B. Tauris.
If it's not broken no reason trying to fix it. (2007, July 23). *Taranaki Daily News*, p. 8.
Jackson, S., & Scott, S. (1999). Risk anxiety and the social construction of childhood. In D. Lupton (Ed.), *Risk and socialcultural theory: New directions and perspectives* (pp. 86–107). Cambridge, England: Cambridge University Press.
James, A., & Jenks, C. (1996). Public perceptions of childhood criminality. *British Journal of Sociology, 47*(2), 315–333.
James, A., & James, A. L. (2004). *Constructing childhood: Theory, policy and social practice.* Houndmills, England: Palgrave Macmillan.
Jenks, C. (1996). *Childhood.* Milton Keynes: The Open University.
Jewkes, Y. (2004). *Media and crime*. London, England: Sage.
Jones, P., & Wardle, C. (2010). Hindley's ghost: The visual construction of Maxine Carr. *Framing crime: Cultural criminology and the image* (pp. 53–67). Oxon: Routledge.
Kay, M. (2003, October 4). Questions over young killer's behaviour. *The Dominion Post*, p. A5.
Law and Order Committee. (2007). *Young Offenders (Serious Crimes) Bill: Report of the Law and Order Committee 28-1* (Select Committee report) (p. 15). New Zealand. Retrieved from http://www.parliament.nz/resource/en-nz/48DBSCH_SCR3912_1/a51ee9c485fd02299ccfb3cb1d9c0d-3383ceb1b4.
Let's screen early for offending. (2008, January 25). *The New Zealand Herald.* Retrieved from http://www.nzherald.co.nz
Lining up to kill? (2002, August 27). *The Timaru Herald*, p. 4.

Lister, M., & Wells, L. (2001). Seeing beyond belief: Cultural studies as an approach to analyzing the visual. *Handbook of visual analysis* (pp. 61–91). London, England: Sage.

Loto, R., Hodgetts, D., Chamberlain, K., Nikora, L. W., Karapu, R., & Barnett, A. (2006). Pasifika in the news: The portrayal of Pacific peoples in the New Zealand press. *Journal of Community & Applied Social Psychology, 16*(2), 100–118. doi:10.1002/casp.848.

Lynch, N. (2010). A change in the law for child offenders: The children, young persons, and their families (Youth Courts Jurisdiction And Orders) Amendment Act 2010. *New Zealand Family Law Journal, 6*, 289–292.

Lynch, N. (2012). Playing catch-up? Recent reform of New Zealand's youth justice system. *Criminology and Criminal Justice, 12*(5), 507–526.

Macdonald, M. (2003). *Exploring media discourse*. Oxford, England: Oxford University Press.

McDonald, G. (2008, February 2). Teens on the knife edge of society. *The Dominion Post*, p. A17.

Mirams, C. (2002, August 26). Children who kill: Stand by for more. *The Dominion Post*, p. A1.

Muncie, J. (2004). *Youth and crime* (2nd ed.). London, England: Sage.

NZ's youngest killer fails in bid for early release. (2007, July 13). *The New Zealand Herald*. Retrieved from http://www.nzherald.co.nz.

O'Conner, T. (2002, September 24). Retribution gets us nowhere. *The Nelson Mail*, p. 7.

Parole board got it right. (2004, January 23). *The Southland Times*, p. 6.

Phillips, H., & Mitchell, M. (2010). *'It's all about feeling the aroha': Successful Maori and Pasifika providers*. (No. EEL report number 7). Lincoln, New Zealand: AERU Research Unit of Lincoln University.

Pogliano, A. (2015). Evaluating news photographs: Trust, impact and consumer culture in the digital age. *Journalism Practice, 9*(4), 552–567. doi:10.1080/17512786.2015.1030141.

Pratt, J. (2006). *Penal populism*. London, England: Routledge.

Pratt, J. (2008). Penal scandal in New Zealand. *Penal populism, sentencing councils and sentencing policy* (pp. 31–44). Sydney, Australia: Hawkins Press.

Pratt, J., & Anderson, J. (2016). "The Beast of Blenheim", risk and the rise of the security sanction. *Australian and New Zealand Journal of Criminology, 49*(4), 528–545. doi:10.1177/0004865815590842.

Pratt, J., & Clarke, M. (2005). Penal populism in New Zealand. *Punishment and Society, 7*(3), 303–322.

Purdy, K. (2001, September 16). Pizza delivery murder brings fear. *Sunday Star Times*, p. A6.

Roberts, J. V., Stalans, L., Indermaur, D., & Hough, M. (2003). *Penal populism and public opinion*. New York: Oxford University Press.

Robson, M. (2002, September 15). Early prevention of criminality more effective than cure. *The New Zealand Herald*. Retrieved from http://www.nzherald.co.nz.

Rudman, B. (2002, August 28). Textbook case of child fated to go off the rails. *The New Zealand Herald*. Retrieved from http://www.nzherald.co.nz.

Scraton, P. (Ed.). (1997). *"Childhood" in crisis?* London, England: UCL Press Limited.

Smith, L. (1996). *Nga aho o te kakahu matauranga: The mulitple layers of struggle by Maori in education* (Ph.D.). University of Auckland, Auckland, New Zealand.

Sorting out children before they turn on the adults. (2002, August 26). *Taranaki Daily News*, p. 8.

Statista. (2017). Incarceration rates in OECD countries 2012/13. Retrieved from www.statista.com.

Tagg, J. (1988). *The burden of representation: Essays on photographies and histories*. London: Macmillan.

Time to act on child crime. (2002, August 25). *Sunday Star Times*, p. 8.

Valentine, G. (1996). Angels and devils: Moral landscapes of childhood. *Environment and Planning D: Society and Space, 14*, 581–599.

Victim's mum "exploited"—Prison aid group. (2008, March 10). *Stuff*. Retrieved from http://www.stuff.co.nz/national/308738/Victims-mum-exploited-prison-aid-group.

Why no inquiry on BJ Kurariki case? (2002, August 28). *The Nelson Mail*, p. 11.

Wall, T. (2002a). Welfare failed boy killer says police officer. *The New Zealand Herald*. Retrieved from www.nzherald.co.nz.

Wall, T. (2002b, August 26). Cherub's long, ruthless criminal career in 13 short years. *The New Zealand Herald*. Retrieved from http://www.nzherald.co.nz.

Watt, E. (2007, May 31). Pizza killer allowed out of jail to work. *The Dominion Post*, p. A3.

Wellwood, E. (2002, August 25). Our youngest killer. *Sunday Star Times*, p. A1.

Who is responsible? (2002, August 29). *The Otago Daily Times*, p. 16. Dunedin, New Zealand.

Workman, K. (2008). *Politics and punitiveness - overcoming the criminal justice dilemma*. Presented at the Lunchtime Series, School of Government and Institute of Policy Studies. Retrieved from http://www.rethinking.org.nz/assets/Media%20and%20Crime/Politics%20and%20Punitiveness%20.pdf.

Wright, S. (2016). "Ah … the power of mothers": Bereaved mothers as victim-heroes in media enacted crusades for justice. *Crime, Media, Culture, 12*(3), 327–343. doi:10.1177/1741659015623597.

Wright Monod, S. (2016). Portraying those we condemn with care: Extending the ethics of representation. *Critical Criminology*. doi:10.1007/s10612-016-9348-1.

Young, A. (1996). *Imagining crime: Textual outlaws and criminal conversations*. London, England: Sage.

Young and bad. (2002, September 2). *The Press*, p. A8.

Young Killer Applies for Home Detention. (2003, September 9). *The New Zealand Herald*. Retrieved from http://www.nzherald.co.nz.

Young killer is no star. (2002, September 2). *The Southland Times*, p. 6.

7

Gangster Guns—A Case Study

The issue of gun control has been at the centre of several moral panics. Most are centred on making a distinction between who should have access to guns and who should not. Critcher (2008) observes that concerns relating to urban spaces, drugs and disaffected young black men in the late 1980s and early 1990s merged into the perceived problem of gun crime related to crack cocaine. Chiricos (2006) interpreted these concerns as politically manufactured in order to distract the public from the dire consequences of neo-liberal social policies upon urban inner city youth and to justify, in turn, the expansion of the state's repressive apparatus (see also Chambliss, 1995). Public reactions after shooting rampages have also been steered in particular directions by those wanting to protect their own access to guns. Shooting rampages are shocking, unexpected events, and as a result very quickly become the centre of media and political attention (Hurka & Nebel, 2013). However, despite the fact that guns enact lethal violence and that shooting rampages would be impossible without them, increased restrictions on access to guns following such events are rare. There have been shooting rampages on many academic campuses in many countries and across time.[1] However, it is the profound, fearful reactions to shootings in the

S. Wright Monod, *Making Sense of Moral Panics*, Palgrave Studies in Risk, Crime and Society, DOI 10.1007/978-3-319-61821-0_7

USA which single out the USA as a context to focus on when making general statements about disproportional responses to school shootings.

Gun Control

Gun control was a hot political topic in the immediate aftermath of the Columbine High School shooting in Colorado in 1999, and many bills relating to firearms were introduced (over 800) (see Schildkraut & Hernandez, 2014). However, only a few 'token' laws were ever passed.[2] Communities were keen to take action nevertheless. School administrators erected gates on campuses, installed security cameras and guards, and implemented randomized checks for contraband held by students (Addington, 2009; Burns & Crawford, 1999; Muschert & Peguero, 2010). There was also a range of efforts to restrict the sale of violent books, movies and video games to children (Carvajal, 1999; Wright, 2000). Each of these actions was the kind that wouldn't pose any substantial challenge to the social order but would demonstrate that *something was being done* to address the problem (Ferguson, 2008; Wright, 2000). Muschert (2007) argues that the Columbine shooters Harris and Klebold were framed by the media narrative about the event as 'juvenile superpredators'; mythic, villainous caricatures who were detrimentally influenced by video games (especially *Doom*) and death metal music (particularly that of Marilyn Manson). This framing served to support the efforts to restrict popular culture material depicting violence.

Gun control was again a hot topic in the aftermath of the Sandy Hook Elementary school shooting in Newtown, Connecticut, in 2012. Following the massacre, one of the most deadly mass shootings in US history, President Obama called for a raft of gun control measures (Koenig & Schindler, 2016). The media too focused its coverage on gun control (Schildkraut & Muschert, 2014). However, to date, not one federal law has been passed (Svokos, 2015; Koenig & Schindler, 2016). Whilst there was some focus, once again, upon the effects of violent video games, it didn't take the kind of hold that it did after Columbine (see Ferguson & Olson, 2014).[3] Concerns coalesced instead on the mental well-being of Adam Lanza and other potential shooters (Koenig & Schindler, 2016). Indeed, the focus of gun control in the USA since Sandy Hook has been concentrated on the access to guns by 'deranged' individuals and other 'monsters' (Vicaro & Seitz, 2015).

What marks each of the responses to these school shootings in the USA is an initial question relating to a need for the control around access to guns, which is then very quickly followed by efforts to swing a shift towards controlling *some people's* access to guns (those who are deemed to be dangerous) or towards controlling something else entirely (that which evokes dangerousness) (Schildkraut & Hernandez, 2014). This shift is typical of moral panics and is what can be seen in the issue of gangster guns, to which I turn my attention now.

The Kawerau Event

On the evening of the 9th of March 2016, the New Zealand media reported that a siege involving a gunman in the Bay of Plenty town of Kawerau was underway. Police had engaged in a cannabis recovery operation in Kawerau, using a spotter aircraft. They heard gunshots, which they believed were being aimed at the plane. The shooter was soon identified to be a single individual with a gun in a house in Kawerau and police would cordon off a rural property after hearing another shot. The Armed Offenders Squad, a specialist unit of the New Zealand Police who are armed to deal with situations in which firearms are being used by suspects, were called into attend the scene from nearby Rotorua. Officers had entered the house and shots were exchanged between police and the gunman. Four officers suffered injuries in this exchange and were airlifted to hospital.

Police attempted to coax the gunman, 27-year-old Ray Warren, from the house. Approximately 100 armed police were present, as were media and some military vehicles. Warren's family, who had arrived on the scene, said that he was terrified of being shot and of returning to prison where he'd spent some time a few years earlier after a conviction for assault. A police commander from another district who knew the family was called upon to act as a liaison. After 23 hours, the siege came to an end as Warren was escorted out of the house and driven away in a police vehicle. The next day he would appear in court facing four charges of using a firearm against a law enforcement officer.

All in all, this was a single event involving tension between a lone gunman and armed police over a period of time during which negotiations were successful in reaching a peaceful conclusion. The events were newsworthy nonetheless. Police had been shot and injured. Locals were reported to be 'shocked' that the siege had taken place on one of the quietest roads in Kawerau where people live on lifestyle blocks, are kiwifruit growers or are retired ('Police injured in rural shooting', 2016). The events of the siege also transpired over a 23-hour period, meaning the press was able to offer a blow by blow account of a 'live situation' where the outcome was unpredictable. The events also lent themselves to a narrative frame. The lone gunman, the exchange of gunfire and the eventual taking of Warren into police custody were akin to scenes of a Western film genre.[4] Indeed, the headline 'A shootout, a siege, a surrender' (Wall, 2016) appeared on the day after the siege had ended.

The day after the siege had come to an end, opposition politicians called for an urgent inquiry into the 'gun problem'. The media, following a statement by the Minister of Police, began to associate the events in Kawerau with an unrelated police raid in Auckland, where a number of weapons had been discovered at a gang stronghold, repeatedly referring to them together as the double-barrelled rationale behind the need for an inquiry. The media also suggested that the 'issue' was potentially out of control and that public safety was at risk ('Time for a look at firearms', 2016; Milne, 2016). All of this served to suggest that there was a much larger problem at hand than one isolated event in Kawerau.

At the same time, several pro-gun organizations made public statements warning that any gun control measures would negatively affect New Zealand's 'inclusive firearms culture' (Sachdeva, 2016a) and that firearms were only a problem when in the 'wrong hands' ('Firearms sports', 2016). Blogger Cameron Slater, who writes on his site *Whale Oil*, also claimed:

> Criminals will get hold of guns if they want them. They will either steal them… or they will just apply copious amounts of illegal cash to buying

> them... Any law changes will simply further infringe the rights of law-abiding and responsible gun owners. (Slater, 2016a)

On March 16, it was reported that the Parliamentary Law and Order select committee had unanimously agreed to hold an inquiry into the *illegal possession of firearms* in New Zealand. The inquiry's draft terms of reference would be a specific focus on how guns were getting into the 'wrong hands', that is, the hands of criminals and gang members. These draft terms would later be formalized as:

- How widespread firearm possession is *amongst criminals, including gangs*?
- How *criminals, gangs* and those who do not have a licence come into possession of firearms?
- What changes, if any, to the current situation might further restrict the flow of firearms to criminals, gangs and those who do not have a licence (Law and Order Committee, 2016)?

Therefore, in less than a week after the events at Kawerau, a problem of criminals and gangs getting access to military-style weapons had been constructed and an inquiry had been initiated to 'do something' about it. This was a fairly swift sequence of events, even by moral panic standards, and it immediately caught my attention. However, was there evidence of disproportionality? Was there a folk devil?

A Moral Panic?

I found no available evidence that there were in fact *masses* of military-style semi-automatic weapons in criminal and/or gang hands. New Zealand, unlike Australia and Canada, only requires that gun owners are registered, not guns per se. There had been an increase in the numbers of *confiscations* of semi-automatic military-style weapons, but there has also been a marked increase in gun *licences* issued that was well over and above the increase in confiscations (Taylor, 2016). The proposed inquiry did not focus on 'rouge' licenced gun owners who are licenced to own guns who then import and then modify guns to sell to unlicensed individuals and groups, some of whom may be part of or have links to criminal activities, despite that two such individuals have been prosecuted in the recent past (Savage, 2014; Taylor, 2016). There was also a lack of discourse about the well-established associations in the literature about firearm crime between a lack of firearm security by owners and the theft of firearms and acts of violence that can follow (see Alpers & Walters, 1998; Walters, 2000).

The distinction between legal possession as unproblematic and illegal possession as problematic was also flawed. Literature concerned with the associations between firearm legislation and firearm deaths found that permissive laws were more likely to result in firearm deaths (Santaella-Tenorio, Cerda, Villaveces & Galea, 2016). The focus on military-style weapons was also without substance. McPhedran and Baker (2011) found that the banning of certain types of firearms has no demonstrable impact on the likelihood of mass shooting events (see also Santaella-Tenorio et al., 2016).

Indeed, like killer kids, the matter of 'gangster guns' appeared to have unfolded as a typical panic could be expected to. There had been a trigger event, intense media attention, the presence of moral entrepreneurs laying claim to a *problem* and pronouncing diagnoses (politicians, police, lobby groups, editors, bloggers, letter writers and posters) and the introduction of state measures to deal with the said problem (an inquiry into gun laws, with a focus on gun acquisition by criminals and gangs), which could be seen to be disproportional to any actual established threat. The lack of evidence, the absence of discourses and the misguided distinction between legal possession as unproblematic and illegal possession as problematic suggested that a moral panic had occurred, and thus, the sequence of events that took place between the time of the Kawerau event and the initiation of an inquiry into how guns were getting into the 'wrong' hands required further investigation.

To commence this investigation, I employed a research assistant to help me retrieve data. To produce a sample, we collected news media articles via the database Newztext between the dates 9 March 2016–30 May 2016. We used the following keyword strings: 'gun control', 'siege', 'gun law' and 'Kawerau + gun', and we limited our search to newspapers and news sites that were owned by New Zealand's largest media company 'Fairfax', to the independent news site 'Scoop' and to Radio New Zealand (RNZ) (the only national broadcaster with public responsibilities). The resulting data set consisted of 104 news articles, 70 RNZ newswires and two letters/commentaries. We scanned various sites in the media ecosystem for evidence of where else there was discourse relating to the Kawerau event and the developing problem relating to gun control. Whilst we found some discourse on Twitter and on Facebook, we found significantly more material on three blog sites: Whale Oil, Kiwiblog and the Daily Blog. We decided to focus on this evidence and not on tweets and Facebook posts after an initial analysis revealed that the discourse unfolding across these was relatively fragmented and often unrelated. To gather blog data, we accessed the three blog sites directly. We used the keywords 'gun', 'gun control', 'gun law' and 'Kawerau' in the March, April and May archives of each of the blogs. This search produced 18 blog posts and 760 comments.

Both my assistant and I independently immersed ourselves in the sample to familiarize ourselves with the overall narrative and emerging thematic structures. We coded the data using codes developed inductively as we read and identified key patterns and discursive formations. We considered functions of the text (definitions, rhetorical strategies and speech genres), of speakers (who said this and why does it matter?) and of sites (what affordances would this platform allow for?). Our findings were remarkably consistent, which assured me that our analysis was sound. The next section describes what we discovered.

Two Discourses, Two Interests, One Panic

Like 'killer kids', when interrogated more closely, the material panic revealed many nuances that the concept of panic, if applied alone, would be unable to pick up. Gangster guns can be defined as a panic of one discourse—that illegal, military-style weapons were ending up in the 'wrong' hands—which very swiftly emerged from the interaction of *two* discourses, each of which was associated with a distinct interest. The events at Kawerau, when associated with the police raid in Auckland, provided for a group of politicians (from both the governing party and from the opposition) an opportunity to develop an 'armed gangs are bad' discourse which justified and furthered their interest in controlling the movements of gangs. Individuals claiming to represent licenced gun owners developed a 'legal guns are good' discourse, aware, it seemed, of the potential for an ongoing debate about guns to affect the liberties of those who used guns for hunting and sporting purposes. These individuals can be seen to have actively supported the 'armed gangs are bad' discourse to develop a specific focus on criminals and gangs. In turn, the 'armed gangs are bad' discourse served and promoted the 'legal guns are good' discourse. From these, one 'gangster guns' panic discourse materialized.

The next two sections present the ways in which the 'armed gangs are bad' and the 'legal guns are good' discourses unfolded. I then discuss how the 'gangster guns' discourse was able to emerge by considering the interfaces between the discursive sites as well as the relationships between the discursive agents.

Armed Gangs Are Bad

A number of political figures were active in contributing to the 'armed gangs are bad discourse'. Most of their statements were made by way of the mainstream media, so media practices would have inevitably impacted upon how the statements were 'storied'. The media contributed in its own way to the making of the case for an inquiry as well, by discursively augmenting the claims that had been made in the statements by political figures.

On March 11, it was reported that Stuart Nash, the law and order spokesperson for the opposition, was renewing an earlier call that he had made for an inquiry into the availability, use and control of firearms ('Labour renews calls for gun inquiry', 2016). The rationale for Nash was the rising number of guns being confiscated by police in addition to a lack of police confidence in the level of firearms training they received (New Zealand Labour Party, 2016). He argued that the number one priority was the safety of police as well as the safety of the community (Nash cited in New Zealand Labour Party, 2016). Police association president

Greg O'Connor also stressed the urgency for an inquiry and began to speak about a specific problem of *criminals* getting their hands on *military-style* guns ('Time for a Look at Firearms', 2016). Justice Minister Judith Collins was also reported to be in support, and in expressing so, she connected the event in Kawerau with the police discovery of illegally held weapons at a gang pad in Auckland in the previous week:

> It's actually quite urgent: we've got police officers being shot, we've got massive numbers of firearms being found in very strange circumstances that you couldn't necessarily say look legitimate from the outside. (Collins cited in Sachdeva, 2016b)

This action was akin to Hall et al.'s (1978) notion of convergence, where issues are linked in order to draw parallels between them. This serves to amplify one or both of the issues in question. In this case, the media, in turn, furthered the convergence by repeatedly stating the rationale for the inquiry was the combination of both events:

> The Labour Party is renewing calls for an independent inquiry on guns following the *Kawerau police shootings* and the discovery of *several military style weapons* in Auckland. ('Labour renews calls for gun inquiry', 2016, emphasis added)

> Labour is calling for an independent inquiry into the availability, use and control of guns in New Zealand following the *Kawerau police shootings* and the *huge haul of firearms* and drugs this week. (New Zealand Labour Party, 2016, emphasis added)

The media also suggested that the issue was growing and was potentially out of control:

> …the surge in offenders carrying guns. (Gaffaney, Nichol, Makiha & Dawson, 2016)

> …a string [of incidents] involving gun violence. (Mass & van Beynen, 2016)

> …a spate of shootings and weapons seizures. (Kirk, 2016)

And warned their audiences that they were unquestionably under threat:

> ...an inquiry should be held now, rather than waiting for a tragedy to happen. ('Time for a look at firearms', 2016)
>
> People seem to assume international trends, such as mass shootings, won't happen here. ('Firearms support', 2016)
>
> As long as more gangsters are stockpiling weapons for use in the ruthless industry, the public will be in mounting danger. (Milne, 2016)

As in the case of killer kids, the media here was active in amplifying the problem and shaping up the folk devil. Collins also stated that there were 'lots of law-abiding gun owners' who posed no danger, and so it was critical that the inquiry did not propose measures that would penalize legitimate gun owners and sellers of firearms:

> They're not the ones racing around selling methamphetamine and using these guns as a means to protect their stash. (Collins cited in Sachdeva, 2016b)

This was a turning point in the discourse, and it firmly assigned folk devil status to criminal groups. It also exhibits a point of alliance between the 'armed gangs are bad' discourse and the 'legal guns are good' discourse. The law and order spokesperson for the political party NZ First Ron Mark was also concerned that gun owners might be affected.[5] He was cited to say:

> ...how about smashing the organised crime rings that are involved in these sorts of things to start with? (Mark cited in Sachdeva, 2016b)

At this point, the Green Party expressed support for the inquiry, as did the then Prime Minister John Key:

> For the most part, we've got good, law-abiding gun owners in New Zealand... some of those guns get into the criminal underworld—gangs in particular. (Key cited in Sachdeva, 2016b)

The agenda by now was firmly set. Indeed, the link that was made between the Kawerau event and the police discovery of guns at an Auckland gang pad, and the distinction that was made between the illegal possession and legal possession, was maintained, despite that both the link and the distinction are tenuous. This can be seen in a press statement released by Tim Macindoe, National MP for Hamilton West on 8 April 2016, almost one month after the Kawerau event, and several weeks after the draft terms of reference for the inquiry into the gun problem had been first announced. The statement also draws into the discourse a focus on gangs:

> Like most New Zealanders, I was appalled by the shooting of four police officers in Kawerau last month. Along with other recent violent offences, and the discovery of a large cache of illegal military style weapons in Auckland, the incident confirms the need to investigate how criminals are able to obtain illegal firearms... The inquiry will investigate the relationship between organised criminal gangs and illegal firearm possession.... Gangs are an insidious problem in New Zealand, and gang members are disproportionality responsible for serious offending, particularly family violence and the manufacture and distribution of methamphetamine. (Macindoe, 2016)

In fact, the statement achieves several things. First, it hails the subject by denoting that *most New Zealanders* were appalled, and so anyone not appalled is not one of the wider community (see Hay, 1995; Hier, 2003). Second, it positions the Kawerau event and the Auckland raid as part of a wider issue of 'violent offences', signifying them as 'tip of the iceberg' events. Third, it furthers the links between *gangs* and illegal firearm possession made up to that point by focusing solely in the second half of the release on offending by gangs.

Overall, the 'armed gangs are bad' discourse developed from practices of making sense of the Kawerau event on behalf of political figures and the media. The focus on how criminal groups were acquiring illegal guns, whilst sparked by a statement that linked the Kawerau event with a police raid on a gang pad a week earlier, would be solidified by the 'legal guns are good' discourse, which I turn the discussion to now.

Legal Guns Are Good

The set of individuals who were active in constructing the 'legal guns are good' discourse could be mainly seen to be contributors to three blog sites: *Whale Oil*, *Kiwiblog* and *The Daily Blog*. Each of these blogs can be termed 'elite blogs' that are read by journalists looking for an 'opinion' or an angle to direct their story and by politicians searching for a sense of the significance of current events (Maratea, 2008). *Whale Oil* is the site of blogger Cameron Slater and *Kiwiblog* is the site of David Farrar. Both of these bloggers lean towards the Right end of the political spectrum. They and their commentators all spoke *for* guns and *against* any moves towards increased 'gun control'. Martyn 'Bomber' Bradbury of *The Daily Blog* also defended guns at some intervals. Commentators on his blogs can be seen to be more active as contributors to the discourse, as they often disagreed with Martyn, who is a Left-leaning blogger.

The bloggers and blog commentators did several things as the 'legal guns are good' discourse emerged amongst their posts. First, they attempted to cool down the energy and redirect the focus of the talk that was emerging during and immediately after the Kawerau event. Second, they sustained the focus of the inquiry on the illegal acquisition of guns by criminal groups as the discourse continued into the following weeks. This can help to explain why the links that were made between the Kawerau event and the discovery of guns at an Auckland gang pad, and the distinction was made between the illegal possession and legal possession, were both upheld.

The bloggers and commenters attacked the practices of media and questioning the credibility of various police and political figures who were making statements in relation to the Kawerau event and the proposed gun inquiry. Plumington, for example, argued:

> While a kneejerk reaction in these situations is expected without proper analysis and thought, [it] will lead to hysterical and unbalanced decisions. (Plumington, 2016)

Slater (2016a), on the other hand, employed various expletives to describe the political figures who were calling for the inquiry, including 'idiot', 'tool' and 'muppet'. Etrex was concerned about the police lying to the 'ignorant' to push an anti-gun agenda. In relation to the haul of weapons the police had confiscated in the Auckland raid, he stated that:

> There was not one assault rifle in that haul of illegally held firearms seized by police raid. All good to police effort… but please guys don't lie to the ignorant about what you found. Can we please rely on the police to tell the truth !!!! (Etrex, 2016)

Bloggers and commenters also argued that levels of gun violence in New Zealand were low and that violence enacted with other objects, such as cars and knives, was far more problematic:

> There have been no massacres or significant gun rampage issues in NZ for a very long time. (Slater, 2016b)

> When there is a car accident nobody calls for a ban on cars even if the accident is called by some half witted twit doing a runner from the Police. If there is a stabbing again there is no outcry from an anti knife sector. (Huia, 2016)

If there was a problem, it wasn't one of the guns themselves, but of who had access to them. A distinction between law-abiding citizens and criminals was for most commentators central to properly directing an inquiry, should one go ahead. Indeed, the focus needed to be on *criminals*, not law-abiding citizens:

> Confiscating guns, more draconian gun laws are just some of these ideas but when you actually think about what you are doing by suggesting such a thing is that YOU INHIBIT THE FREEDOMS OF LAW ABIDING CITIZENS. Criminals and lunatics DON'T OBEY THE LAW pure and

> simple so more laws and confiscation only helps the criminal NOT THE LAW ABIDING (sic). (Plumington, 2016)

> The latest purported gun issue in NZ isn't about the type of guns or gun-licenced law-abiding firearms owners. The issue is scumbag criminals who are neither licensed nor following any laws and who are managing to obtain guns. How? So an enquiry must focus on that: how are they getting guns? (Slater, 2016b)

Part of this argument relied on identifying criminals as the agential force behind shootings, and the gun as only one of several tools for achieving both criminal *and* legal goals. OldmanNZ, for example, compared guns to cars, seeing both as dangerous in the hands of criminals:

> Whencriminals flee the police, the vehicle then becomes the weapon. It has killed or injured many more people, some deliberately, than guns. Some people take a gun to rob a shop, some use a car to ram raid a shop. Some people use a gun to threaten people, some people use a car to try run them over. It's not the weapon of choice, but the user, focus on them. (OldmanNZ, 2016)

Thus, criminals could use neutral guns to hurt innocent people. The objective, therefore, for most commenters, was to keep guns out of the hands of *dangerous* criminals. Only appropriate people should have access to guns.

Appropriate people included farmers, as they had (and have) a series of practical and legitimate reasons for 'needing' firearms. Waldopepper, for example, stated that:

> …rifles, used correctly, for their intended purpose, hurt no one. They put food on the table and keep pests at bay. (Waldopepper, 2016b)

Indeed, the argument that farmers required firearms was accepted across the political spectrum. Even commenters considered 'anti-gun' acknowledged that there were legitimate, practical reasons for possessing a firearm. Martyn Bradbury, for example, said:

> Now let's be clear, I don't have a problem with Farmers and Hunters having their access to 'appropriate' firearms protected. They are tools for Farmers and Hunters. (Bradbury, 2016b)

Farmers were also seen as a politically significant block who would oppose any changes to gun legislation. As Miguel stated:

> Don't forget that National has strong farming support and has farmers in their ranks, so hopefully they'll tread carefully on hacking off this support base who has a legitimate need for firearms for pest control and the like. (Miguel, 2016)

Collectors were also seen as an unproblematic and legitimate group of gun owners. Old Dig, for example, argued:

> It is interesting that there are gun collectors in NZ who own fully operational machine guns (Brens, MG42s, Vickers, etc.) but when was the last time a nutter went on a shooting spree with one? That's right, NEVER. Because licenced gun owners are not criminals. (Old Dig, 2016)

Some advocated gun ownership for the need to protect civil liberties against a potential dictatorship or communist government. Waldopepper (2016a), for example, provided a series of historical cases, including Soviet Russia, Nazi Germany, Khmer Rouge Cambodia and others where dictators supposedly disarmed the population in order to facilitate the crushing of civil liberties. Mark also stated that:

> History teaches us that in every part of the world where it did become valid, guns were first banned. (Mark, 2016)

Bloggers and commenters additionally presented themselves as knowledgeable gun owners. The figure of the knowledgeable gun owner was the antithesis to liberal police and left-leaning politicians, who were deemed unqualified to speak about, let alone regulate against, guns. Etrex, for example, argued:

> What I am saying is the police and politicians have no right to medal with law regarding firearms without the input of the wealth of knowledge firearms owning community has to offer. (Etrex, 2016)

Commenters also engaged in a display of expertise to identify themselves as knowledgeable gun owners who, unlike the police, *were* qualified to have an opinion about guns. Expertise about guns relied in particular on the ability to distinguish between the capability, appearance and calibre of various guns. The appearance of guns, particularly modern black-coloured rifles such as the AR15, was seen as misleading the debate because:

> Gun design has like everything else been refined over time and AR's if painted white probably would be much less threatening to the uninformed. They are a modern design and the military use their particular variants for the same reasons civilians do—accuracy, balance, serviceability, and economical ammo. (Dairy_Flat, 2016)

The ability to show expertise was also seen to be central to the right/ability for people to comment on posts. Seriously?, for example, acknowledged his lack of knowledge about guns, but still engaged with a discussion from an 'anti-gun' perspective. His *lack of* knowledge was repeatedly brought up by other commenters, either as a way of educating Seriously? or to delegitimize his position. At one stage, Seriously? stated that the primary issue was the importation of military assault rifles for private sale (Seriously? 2016). This resulted in a long discussion about the definition of assault rifles, MSSAs and gun types. Metalnwood told Seriously? that:

> Youdon't know your terminology. There is a definite difference between what you can do with a m16 assault rifle and a AR15 semi-automatic rifle. It's not just terminology, it's what they can do. The AR15 is just like any other sporting looking rifle as far as capability and not in the same league as an assault rifle for how much lead it can put down range in a short period of time. A lot of this blog is about understanding what the media are telling you, in this case you are not. Why do you believe what

the media telling you on this correct when you know they tell half-truths on everything else? (Metalnwood, 2016)

Eventually Seriously? accepted defeat and suggested that bans should be connected to capability rather than appearance. The discussion involving Seriously? was, overall, a civil one, with both sides complementing the other's willingness to engage in the debate. Several commenters also praised Seriously?'s open-mindedness. The knowledgeable gun owner is positioned in this dialogue as a calm and rational individual, in stark opposition to the hysterical media and police and political figures making ignorant, ideologically based statements.

All in all, the 'legal guns are good' discourse emerged from the conscious efforts of bloggers and blog commenters to cool down and redirect the discourse that emerged in the days following the Kawerau event. That the focus of the inquiry did very quickly take a formative shape, one that served the needs of the bloggers and commenters, suggests that the 'legal guns are good' discourse achieved much of its intentions. In the next section, I discuss *how* it can be seen to have achieved them.

A Most Productive Interaction

I argued above that *Whale Oil*, *Kiwiblog* and *The Daily Blog* can be termed 'elite blogs'. As discussed, an elite blog is one that is regularly read by journalists looking for an 'opinion' or an angle to shape their story and by politicians searching for a sense of the significance of current events (Maratea, 2008). Comments made about a number of issues on each of these blogs are often repeated in the press. In a recent example, Slater's views about New Plymouth Mayor Andrew Judd following a referendum on the establishment of Maori wards in the area that he blogged about on *Whale Oil* made headlines and were quoted at length in the region's daily paper, the *Taranaki Daily News* (Smith, 2015). *Whale Oil* was also at the centre of a political scandal in which it was claimed that ministers of the governing National Party paid bloggers, notably Cameron Slater, who runs *Whale Oil*, to regularly contribute to the site attacking public figures who opposed their policies (Hager, 2014). The scandal illustrates that a backstage intimacy can occur between elite bloggers and other powerful public figures. This intimacy, along with regular references made to blog posts in the mainstream press, has important implications for how discourses develop in the public arena, on the front stage, particularly when those discourses can be seen to be instrumental in the development of a moral panic (see Maratea, 2008).

Whether the relationship already established between the governing National Party and Cameron Slater came into play in the gangster guns episode is unknown, but it is highly conceivable that it may have given that each of their respective interests could be met with a focus on gangs and guns. Irrespectively so, calls for political figures to remain calm and to think carefully about any policy response to the Kawerau event and the Auckland raid arguably provided the opportunity for bloggers and blog commentators to exert substantial influence on the directions in which responses were focused. Both the Council of Licenced Firearm Owners president Paul Clark and Sporting Shooters Association spokesperson Phil Cregeen had made public statements shortly after the siege at Kawerau had ended warning politicians to *not overreact* in calling for an inquiry into gun control. Editors also cautioned against any knee-jerk response based on ill-informed decision-making:

> There are always lessons to be learned, but any potential policy changes, such as arming the police, *should not be rushed into*. ('Dangers at the Frontline' 2016, emphasis added)

> …there will no doubt be calls for all manner of modifications and amendments to the law and the way we deal with such dangerous events… there will *predictably be ill-informed calls* for tougher firearms legislation or an outright nationwide ban, for police to be routinely armed while on duty and for marijuana to be decriminalised to avoid the need for such investigations. (O'Connor, 2016, emphasis added)

The need for political figures to appear to be making informed decisions, when coupled with the claims by bloggers and blog commenters that their opinions were the *most* informed as they were knowledgeable gun owners participating in rational dialogue about guns, regardless of any backstage intimacy between the parties, was a most productive mix. This can explain why it only took a total of six days to construct a specific problem from initial reactions relating to an extraordinary event, achieve agreement between parties and arrive at a distinct set of terms of reference (though in draft) for an inquiry into that problem. A raft of different needs had been met cohesively and concurrently at this juncture. Indeed, it can be argued that several sets of interests would be ultimately served by the development of the gangster guns discourse: (i) the ability to legitimize and increase regulation of gangs, (ii) the safety of the rights of licenced gun owners, (iii) the ability of political figures to appear informed and (iv) the recognition of the knowledgeable gun owner.

This now brings me to the third phase of the framework that I have proposed for the study of material moral panics. The question at this phase is: what, in this place, and at this time, supports the development of these meanings?

Gangs, Blokes and the Bush

A number of scholars have sought to understand the contexts in which gun control happens. As discussed earlier, gun control in the USA has moved from a focus on controlling *some people's* access to guns (disaffected black youth in urban spaces) to a focus on violent video games following the Columbine High School shooting, to once again focus on *some people's* access to guns, this time those with 'deranged minds'. Vicaro and Seitz (2015) attribute this latter shift to a confluence of three social governance technologies: risk management approaches to mental health care, prospective preventative approaches in criminal justice and a wider shift towards the criminological view of civic identity, where one is either a potential victim (who has the right to protect oneself) or a potential offender (who must be monitored). This confluence enabled public and political discourse that emerged after the events in Newtown, Connecticut, to centre upon the potential problem that mentally unwell individuals with access to guns might engender (see also Guest Pryal, 2015; Metzi & MacLeish, 2015). Whilst each of the three social governance technologies described above can be seen to be operative in New Zealand, there are fundamental differences between New Zealand and the USA which may have circumvented the emergence of a 'deranged mind' discourse in relation to gun control here. In New Zealand, one does not have the second amendment right to own a gun. One must hold a gun licence to own a gun, and in acquiring such a license, one is subject to a mental health check. This means that there is an assumption that those with mental health issues will *not* have access to guns. Notably, too, as discussed earlier, New Zealand has not had any recent mass shooting events which might prompt questions to do with the mental health status of the shooter, like the USA has. There are, however, two features of the New Zealand context that can assist in understanding how the specific discourse of 'gangster guns' was able to emerge in this space and time. The first feature is a recent increase in regulatory measures to control the activities of gangs on behalf of the New Zealand Government. The second feature is the figure of the authentic, kiwi male in New Zealand, which is linked to a frontier imagination (Figgins & Holland, 2012; Kane, 2010; Melzer, 2009; Reis, 2009). I discuss each of these features in more detail below.

A Sustained Gang Panic?

The 'gang problem' has been seen as a recurrent moral panic in the New Zealand context (and elsewhere). Kelsey and Young (1982), for example, argued that during the two year period 1978–1980, the activities of young Maori and Pacific Island gangs were talked about in exaggerated ways by the media and presented as a new type of threatening social problem. Changes to the penal code followed and gang members had severe sentences handed down to them in several cases. Kelsey and Young (1982) propose that these groups were singled out as scapegoats and employed to divert attention from an economic crisis primarily as they were socially visible as 'outsiders'. Roguski and Tauri (2012) document another, more recent episode which occurred during 2005–2007.

The authors describe how media and political figures pronounced that there was a sharp escalation in inter-gang conflict within the South Auckland region following an event of a murder of a man believed to be a father of a youth who belonged to a gang. Interpretations of the issue by the community, however, were markedly different, revealing a 'discursive chasm' between the two groups. Moreover, statistical data were unable to support claims that youth violence was out of control. Roguski and Tauri (2012) argue that driving this latest episode was a police desire for more public resources coupled with 'tough on crime' political interests and a media who was keen on a good story.

Another episode in this saga has possibly been under way since 2009. Certainly, concern has been present as various pieces of legislation have been passed in order to control the movement of gangs across this time. In 2009, for example, a Gangs and Organised Crime Bill was introduced into parliament which proposed to remove gang forts, expand police surveillance powers when it was suspected that an individual was participating in an organized group and to make participation in an organized group an aggravating factor at sentencing. The bill made it to a third hearing but wasn't passed into law. However, the proposals I've just described would subsequently reappear in three other acts: the Local Government Amendment Act 2009, the Crimes Amendment Act 2009 and Sentencing Amendment Act 2009. In 2013, legislation to restrict the wearing of gang insignia on or near government premises was passed. Government premises include the buildings and grounds of schools and hospitals, and other public amenities such as swimming pools. In 2014, the government announced that it had in planning a 'whole of government action plan on gangs'.

In 2016, it was announced that this plan was now operational and that a new Gang Intelligence Centre had been established. The aim of the centre is to collate information about known gang members that is held by the Ministry of Social Development, Customs, the Department of Corrections, Internal Affairs, Immigration and the Police in order to 'disrupt and dismantle illegal gang activities' (Collins, 2016). Critics argue that the government was fiddling the numbers to make its case for the action plan (see, for example, Gilbert, 2014). Critics also say the centre is a misguided response to gang membership and that an address of the conditions in which gangs thrive would be more appropriate (Bradbury, 2016a; Leslie, 2016). The announcement by the government with regard to the establishment of the intelligence centre was made nine days prior to the Kawerau event.

I suggest that, in light of the recurrent nature of concern about gangs in this context, there is a *sustained moral panic* about gangs in New Zealand (Calleja, 2016; see also Martin, 2015 on *permanent* panics). A sustained moral panic is one that fulfils the criteria of Good and Ben-Yehuda's (1994a, 1994b) attributional model, excepting that of volatility. In a sustained panic, there is *always* concern, hostility, consensus and disproportionality with regard to the person, object or set of conditions that is folk devilled (Calleja, 2016). A sustained panic is continued (sustained) by illustrative cases that serve its construction of a problem. The events at Kawerau were employed by political figures to further a 'crackdown' on gang activity.

The Authentic Kiwi Male and the Frontier Imagination

In New Zealand, the most authentic masculinity is known as the 'kiwi bloke'. Kiwi blokes drink lots of alcohol, they enjoy playing and watching rugby, and they wear gumboots (Law, Campbell & Schick, 1999; Phillips, 1996). The figure of the kiwi bloke largely stems from particular understandings of what it meant to be a settler in this country (male, rural). Settlers in New Zealand were frontier men, as were settlers in other 'settler societies' such as the USA, Canada and Australia, on the boundaries between 'civilization' and nature. Indeed, their task was to *conquer* nature using aggression (Carrington & Scott, 2008). Scholarship has explored in depth the ways in which components of this understanding resulted in multiple atrocities against multiple groups of indigenous peoples (see, for example, Lester, 2002; Lightfoot, 2006; Moon, 2016; Rifkin, 2013; Rollo, 2016; Wolfe, 2006) as well as how it still largely informs notions of an authentic masculinity to which men in both rural and urban settings aspire to (and are held accountable to) (see, for example, Hogan & Purcell, 2008; Leipins, 2000; Pease, 2010; Phillips, 1996).

Thus, whilst the image of the kiwi bloke is not one that can be immediately associated with gun ownership, Phillips (1996, p. 288) notes that the most distinctive element of mythic kiwi bloke is having 'backblocks experience and outdoor strength', for which having a gun is inevitably associated. The bush (the wilderness) is where men become *men.* This implicit understanding can be seen in the ways that kiwi blokes are depicted culturally. The 'kiwi bloke' has a long history of representation in literature and film and is epitomized by gun-toting characters such as Barry Crump in his autobiographic novel *A Good Keen Man* (Bannister 2005). A more recent illustrative figure is the fictional character 'Uncle Hec' in the 2016 film *Hunt for the Wilderpeople.*

The figure of the authentic, settler male in the New Zealand context is also integral to two primary industries: dairy farming and adventure tourism (Woods, 2011). New Zealand's economy has long been agriculturally dependent, and this remains the case today. Indeed, agriculture is described as the 'backbone' of the New Zealand economy, with dairy being the biggest export product (New Zealand Trade and Enterprise, 2017; see also Foote, Joy & Death, 2015). This historical and contemporary dependence on farming has afforded New Zealand farmers a significant degree of political sway, something that was not lost on the bloggers and blog commenters as seen in the excerpts offered above. Farmers are exempted, for example, from many laws which govern the impacts of industry on the environment in New Zealand, and this includes an exemption from the Emissions Trading Scheme, an initiative designed to assist New Zealand industries to reduce carbon emissions.[6] Thus, it can be said that the farmer is not only a quintessential kiwi bloke, insofar as he is living rural and working the land, but he is also economically fundamental to the nation and thus politically powerful. His say on carbon emissions, and his being exempt from laws that regulate other industries, provides evidence of that. His say on guns is very likely to hold sway too.

New Zealand's economy is also heavily dependent on adventure tourism. Woods (2011) traces the development of the Queenstown district from gold rush town to a 'global playground' to illustrate this. Queenstown is a place where amenity migrants seeking a 'better life' and tourists seeking thrilling activities coalesce. The latter group contribute hundreds of millions to the local community and make up a significant part of New Zealand's $30 billion tourist industry income. Moreover, the town actively promotes itself as 'the adventure capital of the world'. This understanding of Queenstown as a playground sits alongside another tourist good—its unique natural beauty and its raw, untouched environment. Indeed, New Zealand has an international reputation as a rural paradise, as showcased in Peter Jackson's *Lord of the Rings* trilogy (Bell, 2008; Buttle & Rodgers, 2014). This has proven to be a valuable tourist commodity for our big game estates who sell trophy hunting ventures in international markets (Figgins & Holland, 2012).

Hunting is something of a cultural phenomenon amongst New Zealanders themselves (see Walters, 2000). Reis (2009) argues that hunting, from the perspective of the hunter, is a sensual experience whereby there is a set of particular relations that occur between the hunter and the environment, between the hunter with other hunters and between the hunter and the prey. The relation between the hunter and the environment is seen as a challenge, the feeling that one is conquering nature, civilizing nature. The sense of danger and isolation also feeds into the drama of the experience, which can be interpreted as a very masculine drama, where one conquers his own fear and becomes a man in the process of that—a kiwi bloke amongst other kiwi blokes. The hunter is connecting with, and re-enacting, a very New Zealand past, where kiwi blokes worked together in the bush (Reis, 2009). A substantial number of tourists seeking the same kind of sensual experience visit New Zealand each year and are thought to contribute tens of millions of dollars to New Zealand's economy. Indeed, recreational hunting can be seen as a form of adventure tourism insofar as visitors arrive with an intention to 'trophy hunt', where they can return to their home country with skins and antlers (Figgins & Holland, 2012). Most other countries, even those with similar hunting customs, limit hunters to seasons and to particular locales (Gary Herbert's New Zealand Hunting, 2016). However, many species in New Zealand (and in particular, deer) can be hunted year round and in multiple different spaces (Department of Conservation, 2017). Trophy hunting tourists are instead advised of mating seasons—the deer 'roar', for example—when the hunt is best.

Implications

The context in which each of the 'armed gangs are bad' and the 'legal guns are good' discourses made sense, resonated and effortlessly came together again illustrates the significance of why context matters in moral panic analysis. It was a context in which concern about gangs and gang activities had served in the past, and continues to serve, a variety of interests. It was also a context where an understanding of the frontier man was (and is) not only culturally iconic but also economically powerful. Rural men working the land generate income and tourist men seeking a rural man sensual experience also generate income. In both the routine practices of the farmer and the temporal experiences of the frontier tourist, guns are central. Any increased restrictions on guns in would, therefore, have affected, perhaps irreversibly, two primary income streams—dairy farming and recreational hunting by tourists. Guns, it can be said, are an essential prop in New Zealand's economy. A discourse about *gangster* guns, therefore, was not only a politically valuable discourse but it was also perhaps the only politically viable discourse that could have emerged in this context. Another discourse may well have prompted some difficult conversations, perhaps along the lines of the need for a new identity and a more diverse economy. This helps to explain why the panic erupted so quickly, and a solution, by way of an inquiry, was promptly initiated.

Over the last two chapters, I have examined two cases of moral panic using the framework for panic research proposed in this book. Each of these two panics was unique in terms of its subject matter and in terms of how it unfolded. Yet, both of them were panics in the sense that each of them can be seen to fulfil the basic criteria for a panic. In the next and last chapter, I consider how the contextual features of these panics—what supported them to develop in the places and times that they did (and what was brought forth from them by the panic in question)—might be imagined in a more abstract way. This demonstrates my aim to pave the way for an inductive approach to the study of panics, where cases inform the concept, and where the concept (so informed) can support us to make connections with social theory. It is my position, as I have argued throughout this book, that we will be better equipped to consider the wider social significance of the concept of moral panic with the empirical data firmly steering us.

Notes

1. These include shooting rampages in Canada (the Ecole Polytechnic Massacre in 1989 and the La Loche shootings in 2016); Scotland (the Dunblane massacre in 1996); Germany (the Erfurt massacre in 2002 and the Winnenden school shooting in 2009); France (the Toulouse school shooting in 2012); Finland (The Jokela High School shooting in 2007 and the Kauhajoki shooting in 2008); Brazil (the Realengo massacre in 2011); Australia (the Monash University shooting in 2002); and even one in New Zealand (the Waikino Schoolhouse shooting in 1923).
2. Commentators argued that these measures were the ones the NRA approved of (Colorado Kills Gun Laws, 2000, February 16).
3. Adam Lanza was said to be an avid player of 'Call of Duty' (Ferguson & Olson, 2014).
4. Rowe (2013) demonstrates the salience of an unfolding drama in his account of the Mouat case in the UK, where police chased and captured a lone gunman on the loose, affording, in turn, the media with an opportunity to deliver 'rolling coverage' from the scene itself. Media reports of the Mouat case in the UK also employed the 'Western' frame (Rowe, 2013).
5. Readers will note that it was Ron Mark who proposed the Young Offenders (Serious Crimes) Bill in the killer kids panic (see Chap. 6).
6. At time of writing, this scheme is under review.

References

Addington, L. A. (2009). Cops and cameras: Public school security as a policy response to Columbine. *American Behavioural Scientist, 52*(10), 1426–1446.

Alpers, P., & Walters, R. (1998). Firearms theft in New Zealand—Lessons for crime and injury prevention. *Australia New Zealand Journal of Criminology, 31*(1), 85–95.

Bell, C. (2008). 100% PURE New Zealand: Branding for back-packers. *Journal of Vacation Marketing, 14*(4), 345–355.

Bradbury, M. (2016a, March 4). Beware a government using big data to crack down on "gangs" plus a question to ask Judith Collins. [Web log message]. Retrieved from http://thedailyblog.co.nz.

Bradbury, M. (2016b, March 14). Sweet Jesus—I agree with Judith Collins—It's time to crack down on guns. [Web log message]. Retrieved from http://thedailyblog.co.nz.

Burns, R., & Crawford, C. (1999). School shootings, the media, and public fear. Ingredients for a moral panic. *Crime, Law and Social Change, 32,* 147–168.

Buttle, J., & Rodgers, J. (2014). Panic about crime in New Zealand's rural paradise. *New Zealand Sociology, 29*(2), 31–54.

Calleja, N. G. (2016). Deconstructing a puzzling relationship: Sex offender legislation, the crimes that inspired and sustained moral panic. *Justice Policy Journal, 13*(1), 1–17.

Carrington, K., & Scott, J. (2008). Masculinity, rurality and violence. *British Journal of Criminology, 48,* 641–666.

Carvajal, D. (1999, June 20). Ideas & trends; full metal dust jacket: Books are violent, too. *The New York Times.*

Chambliss, W. J. (1995). Crime control and ethnic minorities: Legitimizing racial oppression by creating moral panics. In D. F. Hawkins (Ed.), *Ethnicity, race, and crime: Perspectives across time and place* (pp. 235–258). Albany, NY: State University of New York Press.

Chiricos, T. (2006). Moral panic as ideology: Drugs, violence, race and punishment in America. In C. Critcher (Ed.), *Critical readings: Moral panics and the media* (pp. 103–123). Maidenhead: Open University Press.

Collins, J. (2016, January 3). New Gang Intelligence Centre will reduce gang harm. *Beehive.govt.nz.* Retrieved from www.beehive.govt.nz.

Colorado kills gun laws. (2000, February 16). *CBSNews.* Retrieved from http://www.cbsnews.com.

Critcher, C. (2008). Moral panic analysis: Past, present and future. *Sociology Compass, 2*(4), 1127–1144.

Dairy_Flat. (2016, March 17). Considerations for the gun inquiry. [Web log message]. Retrieved from www.whaleoil.co.nz.

Dangers at the frontline. (2016, March 11). *The Nelson Mail.* Retrieved from http://www.stuff.co.nz

Department of Conservation. (2017). Hunting. Retrieved March 11, 2017, from http://www.doc.govt.nz/parks-and-recreation/things-to-do/hunting/.

Etrex. (2016, March 17). Considerations for the gun inquiry. [Web log message]. Retrieved from www.whaleoil.co.nz.

Ferguson, C. J. (2008). The school shooting/violent video game link: Causal relationship or moral panic? *Journal of Investigative Psychology and Offender Profiling, 5*, 25–37.

Ferguson, C. J., & Olson, C. K. (2014). Video game violence use among "Vulnerable" populations: The impact of violent games on delinquency and bullying among children with clinically elevated depression or attention deficit symptoms. *Journal of Youth Adolescence, 43*, 127–136.

Figgins, G., & Holland, P. (2012). Red deer in New Zealand: Game animal, economic resource or environmental pest? *New Zealand Geographer, 68*, 36–48.

Firearms support. (2016, March 12). *Radio New Zealand News*. Radio New Zealand.

Foote, K., Joy, M., & Death, R. (2015). New Zealand dairy farming: Milking our environment for all its worth. *Environmental Management, 56*(3), 709–720.

Gaffaney, C., Nichol, T., Mahika, K., & Dawson, K. (2016, March 10). Armed forces gather at scene of police shooting. *The New Zealand Herald*, p. A002.

Gary Herbert's New Zealand Hunting. (2016). Retrieved December 22, 2016, from http://www.nzhuntingsafaris.com/.

Gilbert, J. (2014). Guest blog: Dr Jarrod Gilbert—Proof of David Farrar's deception: My own experience of Dirty Politics. [Web log message]. Retrieved from http://www.jarrodgilbert.com.

Goode, Erich., & Ben-Yehuda, N. (1994a). Moral Panics: Culture, Politics, and Social Construction. *Annual Review of Sociology, 20*, 149–171.

Goode, Erich., & Ben-Yehuda, N. (1994b). *Moral panics : the social construction of deviance*. Cambridge: MA: Blackwell.

Guest Pryal, K. (2015). Heller's scapegoats. *North Carolina Law Review, 93*, 1440–1474.

Hager, N. (2014). *Dirty politics: How attack politics is poisoning New Zealand's political environment*. New Zealand: Craig Potton Publishing.

Hall, S., Critcher, C., Jefferson, T., Clarke, J., & Roberts, B. (1978). *Policing the crisis: Mugging, the state, and law and order*. London: Macmillan.

Hay, C. (1995). Mobilisation through interpellation. *Social and Legal Studies, 4,* 197–223.

Hier, S. (2003). Risk and panic in the late modernity: Implications of the converging sties of social anxiety. *British Journal of Criminology, 54*(1), 2–20.

Hogan, M., & Purcell, T. (2008). The real Alaskan: Nostalgia and rural masculinity in the "last frontier". *Men and Masculinities, 11*(1), 63–85.

Huia. (2016, March 11). Usual suspects calling for gun control after Kawerau. [Web log message]. Retrieved from www.whaleoil.co.nz.

Hurka, S., & Nebel, K. (2013). Framing and policy change after shooting rampages: A comparative analysis of discourse networks. *Journal of European Public Policy, 20*(3), 390–406.

Kane, M. J. (2010). Adventure as a cultural foundation: Sport and tourism in New Zealand. *Journal of Sport & Tourism, 15*(1), 27–44.

Kelsey, J., & Young, W. (1982). *The gangs: Moral panic as social control.* Wellington: Victoria University Press.

Kirk, S. (2016, March 16). Parliament to hold inquiry into New Zealand gun laws. *The Press*. Retrieved from http://www.stuff.co.nz.

Koenig, C., & Schindler, D. (2016). Dynamics in gun ownership and crime: Evidence from the aftermath of Sandy Hook. Retrieved from http://davidschindler.de/JMP%20David%20Schindler.pdf.

Labour renews calls for gun inquiry. (2016, March 11). *Radio New Zealand News*. Radio New Zealand.

Law, R., Campbell, H., & Schick, R. (1999). Introduction. In R. Law, H. Campbell, & J. Dolan (Eds.), *Masculinities in Aotearoa/New Zealand.* Palmerston North: Dunmore.

Leipins, R. (2000). Making men: The construction and representation of agriculture-based masculinities in Australia and New Zealand. *Rural Sociology, 65*(4), 605–620.

Leslie, D. (2016, March 2). Gang plan could harm some whanau—Marama Fox. *Radio New Zealand.*

Lester, A. (2002). British settler discourse and the circuits of empire. *History Workshop Journal, 54,* 24–48.

Lightfoot, K. (2006). Missions, gold, furs, and manifest destiny: Rethinking an archaeology of colonialism for Western North America. In M. Hall & S. Silliman (Eds.), *Historical archaeology*. London: Blackwell.

Macindoe, T. (2016, April 8). Cracking down on gangs and firearms. *Bay of Plenty Times*, p. A010.

Maratea, R. (2008). The e-rise and fall of social problems: The blogosphere as a public arena. *Social Problems, 55*(1), 139–160.

Mark. (2016, April 6). Irrational argument ignores reality of gun crime. [Web log message]. Retrieved from www.whaleoil.co.nz.

Martin, G. (2015). Stop the boats! Moral panic in Australia over asylum seekers. *Continuum Journal of Media & Cultural Studies, 29*(3), 304–322.

Mass, A., & van Beynen, J. (2016, March 13). Gunfight witness describes sudden shots in darkness. *Sunday Star Times*, p. 2. Auckland, New Zealand.

McPhedran, S., & Baker, J. (2011). Mass shooting in Australia and New Zealand: A descriptive study of incidence. *Justice Policy Journal, 8*(1).

Melzer, S. (2009). *Gun crusaders: The NRA's culture war*. New York: New York University Press.

Metalnwood. (2016, March 17). Considerations for the gun inquiry. [Web log message]. Retrieved from www.whaleoil.co.nz.

Metzi, J. M., & MacLeish, K. T. (2015). Mental illness, mass shootings, and the politics of American firearms. *Framing Health Matters, 105*(2), 240–249.

Miguel. (2016, March 14). Bi-partisan approach to illegal firearms needed. [Web log message]. Retrieved from www.whaleoil.co.nz.

Milne, J. (2016, March 13). Editorial: We have too many guns on our streets. *Sunday Star Times*, p. 2.

Moon, P. (2016). Nietzschean interpretation of the language of Britain's colonisation of New Zealand. *Settler Colonial Studies, 6*(1), 45–60.

Muschert, G. W. (2007). Research in school shootings. *Sociology Compass, 1*(1), 60–80.

Muschert, G. W., & Peguero, A. A. (2010). The columbine effect and school antiviolence policy. *New Approaches to Social Problems Treatment, 17*, 117–148.

New Zealand Labour Party. (2016, March 11). Labour calls for independent gun inquiry. *Scoop.co.nz*. Retrieved from http://www.scoop.co.nz.

New Zealand Trade and Enterprise. (2017). *Dairy*. Retrieved from https://www.nzte.govt.nz.

O'Connor, T. (2016, March 15). Kawerau siege could easily have ended in funerals. *Waikato Times*. Retrieved from http://www.stuff.co.nz.

Old Dig. (2016, March 14). Bi-partisan approach to illegal firearms needed. [Web log message]. Retrieved from www.whaleoil.co.nz.

OldmanNZ. (2016, March 17). Considerations for the gun inquiry. [Web log message]. Retrieved from www.whaleoil.co.nz.

Pease, B. (2010). Reconstructing violent rural masculinities: Responding to fractures in the rural gender order in Australia. *Culture, Society & Masculinity, 2*(2), 154–164.

Phillips, J. (1996). *A man's country? The image of the Pakeha male (revised).* Auckland: Penguin Books.

Plumington. (2016, March 14). Sweet Jesus—I agree with Judith Collins—It's time to crack down on guns. [Web log message]. Retrieved from http://the-dailyblog.co.nz.

Police injured in rural shooting. (2016, March 10). *The Press*, p. 1.

Reis, A. C. (2009). More than the kill: Hunters' relationships with landscape and prey. *Current Issues in Tourism, 12*(5–6), 573–587. doi:10.1080/13683500903042881.

Rifkin, M. (2013). Settler common sense. *Settler Colonial Studies, 3*(3), 322–340.

Roguski, M., & Tauri, J. M. (2012). The politics of gang research in New Zealand. In K. Carrington (Ed.), *Crime, justice and social democracy: An international conference proceedings* (2nd ed., pp. 26–44). Brisbane, Australia: School of Justice, Queensland University of Technology.

Rollo, T. (2016). Feral children: Settler colonialism, progress, and the figure of the child. *Settler Colonial Studies*, 1–20.

Rowe, M. (2013). Just like a TV show: Public criminology and the media coverage of "hunt for Britain's most wanted man". *Crime, Media, Culture, 9*(1), 23–38. doi:10.1177/1741659012438298.

Sachdeva, S. (2016a, March 11). Gun inquiry shouldn't eliminate "inclusive" NZ firearms culture. *Stuff.co.nz.* Retrieved from http://www.stuff.co.nz.

Sachdeva, S. (2016b, March 14). Judith Collins: Inquiry into NZ's gun laws could move ahead this week. *Stuff.co.nz.* Retrieved from http://www.stuff.co.nz.

Santaella-Tenorio, J., Cerda, M., Villaveces, A., & Galea, S. (2016). What do we know about the association between firearm legislation and firearm-related injuries? *Epidemiologic Reviews, 38,* 140–157.

Savage, J. (2014, April 29). Firearms cut down and sold to criminals. *The New Zealand Herald.* Retrieved from www.nzherald.co.nz.

Schildkraut, J., & Hernandez, T. C. (2014). Laws that bit the bullet: A review of legislative responses to school shootings. *American Journal of Criminal Justice, 39,* 358–374.

Schildkraut, J., & Muschert, G. W. (2014). Media salience and the framing of mass murder in schools: A comparison of the Columbine and Sandy Hook massacres. *Homicide Studies, 18*(1), 23–43.
Seriously? (2016, March 17). Considerations for the gun inquiry. Retrieved from www.whaleoil.co.nz.
Slater, C. (2016a, March 11). Usual suspects pushing for gun control after Kawerau. [Web log message]. Retrieved from www.whaleoil.co.nz.
Slater, C. (2016b, March 17). Considerations for the gun inquiry. [Web log message]. Retrieved from www.whaleoil.co.nz.
Smith, B. (2015, May 18). Whale oil blogger calls New Plymouth mayor Andrew Judd a "Halfwit." *Taranaki Daily News*. Retrieved from http://www.stuff.co.nz.
Svokos, A. (2015, December 14). Congress has not passed a single gun control law since Sandy Hook. *Elite Daily*.
Taylor, P. (2016, April 9). In their sights—Criminals. *The New Zealand Herald*, p. A25. Auckland, New Zealand.
Time for a look at firearms—Police Association. (2016, March 11). *Radio New Zealand News*. Radio New Zealand.
Vicaro, M., & Seitz, D. (2015). Guns, crime, and dangerous minds: Assessing the mental health turn in gun policy discourse. *Cultural Studies <=> Critical Methodologies*.
Waldopepper. (2016a, March 11). Usual suspects pushing for gun control after Kawerau. Retrieved from www.whaleoil.co.nz
Waldopepper. (2016b, March 17). Considerations for the gun inquiry. [Web log message]. Retrieved from www.whaleoil.co.nz.
Wall, T. (2016, March 10). A shootout, a seige, a surrender—How the Bay of Plenty standoff unfolded. *Stuff.co.nz*. Retrieved from http://www.stuff.co.nz.
Walters, R. (2000). Serious firearm offending in New Zealand—Issues for gun controls and public safety. *Australia New Zealand Journal of Criminology, 33*(1), 64–76.
Wolfe, P. (2006). Settler colonialism and elimination of the native. *Journal of Genocide and Research, 8*(4), 387–409.
Woods, M. (2011). The local politics of the global countryside: Boosterism, aspirational ruralism and the contested reconstitution of Queenstown, New Zealand. *GeoJournal, 76*, 365–381.
Wright, R. (2000). 'I'd sell you suicide': Pop music and moral panic in the age of Marilyn Manson. *Popular Music, 19*(3), 365–385.

8

Conclusions and Conjectures

Making sense of panics, in new or different ways to how they have been made sense of in the past, is important for renewing the concept of moral panic and reconfirming its place as a central idea for the social sciences (and criminology in particular). I have proposed in this book that panic studies should always be a study of a material on-the-ground-happening reaction first. Researchers examining an episode of moral panic should employ Cohen's (1972) concept as a general guide but approach the case inductively and ultimately let 'the case decide the concept' (Becker, 1998). Researchers should also locate an episode within its particular social, cultural and political context, and consider the relationship between the processes of the reaction and its contextual backdrop. Researchers should then examine how their particular episode challenges or supports the parameters of the concept of moral panic (the analytical model that social scientists use to interpret their data) as it was understood by Cohen (1972). Does this case unfold as Cohen suggests it might? What explains any variances? Are these critical to understanding the unfolding of this particular social reaction? Would a model based on this particular episode look dramatically different to Cohen's one?

S. Wright Monod, *Making Sense of Moral Panics*, Palgrave Studies in Risk, Crime and Society, DOI 10.1007/978-3-319-61821-0_8

If this inductive approach is practiced across many types of material panics, three things could be achieved. First, it would allow for a view of what features of panic remain salient across all cases and where the model may need adjusting. Second, it would enable us to 'group' cases that have similar variations about them and to decide whether another analytical concept might be more appropriate for the analysis of these, whether another level of abstraction is required or the inclusion of another idea might be helpful. Third, a developed understanding of the contexts in which material panics emerge can help us to explain what the conceptual model reveals (see Dandoy, 2014). An understanding of the specific contexts in which episodes unfold could then allow for a much more stable connection with broader ideas to be made. A comparative analysis of moral panics, each of which has been investigated as a situated material episode, would enable scholars to theorize about why a panic might emerge about an event, object or person in one space (or at one time) but not another, and thus where the focus of the concept of moral panic is (or should be).

In Chap. 1, the introductory chapter, I made the case for why this approach is necessary. Given the diversity of the field today *and* the drive to consider where the focus of the concept of moral panic is (or should be), it is critical that panic scholars establish (as far as it is possible to do so) some common ground about the shape of the concept, and how it can be used in the present day. I also argued that a concept to unpack volatile social conflicts that give rise to untenable practices of exclusion and excessive practices of criminalization is now needed more than ever as we face social and political upheaval from climate change, alarming levels of social and economic inequality and a profound shift in social consciousness that Brexit and Donald Trump's presidency both testify to. This concept must be *able* to capture the complexities of contemporary social reactions. The processes of panic described by Cohen (1972) in *Folk Devils* were intimate with their subject matter—the Mods and Rockers—and his idea for a concept that could deconstruct the nuances of other cases was drawn from processes specific to the reaction *in that case*. Studies using Cohen's model are therefore 'letting the concept decide the case' rather than the other way around (Becker, 1998). I then outlined a research framework for the inductive study of material on-the-ground-happening social reactions. The framework has five phases. The first phase justifies why a particular episode warrants consideration as a moral panic; the second phase explores the meanings that are developing (and how they are developing); the third phase examines the context (space and time) in which those meanings are made salient; the fourth phase draws a concept from the empirical data (lets the case decide the concept); and the fifth and final phase considers how the relationships between a panic and the features of its context point to links that might be made between the concept of moral panic and social theory.

In Chap. 2, I documented the development of the concept of moral panic in the 'original project' of panic. The studies at the centre of this project are Cohen's (1972) *Folk Devils and Moral Panics*, Hall, Critcher, Jefferson, Clarke, & Roberts (1978) *Policing the Crisis* and Good and Ben-Yehuda's (1994) *Moral Panics: The Social Construction of Deviance*. Chapter 3 examined and evaluated the nature of the critiques that have been directed at moral panic since its inception and the responses to these by Cohen (2002, 2011) and other key scholars in the field. Chapter 4 critically examined the connections made between panic and developments in social theory over the recent past. It looked specifically at the work of Ungar (1992, 2001), Hier (2002a, 2002b, 2003, 2008, 2011, 2016a, 2016b), Critcher (2003, 2006, 2008, 2009a, 2009b, 2011) and Rohloff (2008, 2011), and positioned my argument for an inductive approach to panic case studies amongst their ideas. Chapter 5 discussed the central role of the media in panic development. I outlined the ways by which the news media is critical in amplifying a panic, shaping up a folk devil and setting an agenda. I also considered how social media has affected the ways in which news is now produced and received, which, in turn, can affect the ways in which moral panics develop. Chapter 6 employed the framework to examine the case of 'killer kids', a panic which emerged in New Zealand in 2002. This was a case that had all the ingredients of a typical moral panic: a horrible crime committed by a group of young people; sensationalist media coverage; a plethora of opinions, diagnoses and remedies; and the development of a proposal to make a knee-jerk law change. Chapter 7 explored the case of 'gangster guns', which occurred in New Zealand in 2016.

This case, like killer kids, could also be seen as a classic moral panic. It involved a trigger event involving a standoff between police and a gunman; dramatic media accounts of unfolding events; an array of sentiments and analyses from politicians, editors, blogging communities and gun lobbyists; and the establishment of an urgent governmental inquiry.

Despite their typicality, each case also followed a unique trajectory. Working my way through each phase of the framework, I found, for example, that killer kids was marked by the presence of three very different discourses which emerged across two phases. A discourse of *moral reprisal* defined the 'problem' in terms of malevolent children, social disorder at the hands of dysfunctional families and moral decay in the move towards a more permissive society. A discourse of *social rescue* argued for perspective in relation to the claims that were being made, for 'the system' to be held accountable and for the crime to be seen as an incident arising from the social consequences of the free market. These two discourses emerged in a first phase: an outburst of agitated reaction that appeared immediately after the image of Bailey sitting in court after the trial for the murder of Michael Choy was shown on the front page of New Zealand's national newspaper *Sunday Star Times*. A discourse of *criminal risk* argued that New Zealand's justice system was far too lenient, that 'justice' needed to be served and that community safety needed to be assured. This discourse dominated the episode once the outburst had subsided, ushering in a new phase that resembled a moral campaign. As I considered the questions of the third phase for panic research, the events of Michael Choy and the media coverage of the trial a year later touched on a set of truths assumed of news images and of crime images, a plethora of fantasies about 'criminal others' and a punitive sensibility amongst ordinary folk which was gaining a good deal of political influence in New Zealand at the beginning of the 2000s. It was these contextual features that gave rise to the meanings made in the discourses across the episode.

The gangster guns episode, on the other hand, was a panic of two mutually reinforcing discourses that emerged from two quite distinct sets of interests. Following the Kawerau event, in which a siege between a lone gunman and police had come to a peaceful end, political figures, aided by the mainstream news media, initiated an 'armed gangs are bad' discourse. It was claimed, initially, that gun control in New Zealand required a revamp. Shortly after, it was claimed that criminal groups were acquiring military-style firearms illegally and at an unprecedented pace, and that the police and the wider community were in acute danger. In response to initial talk about the need for tighter 'gun control' regulations, bloggers and commenters claiming to represent the interests of gun owners in New Zealand launched a 'legal guns are good' discourse. It was claimed in this discourse that guns were only a problem when in the 'wrong hands', and that guns were benign objects when in the possession of responsible gun owners, such as farmers, collectors and hunters. These two discourses came together to produce one 'gangster guns' discourse, which provided the rationale for an urgent inquiry into how criminal groups were acquiring illegal guns, a focus that had very little to do with what had transpired in the Kawerau event. I then argued, from my analysis using the third phase of the framework, that the gangster guns episode supported a current peak in a long-standing (sustained) panic about gangs in the New Zealand context. The gangster guns episode also sparked a defence of the identity of the 'kiwi bloke', whose imagery props up two primary income streams: farming and trophy hunting. This defence cemented the focus on gangs.

The task of the fourth phase of the framework for panic research was to consider which features of each of the case or cases examined (here, killer kids and gangster guns) were explicitly *not* captured by Cohen's model. This was, in part, to illustrate that a concept based upon any one case study can be extraordinarily narrow and that Cohen's model, despite its abstractness, reflected the unfolding of the case of the Mods and Rockers. This is a point often missed in panic analyses using Cohen's work and is why we need to collate and map many complex material cases prior to determining how we might revise the concept and connect panic processes (if we can settle on a set of processes) with social theory. With that in mind, I propose that of killer kids, Cohen's (1972) model was unable to capture the news image of Bailey Kurariki in the *Sunday Star Times* as the trigger event, nor could it help to reveal the two qualitatively different phases and the three independent discourses. On the other hand, of gangster guns, the model alone couldn't account for the complex interface between two seemingly disparate discourses. These features could only be captured with an inductive approach to the data of each case. Moreover, killer kids would not have occurred if children were not culturally divided into little angels and mini-monsters, if news images and crime's images were looked upon with scepticism, if Polynesian peoples with brown faces were not subject to a racialized regime of representation and if there was a rehabilitative, restorative approach to criminal acts in New Zealand in 2002. Gangster guns would not have occurred should the New Zealand government not have had an impetus to 'crack down' on gangs, and guns were not integral to the image of the 'kiwi bloke', and the imagery of the kiwi bloke was not integral to two primary sources of national income. Context matters. But context, on its own, cannot explain a panic. It is the *interaction* between processes in a material panic and the features of context that matters. Should, for example, any one of the features of killer kids have been different, then the reaction would have looked *utterly* different. Indeed, whether a panic would have emerged at all is uncertain. To demonstrate why I might infer this, I drew on another, very similar case, which unfolded in the same context but at a different time. In this case, which featured a murder of a shopkeeper by a 14- and a 12-year-old, the reaction was far more subdued than it was in killer kids, despite that it emerged at a time when many of the same contextual conditions were still present or had, in fact, become *ever more* relevant. By 2014, punitive sensibilities were well entrenched into New Zealand's criminal justice practices, for example (Pratt & Anderson, 2016). I argued that the reason no panic emerged was due to the fact that no images of the two youths convicted were ever displayed in the press. The truths assumed of news images and of crime's images had no process to draw them into the light—to 'focus them' (Cohen, 1972). The processes by which panics unfold are also sustained by the contexts in which they are meaningful. This was clear in the gangster guns panic, as New Zealand's economic dependency on industries which valorise guns firmly swayed discourses relating to gun control to focus on the 'wrong people's' access to guns.

Because contextual features are drawn in by and work to sustain a material panic, they are key indicators for thinking about where the focus of the concept is (or should be). There are a number of theoretical possibilities that ensue from the consideration of killer kids and of gangster guns that I want to briefly explore, in part to highlight their degree of distance from the current conjectures of panics as volatile episodes of moral regulation and panics as decivilizing processes emerging from civilizing offensives, illustrating that there are other ideas that might be connected to moral panic. This is the fifth and final phase in the framework for panic research, and the questions here are: what is the nature of the contextual features of this episode? What scholarly ideas can shed light on this nature?

The centrality of the imagery of Bailey Kurariki to the case of killer kids, and the set of truths to which it pertained, is one indicator for interpreting panic as an instance of other broader phenomena. Carney (2010) argues that the forensic, evidential understandings which underpin crime images should always be deconstructed, as they also exist within a 'photographic spectacle' operating within the larger 'theatre' of crime and punishment. Images that belong to this spectacle can be interpreted in terms of an encounter between a performance and a desire. That is, images of crime are produced to perform and enact particular imaginations about crime and criminals, and they are received with a desire to see when we look upon them. This desire is accompanied by a drive to converse, debate, loath, fear and judge about transgressions and deviants (Carney, 2010). On the other side of the coin, images of crime are said to mark criminal bodies with shame. Images of crime arrest, control and identify criminals through the display of them *as* criminals (Carney, 2010). A panic that is sparked by or is dominated by the exhibition of images of an offender or another type of deviant outsider may then be seen in terms of the processes through which the festivity of performance (coupled with desire) and the collective markings of shame come together.

The role that the fantasies of the criminal other played in this episode points to another possibility. Cunneen (2011) argues that the imagined criminogenesis of ethnic others, particularly indigenous others, stems from historical and contemporary practices of colonial imperialism. Historical practices intended to build new nations in new lands and so were exclusionary of the 'others' who already lived there. One of the ways this was achieved was by practices of criminalization. By imagining 'the nation' in particular ways (i.e. New Zealand as a paradisiacal

Britain of the South Pacific, populated by civilized and entrepreneurial European settlers—see Pratt, 2006), moral boundaries about what it is to be a good New Zealander were created. To be outside the moral community (to be anything other than a civilized and entrepreneurial European settler) is to be vulnerable to the violence of the state. The legislation is created that then defends the vision of a nation, and 'others' are then policed and punished as what they do and who they are intrinsically transcend such codes (Cunneen, 2011). Those who are subjected to criminal justice processes come to be seen as *social* threats. As a consequence, the criminal justice system is active in *creating* a society, and it has done so according to racialized lines. In later periods, particularly those of economic or political instability, these 'other' groups are over-policed as the state seeks to reassert its sovereignty (Cunneen, 2011). The processes of moral panic might then be viewed as sets of exclusionary practices that emerge from a particular conjunction where racializing discourses are given a manner of authority not normally afforded to them. In the case of killer kids, fantasies about criminal others were displayed in a way that suggested there was a *truth* about them. This is very much in line with Hall et al.'s (1978) argument about the mugging moral panic, in Britain, in the 1970s. Understanding of inner city black youth as 'threats' to the British 'way of life' was propagated and promoted to preserve capitalist interests in the midst of an economic crisis. It is also in line with assessments made about panics to do with asylum seekers (Martin, 2015; see also Fitzgerald & Smoczynski, 2015).

The significance of penal populism as a social force in the New Zealand context points to yet another possibility. Loader (2009) identifies that responses to crime do not exist outside of and in isolation from other social/cultural/political phenomena. Indeed, one must consider the relations between penal trends and movements with other more general social practices that he argues can be characterized by a tendency towards *excess*:

> Consider for a moment the following features of contemporary social life: cheap air travel; SUVs (coupled with an increase in the size of all types of car); chocolate in breakfast cereals; double-sized Mars bars; rising rates of childhood obesity; the disappearance of 'small' cups of coffee

> (or indeed of any take-away beverage); cheap alcohol; the quick and easy availability of credit; the instant access to information, images, goods and people afforded by mobile phones and the Internet; cosmetic surgery; the social worship of footballers, celebrities and entrepreneurs; the explosion of corporate pay; 20/20 cricket, multi-channel television and so on and so on. What these seemingly disparate things commonly give effect to and symbolise is the idea that the world is—or at least ought properly to be—organized so that one's immediate desires can be instantly satisfied in ways which often permit one to disregard, perhaps even trample over, the interests, feelings and well-being of others. It is a world that pays homage to self-regarding self-fulfilment; where speedy access to what one craves is paramount; where the great enemies are obstacle and delay. (Loader, 2009, p. 242)

For Loader (2009), the excess in all of these things, together with the beliefs underpinning demands for security and punishment in the modern era, is marked by and can be explained by an *appetite* propagated by increased understandings of and sensitivity to risk, a climate of anxiety, increased media attention, an absence of community, political responsiveness to lay desires (in a climate of deference) and so forth. Loader (2009) argues that these contextual features are all-pervasive in the late-modern era because each reinforces another, reflecting a dialectical relationship between social phenomena and its contexts. Perhaps, it is then that moral panic captures the 'flashpoint' at which a set of appetites collide (see Poynting & Morgan, 2007). In a context of penal populism, where an appetite for security is already flourishing, a slightly uncommon criminal event, one that is marked by a set of truths, or one that taps into a set of fantasies, would set off such a collision.

The context in which the gangster guns episode emerged points to another possibility. I mentioned that the focus on the acquisition of illegal guns on behalf of criminal groups allowed the New Zealand government to further its current interests in controlling the practices of gangs, which in turn could be seen as the latest manifestation of long-standing, sustained panic about gangs in the New Zealand context. A material study of each manifestation of this sustained panic, and of the connections between them, would be valuable for making links with broader ideas. What I will focus on here is the discourse of hegemonic frontier masculinity which endorsed the specific episode of gangster guns. Stroud (2012) argues that the meaning of a gun shifts depending on who is holding it, the context in which it is held and by whom is accorded authority to give meaning to the context in which it is being held. In colonial states, such as the USA, Australia, Canada and New Zealand, rural men can control understandings about guns and gun use (Gahman, 2015). This is because rural men in colonial states (the USA, Australia, Canada and New Zealand) are central in performances of hegemonic masculinities which support national imaginations and relations of colonial power, and the gun is a central prop in those performances. To question guns is to question hegemonic masculinity and to threaten the stability of national identity and prevailing power structures. Perhaps, then, moral panics describe moments of instability at which performances of social identification that are essential to maintaining the status quo, or that serve a powerful interest, come into question.

Intersectional risk theory offers another explanation. Embedded in this perspective is the notion that risk is something that is performed. Performing risk, which is a permeable concept, oriented to the future and not certain, serves to stabilize it. However, this performance is always co-articulated with other norms and discourses (Giritli Nygren, Ohman & Olofsson, 2017). When one performs risk (say by avoiding *or* by engaging in a risky activity), one is also performing one's gender, ethnic identity, class and sexuality. In turn, each of these sectional performances affects how one performs risk. A woman will perform risk differently to how a man does, for example. She will also perform different *sets* of risks to what he does as there are different sets of risk assigned to her, based on understandings of her gender. When a woman drinks alcohol, for example, she is expected to manage her drinking so as to avoid being interpreted as a 'bad girl' or as 'tragic' (Hutton, Griffin, Lyons, Niland & McCreanor, 2016; Wright, 2016). A woman is also expected to manage her vulnerability to rape, at all times (Barton, 2017). Similarly, a person of colour is also subject to different sets of risks from what a person of European descent is. Police practices, for example, target minority ethnic groups and communities, who, in turn, must manage the risk of being targeted (Brunson, 2007; Elers, 2012;

Workman, 2016). Intersectional risk theory takes account of structural inequalities as well as the relationship *between* these inequalities. Giritli et al. (2017) focus on the embodied performance of risk by governed actors (citizens). However, *governors* can also be seen to perform risk as they assign risk to practices and situations in policy statements and enactments of law, and as their agents police these practices and situations. Assigning risk is a political, exclusionary act. To assign risk to somewhere (or to someone) is to prevent its assignment to somewhere (or someone) else. To perform risk by assigning it is to also perform inequality in that risk will be assigned to some and not others. Perhaps, then, a moral panic can be seen as a risk assignment process, incited by performances of risk by embodied citizens that threaten to redraw the sectional lines that currently demark risk. In the gangster guns episode, the risk was firmly assigned to illegal guns and 'the wrong people', in order that the 'right people' (farmers, gun collectors and hunters) could freely hold guns. Conceivably, it was no accident that the right people were wealthy farmers and tourists, and the wrong people happened to be urban males already socially estranged.

These conjectures aside, my principal aim in this book was to propose an inductive approach for panic study. It was argued that for moral panic to regain some authority as an analytical concept, the study of panic needs to demonstrate the complexity of individual cases at the same time as it identifies the commonalities or constancies between panics as these shift or remain the same (see Critcher, 2003, 2006). It may be found that there are many different forms of acute panic-like reaction and that moral panic as we know it now will eventually serve as an overarching concept only (see Goode, 2012). At this point, it appears to me that all panic reactions have trigger events, active interests and sensitive contexts and that perhaps this is the holy trinity in panic development which can serve as our umbrella under which sets and subsets of panic reside. Whatever does emerge from future moral panic work, it is essential that the work is done. Because moral panic is inherently a concept that 'allows us to identify and conceptualise the lines of power in any society, the ways in which we are manipulated into taking some things too seriously and other things not enough' (Cohen, 2002, p. xxxv), and we live in a time where taking things seriously has become critically important, moral panic *must* remain a central concept for criminology, sociology and other related disciplines.

References

Barton, A. (2017). *It's the same old story: Rape representation in New Zealand newspapers 1975–2015.* (Masters). Victoria University of Wellington, Wellington, New Zealand.

Becker, H. (1998). *Tricks of the trade: How to think about research while you are doing it.* Chicago: The University of Chicago Press.

Brunson, R. K. (2007). "Police don't like Black people": African-American young men's accumulated police experiences. *Criminology & Public Policy, 6*(1), 71–101.

Carney, P. (2010). Crime, punishment and the force of the photographic spectacle. In K. J. Hayward & M. Presdee (Eds.), *Framing crime: Cultural criminology and the image.* Abingdon, Oxon: Routledge.

Cohen, S. (1972). *Folk devils and moral panics.* Herts, England: Paladin.

Cohen, S. (2002). *Folk devils and moral panics* (3rd ed.). London: Routledge.

Cohen, S. (2011). Whose side were we on? The undeclared politics of moral panic theory. *Crime, Media, Culture, 7*(3), 237–243.

Critcher, C. (2003). *Moral panics and the media.* Buckingham, England: Open University Press.

Critcher, C. (Ed.). (2006). *Critical readings: Moral panics and the media.* Berkshire: Open University Press.

Critcher, C. (2008). Moral panic analysis: Past, present and future. *Sociology Compass, 2*(4), 1127–1144.

Critcher, C. (2009a). Widening the focus: Moral panics as moral regulation. *British Journal of Criminology, 49,* 17–34.

Critcher, C. (2009b, November). *Onto the highway or up a cul-de-sac? The future destination of moral panic analysis.* Presented at the Special research seminar on moral panics, Department of Sociology and Communications, School of Social Sciences, Brunel University, London, England.

Critcher, C. (2011). For a political economy of moral panics. *Crime, Media, Culture, 7*(3), 259–275.

Cunneen, C. (2011). Postcolonial perspectives for criminology. In M. Bosworth & C. Hoyle (Eds.), *What is criminology?* (pp. 249–266). Oxford: Oxford University Press.

Dandoy, A. (2014). Towards a Bourdieusian frame of moral panic analysis: The history of a moral panic inside the field of humanitarian aid. *Theoretical Criminology*.
Elers, S. (2012). Police interactions with Maori: A contributing factor in disproportionate crime statistics. *Australasian Policing: A Journal of Professional Practice and Research, 4*(2), 30–31.
Fitzgerald, I., & Smoczynski, R. (2015). Anti-Polish migrant moral panic in the UK: Rethinking employment insecurities and moral regulation. *Czech Sociological Review, 51*(3), 339.
Gahman, L. (2015). Gun rites: hegemonic masculinity and neoliberal ideology in rural Kansas. *Gender, Place & Culture, 22*(9), 1203–1219.
Giritli Nygren, K., Öhman, S., & Olofsson, A. (2017). Doing and undoing risk: The mutual constitution of risk and heteronormativity in contemporary society. *Journal of Risk Research, 20*(3), 418–432.
Goode, Eric. (2012, November). *The moral panic: Dead or alive?* Seminar presented at the Revisiting moral panics: Moral panics and the family, University of Edinburgh.
Goode, Erich, & Ben-Yehuda, N. (1994). *Moral panics : The social construction of deviance*. Cambridge, MA: Blackwell.
Hall, S., Critcher, C., Jefferson, T., Clarke, J., & Roberts, B. (1978). *Policing the crisis: Mugging, the state, and law and order*. London: MacMillan.
Hier, S. (2002a). Conceptualizing moral panic thought a moral economy of harm. *Critical Sociology, 28*(3), 311–334.
Hier, S. (2002b). Raves, risk, and the ecstasy panic: A case study in the subversive nature of moral regulation. *Canadian Journal of Sociology, 27*(1), 33–59.
Hier, S. (2003). Risk and panic in the late modernity: Implications of the converging sties of social anxiety. *British Journal of Criminology, 54*(1), 2–20.
Hier, S. (2008). Thinking beyond moral panic: Risk, responsibility, and the politics of moralization. *Theoretical Criminology, 12*(1), 73–190.
Hier, S. P. (2011). Tightening the focus: Moral panic, moral regulation and liberal government1: Tightening the focus. *The British Journal of Sociology, 62*(3), 523–541.
Hier, S. (2016a). Good moral panics? Normative ambivalence, social reaction, and coexisting responsibilities in everyday life. *Current Sociology*, 001139211665546. doi:10.1177/0011392116655463.
Hier, S. (2016b). Moral panic, moral regulation, and the civilizing process: Moral panic, moral regulation, and the civilizing process. *The British Journal of Sociology, 67*(3), 414–434.

Hutton, F., Griffin, C., Lyons, A., Niland, P., & McCreanor, T. (2016). "Tragic girls" and "crack whores": Alcohol, femininity and Facebook. *Feminism & Psychology, 26*(1), 73–93.
Loader, L. (2009). Ice cream and incarceration: On appetites for security and punishment. *Punishment and Society, 11*(2), 241–257.
Martin, G. (2015). Stop the boats! Moral panic in Australia over asylum seekers. *Continuum Journal of Media & Cultural Studies, 29*(3), 304–322.
Poynting, S., & Morgan, G. (2007). *Outrageous! Moral panics in Australia.* Hobart TAS: Australian Clearinghouse for Youth Studies Publishing.
Pratt, J. (2006). The dark side of paradise: Explaining New Zealand's history of high imprisonment. *British Journal of Criminology, 46*(4), 541–560.
Pratt, John, & Anderson, J. (2016). "The Beast of Blenheim", risk and the rise of the security sanction. *Australian and New Zealand Journal of Criminology, 49*(4), 528–545.
Rohloff, A. (2008). Moral panics as decivilising processes: Towards an Eliasian approach. *New Zealand Sociology, 23*(1), 66–76.
Rohloff, A. (2011). Extending the concept of moral panic: Elias, climate change and civiliazation. *Sociology, 45*(4), 634–649.
Stroud, A. (2012). Good guys with guns: Hegemonic masculinity and concealed handguns. *Gender & Society, 26*(2), 216–238.
Ungar, S. (1992). The rise and (relative) decline of global warming as a social problem. *The Sociological Quarterly, 33*(4), 483–501.
Ungar, S. (2001). Moral panic versus the risk society: The implications of the changing sites of social anxiety. *British Journal of Sociology, 52*(2), 271–292.
Workman, K. (2016). From a search for rangantiratanga to a struggle for survival: Criminal justice, the state, and Maori 1985–2015. *Journal of New Zealand Studies, 22,* 89–104.
Wright, S. (2016). "Serious public mischief": Young women, alcohol and the New Zealand press. *Continuum, 30*(6), 636–645.

Index

S. Wright Monod, *Making Sense of Moral Panics*, Palgrave Studies in Risk, Crime and Society, DOI 10.1007/978-3-319-61821-0

Printed by Printforce, the Netherlands